NIG. ROCHESTER
The Double-Initial Murders

Michael Benson
With Private Investigator Donald A. Tubman

Copyright © 2018 Michael Benson and Donald A. Tubman

All rights reserved. Except as permitted under the U.S. Copyright Act of 1976, no part of this publication may be reproduced, distributed, or transmitted in any form or by any means, or stored in a data base or retrieval system without the prior written permission of Michael Benson and Donald A. Tubman.

AUTHORS' NOTE

Although this is a true story, some names and locations have been changed to protect the privacy of the innocent. When possible, the spoken word has been quoted verbatim. However, when that is not possible, conversations have been reconstructed as closely as possible to reality based on the recollections of those who spoke and heard the words. In places there has been a slight editing of spoken words, but only to improve readability. The denotations and connotations of the words remain unaltered. In some cases, witnesses are credited with verbal quotes that in reality only occurred in written form. Some characters may be composites. Information based on a published source is footnoted. In some cases, articles have survived the years only in clippings, and original page numbers may be missing from those endnotes.

ISBN 13: 978-1-7901-6809-5

Benson Book #1806

Cover design: Tekla Dobson
Cover photo: Don Tubman
Cover concept: Ethan Moyer

> Come away, O human child!
> To the waters and the wild
> With a faery, hand in hand,
> For the world's more full of weeping than you can understand.
>
> —William Butler Yeats

ACKNOWLEDGEMENTS

The authors would like to thank the following individuals and organizations, without whose help, the writing of this book would have been impossible: Alyssa Alaimo; Kristin Asselta at the Pittsford Barnes and Noble; Tom and Hannah Baumgartner; Carol Beechey; Gail Beers; Donna Bianchi; Randy Bileschi; Barbara Kolb-Cieslewicz; Stacey Coghlan and Cory W. Paine; producer of *Air Wreck Radio*; Angel Colon; Guillermina Colon; George Conboy; Stefanie Conte; Astrid Cortez; New York State Police Investigator Thomas Crowley; Don Cummings; Robert Cummings; Chad Cunningham; Charlie Cuyler; Debbie DiFranco; Mike DiGiorgio; Brita Edman; Robin Fox; Jen Johnson, Doug Emblidge and Norma Holland at *Good Day Rochester*; private investigator and filmmaker Nicholas Fici; James Gillen; Phyllis Murray Godette; Christine Green; Robbie Head; Susan Buhr Hewitt; Bobbi Ingerick at the RIT Inn; Ithaca College; Jennifer Jacob; Renee Kendrot, Local History Division, Monroe County and Rochester Public Library; Curt Kentner; LuEllen Kepler; Lynn King; Diane Kreutzer; Magnus Krystosek; Mary Ann Lang; Kathy Lake; Sandy Zaso Lambert; Maryann Lang; Director of Transportation Joan Lenhard; Laurie Leo at the Scottsville Free Library; Sandy Lewis; Chris Cummings Magliocco; Mark Mariano; Lori Meath; Jane Milliman, editor of *(585) Magazine,* where the introduction to this book was first published in slightly different form; Theresa DeFranco Morris; Ethan Moyer; Jim Munnings; Judith Ellen Naso; Jeannie Porter Nelson; Cynthia Nicoletti; Patrick O'Flynn; Donna O'Keefe; Robert G. O'Keefe; Shannon O'Keefe; Jay Osborne, Supervisor, Local History, Rochester Central Library; Carmel Paradis; Kit Pence; William Phillips; Robert Pusateri; Rochester Murderinos; Dawn Bileschi Roides; Nik Salonikis; Gates Police Lieutenant Donald Sapienza; Frank Solomon; Yolanda Schultz; Shelby Selover; Philip Semrau; Mike Shannon; Deb Sperling; JoAnn and John Spock; Mike Stasi; Dick, James, and Nancy Szczesniak; Trina, Tim, and David Treu; Loren Tripp; Town of Gates Police Chief James VanBrederode; Gene VanDeWalle; Maria Vasquez; Alan R. Warren of the *House of Mystery* podcast; photographer and historian R. Jerome Warren; Michael Wilcox; Judith A. Yates; Ed and Sandy Yaw; Darcy Young; Michele Zuck; Dan Zupansky of the *True Murder* podcast, and all of the journalists who reported upon these events when they were new.

Introduction
Genesee Junction

My fascination with evil stems from childhood trauma. On June 25, 1966, when I was nine, my babysitter George-Ann Formicola and her friend from just down the road Kathy Bernhard went swimming in Black Creek behind the Benson house off Ballantyne Road in Chili, New York, and didn't come home.

It was the first day of summer vacation, a hot and humid Saturday night. At the high school, commencement ceremonies were underway, and almost no one thought about the girls who'd gone to the swimming hole for a quick cool down.

The hole, actually a tranquil section of the creek, was just to the east of my dad's property, yards away from the once thriving Genesee Junction, where the New York Central and Pennsylvania railroads crossed. Now it was an abandoned ghost town.

The girls swam alongside the ancient stone trestle that carried trains across, originally built in the early nineteenth century to accommodate the barge-tugging mules of the long-forgotten Genesee Valley Canal.

A month later the girls were found face up, mummified among elderberry bushes, alongside a lover's lane to the west, horribly mutilated with a knife. A farmer, thinking he might have lost a cow, found them.

George-Ann's throat was cut so deeply that she was almost beheaded. One breast had been removed and she had been stabbed repeatedly in the crotch. Kathy had had both breasts removed, along with a wedge shaped section of her crotch. Her vagina and uterus were gone.

All of the removed parts were missing and never found. Both girls had defensive wounds to their arms, indicating that the initial attack was quick and savage. The surgery was done post-mortem and with a more careful hand.

The killer had partially redressed the girls in their two-piece bathing suits, covering up the parts he had removed. Kathy wore both portions of her suit. George-Ann wore only her top. The bottoms were found nearby.

Monroe County, it seemed, had its own Jack the Ripper, with Genesee Junction serving as a desolate, modern-day Whitechapel, a spot where the devil had visited earth, as always in human form.

The case was never solved, and was too ghastly to be covered in detail in the newspapers of the day. The papers left no doubt that it had been a sex crime, mentioning mutilation and a "mad thrust of the blade." Veteran law enforcement officers called it the worst thing they had seen in their lives.

Although us Bensons heard nothing memorable that night, neighbors heard one blood-curdling scream for help coming from behind our house back where Black Creek and the New York Central ran more or less parallel.

So I grew up knowing that a real-life boogieman had crossed my backfield. Even as a kid, paralyzed by fear, I wanted answers, to solve the crime and identify the monster. I began writing about George-Ann and Kathy when I was twelve, and I grew up to become a true-crime writer.

In the 1990s, I read every true crime book. My Manhattan office where I worked as a magazine editor was a crazy quilt of detective magazines, with their bright, vivid covers of lingerie babes packing heat and newsprint innards as gray as a Monday morning corpse.

I learned plenty about serial killer Arthur Shawcross, convicted of killing eleven women in Rochester during the 1980s. Earlier in life, he killed two children in the Watertown, N.Y. area. The thing most fascinating about Shawcross was the fictional biography he gave a shrink after his Rochester arrest. He recounted his days in Vietnam, alone on jungle patrol, coming upon a pair of "Vietcong chicks" swimming in a stream. He said he killed, mutilated, and cannibalized them.

The man was clearly confessing to something, but his records showed that he had never been in a position to patrol a jungle alone or otherwise. Change jungle to woods and Vietnam to Chili and he could have been describing "my" murders.

By the early 2000s, with true crime already my obsession, I figured I might as well make a living at it. My first true crime book was about a family affair in Penfield, a tragic real-life soap opera that turned into my *Betrayal in Blood*.

In July 2003, diminutive lawyer Kevin Bryant sleepily called the cops to report that he'd been upstairs reading while an intruder came into the house and shot his wife, the beautiful and much-younger Tabatha. The tapes of that 911 call are shocking. Bryant is the calmest man in the history of 911 calls. At one point it sounds as if he yawns.

As the story unfolded, Rochester received a lesson in the depths of human depravity. Bryant had lifestyle issues. Despite a bad ticker, he was into hookers and blow, sometimes in a motel room, sometimes in a strip joint, sometimes right there in his office, while Tabby toiled as a teller at the drive-in window of a branch bank and took care of their two little boys.

One of Bryant's cocaine buddies was Cyril Winebrenner, who was Tabby's half-brother, a guy with mental problems, whose girlfriend Cassie turned tricks. Kevin tried to get Tabatha to become a swinger with him and all that that implied. Instead, Tabatha sought the real love she needed elsewhere and found a boyfriend. When her husband learned he had been cuckold, he proclaimed her dead meat and hired Tabby's brother Cyril to murder her, promising to pay him off in cocaine.

While the couple's boys and Kevin were upstairs in bed, and Tabatha was on the couch downstairs, Cyril entered the home, shot Tabatha in the face, only wounding her, jammed the gun, and finished the job with a knife, which managed to unsparingly spatter the living room ceiling with gore.

Cops immediately suspected the husband, not just because cops always suspect the husband, but because that fuss downstairs must've been noisy as hell, yet Kevin's reaction was somnolent. By the time he got to the top of the stairs and looked down into the horror that was his living room, he said the intruder had gone. He heard a car pull away outdoors. Tabby had a boyfriend, he said softly. Maybe he did it.

Cassie drove the getaway car and she turned out to be the weak link in the conspiracy. Once cops flipped her, the case abruptly fell into place. A jury found Kevin Bryant guilty. Cyril Winebrenner and Cassie copped deals.

I asked Cyril and Tabatha's mom why she hadn't gone to Cyril's trial—before the deal was cut—and the mother of both the defendant and the victim said, "I couldn't go. I wouldn't have known which side of the courtroom to sit in."

My second Rochester investigation began as an examination of the Lyell Avenue hooker killings of the late 1980s and early 1990s. Ladies of the evening were dropping like flies. Arthur Shawcross was arrested, resulting in splash headlines and the moniker "The Genesee River Killer," but the murders didn't stop.

Bizarrely, at one point three serial killers were working the same ward of Rochester, from Edgerton Park down to Lyell Avenue, west of Lake Avenue. And one of those serial killers was Robert Spahalski. The kicker was Robert had an identical twin named Stephen who once killed as well, and he did it identically to Robert.

By the time I got into the act, Robert Spahalski was in prison forever. Nonetheless, he and I hit it off. We became pen pals, discussing our tastes in music. We'd both grown up in the country, on dirt roads, with lots of bored troublemaking in the summertime. We each had our own special herbal garden.

The only difference was he grew up to be a psycho killer and I didn't. But we ignored that at first. I asked him if he knew of a Deep Purple album called *Machine Head*, and he said he wanted me to be the one to tell his story.

It was through Spahalski that I came to understand the absolute selfishness that accompanies a sociopathic personality disorder. I knew it existed—that conscience-free psyche that keeps the blood stunningly cold—but I didn't get it until I asked Robert how he learned to kill. He told me that when he was a teenager he put a gun to the head of his father's favorite pig, blew the pig's brains out.

I asked him, "Were you angry with your father?"

"No," he replied, "I felt like pork chops."

His twin Stephen killed a man in Elmira, N.Y. in 1971, sneaking up behind him on a stairway and hitting him over the head with a hammer. Twenty years later, Robert would identically kill a victim, bludgeoning to death from behind his only male victim.

On New Year's Eve 1990, Robert murdered a Rochester woman Moraine Armstrong. She was exchanging sex for crack, and he killed her by ligature strangulation in her apartment on Lake Avenue in Rochester. Moraine was found in bed, almost naked, wearing only one sock. She had multiple electrical cords wrapped around her neck.

Outside the building, a crowd gathered. One spectator was an antsy unwashed man with his "belly pressed against the police tape." He said he lived across the street. Yeah, he knew Moraine Armstrong. She wasn't a friend but he'd seen her around. The police officer wrote down the guy's name and age: Robert Bruce Spahalski, age 36.

In the summer of 1991, during a heat wave, there was a report of a bad odor coming from a house on Emerson Street, only a block and a half from the Armstrong crime scene. Black flies swarmed the closed apartment windows from the outside.

Tentative police investigated and discovered the decomposed body of the resident, Adrian Berger. The apartment was baked by summer sun into an oven and the body was so far gone that the medical examiner couldn't determine cause of death.

Someone had taken Berger's car and parked it a few blocks to the north, so neighbors would think she was away. Berger, investigators learned, had an on-again/off-again boyfriend named Robert Bruce Spahalski.

Spahalski's fingerprints were found in the apartment. Police picked him up but he didn't have much to say. Sure, he'd seen Adrian a few days earlier, played dice with her, but she was fine when he left.

There followed for Robert a decade of calm. He lived off the street. Pimping. Whoring. Selling cocaine. Had a steady girlfriend. Became HIV positive. Developed a desperate crack addiction, but for the longest time, as far as we know, he didn't kill anyone.

He killed for the last time on November 8, 2005 when he strangled his friend Vivian Irizarry in his own apartment. The murder occurred, he later said, because he'd smoked too much crack and saw Vivian metamorphose into a demon monster that needed to be vanquished.

When he snapped out of it, he was very sad that Vivian was dead. He bathed her tenderly and moved her body into the apartment building's basement where it was cooler and her rate of decomposition would be slowed.

He visited the body, and cried as he told her how sorry he was. The body wore nothing but one sock, as had Moraine Armstrong's 15 years earlier.

Spahalski was in no condition to hide Vivian's body permanently. This was the end. He killed Vivian on a Friday afternoon and, the following Tuesday morning, he turned himself in. Expertly eased along by investigators, he confessed one by one to the four murders.

In 2009, Robert's twin Stephen Spahalski was released from prison after serving every day of his 30-year sentence for armed robbery and kidnapping. He was so thoroughly institutionalized at that point that he considered prison home, so he was only free (and lost) for a few months before he walked into an Elmira bank, handed the teller a note demanding money, and then sat down and waited for the police to arrive.

Unfortunately, instead of institutionalizing him for the rest of his life, no doubt his goal, he only received 300 days in the Chemung County jail, and lived in a halfway house and walked the streets of Elmira until his death in 2017.

In 2011, my mother Rita Benson and Kathy Bernhard's mom Alice were sitting in folding chairs at a summer backyard party on Names Road in Chili. My mom was bragging about her son who wrote about unusually foul murders, and Alice Bernhard said, "It's too bad your Michael can't write a book about my Kathy."

My mom said, "Why don't you ask him?"

So I teamed up with Alice and former Wheatland cop and current private investigator Donald A. Tubman, who knew the girls and graduated from Wheatland-Chili High School on the evening of the murders. Together we conducted a fresh investigation, and acquired records of the sheriff's investigation through Freedom of Information requests.

Alice asked me to do two things for her: 1) Find out what happened to her Kathy, and 2) get people to think about Kathy because she was forgotten way too soon. The first request did not necessarily mean she wanted to know who killed the girls, but rather *what was done* to the girls. Because of the crime's ghastly nature, no one had ever told Alice about the crime scene.

One of my proudest moments came just after the sheriff's office reports arrived in my afternoon mail. I read through everything twice, and in a flash realized Alice's concern. I called her.

"Kathy wasn't tortured. She was killed quickly and the bad stuff all happened after she was gone."

"Oh thank you, thank you. I have been worrying about that for 45 years," Alice said.

Our investigation uncovered a new suspect that we liked even better than Shawcross. We developed a ton of new evidence, folks willing now to admit things—horrible horrible things—they'd kept mum about in 1966.

Abused little girls were now women in their fifties, in some cases telling me what had been done to them for the first time, telling me things they would never say to a police officer. The case was propelled in a startling new direction.

When the book, *The Devil at Genesee Junction* came out in November 2015, assuring Alice that Kathy would be thought of now more than ever, and maybe forever, she thanked me with a big hug and told me she loved me, which was the best part of the investigation by far.

The book is done, I told her. The investigation goes on forever. There are Kathy and George-Ann witnesses still coming out of the woodwork.

At an event to publicize *Devil* in Scottsville, New York, I was asked what I would do for an encore. I gave an answer that seemed to make everyone happy. So, please consider the book you are holding a follow-up to *Devil,* in which Don Tubman and I get inside Rochester's darkest history, the Double Initial Murders...

*   *   *

In 1971, there began in Rochester, N.Y., a series of hideous murders, cases that offered the starkest of contrast between good and evil: perfectly innocent victims, perfectly evil predators. The three victims were little girls, and—reminiscent of an Agatha Christie novel[1]—each had the same first and last initial. Each, or so the story went, had been dumped in a town that also began with that letter.

The initials theory generated intense infamy, as if Rochester had its own Zodiac Killer. The guy had to be a genius, using patient premeditation, researching little girls like an evil scientist, choosing only those with double initials, to commit what otherwise seemed like impulsive crimes of opportunity.

The victims had all been last seen in an urban setting and their lifeless bodies were found raped and carelessly dumped along a rural roadside, strangled by ligature.[2]

I had just turned 17 when the initials angle was popularized, three months into my senior year at Wheatland-Chili, and the effect on the community was intense. Local girls with alliterative names were terrified. All of the Sue Smiths, Judy Johnsons, and Pauline Petersons (and their parents) lived in constant anxiety. It affected girls from five to 25. The little ones didn't quite get it, but they sensed it, something in their mother's tighter grip on their little hand, or the way mom never relaxed when they were out of doors.

The older ones looked at maps and guessed where their own lifeless bodies would be discovered in a ditch. No one wondered why the initials were important, what it all meant. They understood one thing: it was terrifying.

On the other side of the coin, some parents, who had little girls with variant initials, assumed they were off the hook, and let their darlings walk around the streets of Rochester alone.

"Here's fifty cents, honey, go to the corner and buy mommy pack of cigarettes."

It became *the* case: the one that ate away at the community's collective consciousness, bizarre enough to be appreciated globally, one of the things that Rochester, N.Y. became known for. In addition to the alphabet thing, the victims were underpriviledged, poor little girls, adding further poignancy to the tragedy.

The double-initials thing had power, but it didn't convince many close to the investigation. People liked to see patterns in things, sometimes even when no patterns existed: a cloud that looked like an elephant holding a balloon in his trunk, a strategy to beat a slot machine, Paul is Dead clues[3], the DaVinci code, a face on Mars, and double-initials.

But wait…looking at it logically: Was it even possible? Feasible? Why would the initials matter to a killer? If he was trying to send some sort of message, why wasn't there a word of explanation, letters scratched into the dirt or chalked on a wall?

Why were there no letters written to taunt cops and reporters? Why wasn't he letting the world in on his secret? Why only little girls with double initials? Wasn't this primarily a sex crime, the scratching of a perverted itch? Spontaneous, spur of the moment?

If it was actually part libidinous and part super-villain wannabe, one had to wonder how you could have a man with so much control and yet so little control. But it couldn't be a coincidence, either. Right? What *were* the odds?

Many prolific serial killers collected souls in the double digits and never killed *anyone* with the same first and last initial. The guy in Rochester (assuming it was one guy) was three for three.

No study had been conducted, that I knew of, but it was easy to imagine that little girls born in the early 1960s were more prone to alliterative names than those born during other times, due to the popularity of the movie stars Marilyn Monroe and Brigitte Bardot, known as MM and BB in the supermarket movie magazines. It has long been the norm for fictional characters to have alliterative names. Lois Lane. Troy Tempest. They were cute and easy on the ears. Mothers naming their babies in the early 1960s may have thought, subconsciously at least, that double initials enhanced their daughters' chances of success, might even make them movie stars.

*   *   *

When weighing the extraordinary collective trauma these murders cast upon my hometown, we can't overstate the tragic power of the first victim. Years before anyone considered the initials, this case became Rochester's nightmare right off the bat, with the all-too-public last agonizing moments of an angel named Carmen Colon.

—Michael Benson, Fall 2018

The Girl Who Had Bad Dreams

It was November 16, 1971[4], the day after deer season opened. *The French Connection* was the big picture out. Roller derby was coming to town. That afternoon you could watch *Perry Mason*, *The Munsters* or *Sesame Street* on TV. In the NFL, the Patriots had just defeated the local favorites, the Buffalo Bills. The Amerks were playing Hershey at the War Memorial.

In the Bull's Head section of Rochester, southwest of downtown,[5] several major streets—Genesee Street, Main Street West, Chili Avenue, Brown Street, and West Avenue—came together in a hub. As a small child, my first barber had his shop there on Genesee. It was once a thriving shopping district but had deteriorated and was now populated by transients and drug addicts. It was a mostly cloudy day, late afternoon temperature in the mid-fifties.

Ten-year-old Carmen Colon lived her first five years in Guayama, Puerto Rico, and still did not speak much English. She was tiny—four feet tall, 65 pounds. Her long brown hair cascaded over her shoulders and made her look angelic. Her playmates were her cousins, and sometimes neighbor kids. They spoke Spanish, too.

In recent years, she had been living with her grandfather Felix Colon and his wife Candida on Brown Street. Her mother, Guillermina (Gee-jurr-Mee-nah), was only just 14 when she became pregnant with Carmen.

Carmen's father Justiano Colon had been 32. He was married to Guillermina's older sister Carmen, who was simultaneously pregnant by Justiano. Baby Carmen had been conceived without romance.[6]

Guillermina, who lived on Romeyn Street[7], was visiting Carmen's grandparents' home on Brown Street on Tuesday afternoon, November 16, and while there sent Carmen the block and a half to the Jax Drug Store on Main Street West to have a prescription filled.[8] Carmen's baby sister had an earache.

Carmen's official residence is in question. According to Investigator Patrick Crough of the Monroe County Sheriff's Office (MCSO), Carmen officially lived at the Romeyn St. address.

Carmen's Uncle Miguel, the Colon brother closest to her mother's age, the much-younger brother of the man who impregnated Guillermina, moved in with Guillermina. Carmen spent increasing time at and eventually moved into her grandparents' home on Brown Street.[9]

Carmen was wearing white sneakers, a long red wool coat, children's size-ten green pants, and a red sweater with a black collar. As a rule, when Carmen was asked to run an errand, she would tell her grandfather Felix and he would accompany her, walking behind her across Essex Street and Kensington streets. Neither were busy intersections and were easily and safely crossed by a child as long as she remembered to look both ways.

The drug store was on the north side of Main Street West, so she just had to turn the corner and she was there. (Usually when Carmen ventured out, she was going to Morrell's Cigar Store on Brown Street—even closer than the drug store—for a candy bar or a bottle of pop. This was easier on her grandfather as he could watch her go and return from the front of his house.) On her way back from the drug store, she would race past her grandfather and again he'd follow behind until she was home safely. Carmen accrued with these trips a careful and small sense of independence.

But on this day Carmen forgot to tell her grandfather that she was headed out, and she found herself alone on the streets.[10] What a strange and empowering feeling it must've been for the cloistered girl, now alone, in the outside world, outside the fenced-in front yard. Best guess is she looked both ways before crossing Essex Street, perhaps ceremoniously, demonstrating to herself what a big girl she was.

Carmen entered the drug store at 4:30 p.m. On duty was Jack Corbin, who was both the clerk and the storeowner. The girl gave him the prescription and her mother's Medicaid card. He told her it would take a few minutes. Because it was a Medicaid purchase, there were forms that needed to be filled out.

"Come back in a half hour," he said.

There is no way to know how much of that Carmen understood, but she left and never returned home. The druggist later said that this was the third time he had seen the little girl come into the store and that she seemed alert and bright and should have been familiar with the Medicaid procedure. In retrospect, this seems like a drastic overestimation of Carmen's competence.

When Carmen didn't return home, her uncle Antonio Colon searched the neighborhood. Mentioned in initial reports of the girl's disappearance, but forgotten by the public, was the fact that the little girl's family did not call her Carmen. She was called by the nickname "Guisa", which was at first listed in the papers as her middle name, but then forgotten. So, as relatives searched before calling police, it was this name—"Guisa! Guisa!"—that was being called aloud with increasing distress, as this was the name she answered to.[11]

The police were called at 7:50 p.m. Not a single witness in the neighborhood could be found who had seen Carmen after she left the drug store.

Carmen Colon was an outwardly happy girl. Those outside of her home knew her as "always smiling."[12] But there were indications that all was not well in her life. She would kneel beside her bed, say her prayers to the crucifix on her bedroom wall (all of her bedroom's wall decorations were religious), and then wake everyone in the house in the middle of the night with screams of terror.

Sometimes she would fall from her small bed onto the red tiles of her eight-by-ten-foot bedroom floor. The screams were so common in fact that her grandparents had long since ceased reacting to them, and it was up to Carmen to get back into bed and asleep.

MCSO Investigator Patrick Crough, an expert on the victims and predators of child sex abuse, lists frequent nightmares as a symptom of sexual abuse.[13]

In the morning, Carmen's standard breakfast was two cups of coffee light-and-sweet and crackers, eaten while watching TV. Her grandparents would walk her to St. Peter and Paul's Church where a school bus picked her up and took her to John Williams School 5. The bus arrived at ten to nine and was always met by Carmen's teacher, Mrs. Joyce DeMasi, who taught the class of 15 special education students.

There were indications that Carmen's home life was not always a happy one. A relative told a reporter that the uncles and aunts that came to her grandparents' home didn't like or have time for Carmen.

A neighbor, Mrs. Gloria Trott said, "I remember one time a lot of the family was driving to the park. Carmen was all dressed up and ready to go, and she ran out and they told her she couldn't go. She just looked out the window and cried as everyone left."

Though relatives said Carmen spoke little English, she was apparently a different girl at school. The previous year she had been in a special-class program for students who had English as their second language, but starting in the fall of 1971 it was said that she no longer needed the English lessons.

Carmen was becoming more articulate every day, increasingly capable of describing how she felt and recalling communicatively the things that had happened to her during her life. She remained in special education because she was mentally handicapped, with an IQ estimated to be between 50 and 70, well below normal.

Mrs. DeMasi described Carmen as a "bundle of energy" in class, always chattering away and bouncing up and down.

Every few minutes, Mrs. DeMasi would be forced to say, "Carmen, please sit still; your work is not finished."

Carmen would remain still for a time, and then a fresh burst of energy would overcome her.

On Tuesday, Carmen's last day at school, she went through the daily rituals with her classmates, saying "Here!" when her name was called for attendance, saying the Pledge of Allegiance, drinking her morning milk, learning some reading and spelling, and then changing into her gym clothes for a half-hour physical education class that began at 9:45.

Her teacher recalled that this was Carmen's favorite part of the school day: "She always loved that because she could really run around and get rid of her energy," the teacher said.

After gym, there was more reading, and at 11:50 came lunch. That Tuesday she had sloppy joe, potatoes, vegetables, fruit, and milk. Mrs. DeMasi didn't recall if Carmen ate her lunch in the lunchroom on that Tuesday. On some days, Carmen would bring her lunch back to the classroom and eat with her teacher. In the afternoon she studied writing and arithmetic. She could do simple addition and could count and write her numbers up to 20. At 1:50 she had a special speech class.

She was a popular girl. Mrs. DeMasi said, "Everybody liked her, and she played with all the kids. The kids sort of babied her because they knew she was slower than they were."

At 3:00 p.m., on her final school day, Mrs. DeMasi saw

Carmen onto her school bus. She arrived home a half-hour later. Her mother Guillermina was there. Carmen showed off some dance moves she had learned in gym class and told her mother, "You should do them too if you want to be skinny like me."

She changed her clothes and then played with her two cousins next door in their front yard behind a wire fence. She came home 45 minutes later and heard her mother discussing medicine she needed for her sister. Carmen volunteered to pick up the medicine but her mother said no repeatedly.

"Three or four times she said no," a relative recalled.

Carmen insisted and her mother finally gave in. The little girl—four-foot, 65 pounds—grabbed the prescription, donned her full-length red wool coat and left without telling her grandfather where she was going.

Then came the nightmare, the images that burned into Monroe County's collective psyche like a branding iron, so wickedly appropriate for a girl prone to nightmares, who loved to wake up in the morning because she no longer had to worry about bad dreams.

About an hour after her abduction, Carmen wriggled free from her abductor, or abductors, and jumped out of a car. Naked from the waist down, holding her pants in one hand, she ran hysterically down the shoulder of the "Western Expressway"—now known as Interstate 490—toward heavy oncoming rush-hour traffic, screaming for help, waving her arms, trying to hail passing cars.[14]

She was seen by *dozens of motorists* as they approached the Route 36 interchange, Exit 3 to Churchville. As she ran toward traffic, some saw a car behind her backing up toward her. Some saw a parked car and an adult running after her. Scores of cars drove by, observing the child in distress. No one stopped. Carmen was presumably caught and dragged back.

Psychologists were later kind to the motorists who saw some sort of commotion along the roadside but didn't stop. The sight was too bizarre to be processed swiftly by most people. Shrinks correctly predicted the guilt those motorists would feel at the notion that they could have saved Carmen's life but didn't.

The story broke in the city newspapers when three young men reported to authorities that they had been among those who saw Carmen's desperate attempt at flight but had not stopped. One of the men, from the town of LeRoy, tried to explain himself: "It went by so fast," he said. "I couldn't believe what I saw."

Most witnesses agreed it was a luxury car by the side of the road. Some called it a Cadillac, or a Lincoln, or a Ford LTD. Mostly what people saw were the taillights as the car backed up.

Another man, who was from Batavia, remembered saying to his passenger, "Should we go back?" They didn't, feeling that there was probably a car behind them in a better position to help. Stopping and turning around would have presented difficulties. "I was going 65 or 70 miles per hour and there were five or six cars directly behind me." By the time he had thought it through, it was too late. "I didn't expect anything sinister," he said. "I thought at first maybe a parent had stopped to allow a child to go to the bathroom or something." He said he was sick when he read about Carmen in the newspaper and realized that she must have been the little girl he had seen. He estimated that upwards of 100 cars must have passed the fleeing girl. But even before that he was bothered by what he had seen and his own inaction. When he got home he told his wife about it.

One man who was haunted by the memory of that commute was F. Nicholas Zuck, a successful advertising man from Scottsville, N.Y. who was 27 years old at the time. Until his death in 2013, he remained deeply troubled by thoughts of "what if." Years later, his widow[15], Michele, told me that Nick had seen a large car, perhaps a Cadillac, parked at the side of the expressway. Running toward him along the side of the road was a little girl who was either naked or naked from the waist down. In the car were two adults, and, as he passed, he saw a woman get out of the car in presumed pursuit of the unruly child. Nick, she said, did not contact the sheriff about what he had seen, and didn't discuss the matter with law enforcement until the *Rochester Democrat and Chronicle* ran a two-part article on March 1–2, 2009, at which time Nick reported the incident to someone at the state police barracks in Canandaigua. Nick and his wife had talked about the running girl throughout the years and Nick harbored deep regrets and Michele would try in vain to assuage his feelings of guilt. She told him that what he had seen was surreal, and difficult to process.

"More so then than now," she added, "your mind didn't automatically go to the worst."

MCSO Investigator Patrick Crough later acknowledged that descriptions of the car on the shoulder of 490 varied, but that at least one of the descriptions matched the car that Carmen's Uncle Miguel had recently purchased.[16]

The sheriff begged eyewitnesses to come forward, and the slight response was disappointing because he knew there were witnesses to portions of Carmen's ordeal out there, now too embarrassed or suspicious of police to come forward.

There were reports from girls across the area of men lurking and stalking. Two girls from Monroe Junior High School said a man in a white car at the corner of Main and Clinton downtown had menaced them.[17] They also said they were friends of Carmen.

Back at Bull's Head, according to Detective Lieutenant Daniel Gudell, teams of officers and detectives, five detectives, 35 officers in all, were going door to door, giving special attention to vacant houses and other possible hiding places.

Police officers Charles Laffin, Robert Kilpatrick, and John Thyroff searched along the east-west railroad tracks that crossed Brown Street several blocks north of the Colon home. Special attention was paid to the thick underbrush along the tracks off of Taylor Street.[18]

Because the girl was Puerto Rican, attempts were made to determine if she had tried to contact relatives there. Perhaps, the wishful thinking went, she had felt homesick for the island. But, as news of the incident along the Western Expressway spread, wishful thinking went by the wayside.

Miguel Colon's recently purchased car was subsequently searched and it was discovered that the trunk had been recently washed with a cleaning solution. The dealership that sold the car to Miguel said the trunk had not been detergent-washed prior to sale.[19]

One of Carmen's dolls was found in Miguel's car, which investigators thought might be significant until it was explained by the family that Carmen rode in that car frequently and she could have forgotten a doll in there at any time.

On the morning of Thursday, November 18, United Press International reported that two men, one a Scoutmaster, in Jacksonville, Florida, were caught attempting to sell two children from Oklahoma City for $7,000. The mom, they said, had another kid and a drunken husband that took up all her time, so she wanted to get rid of the others.[20]

In Monroe County, that morning, a University of Rochester professor said the area needed more social workers because of the problem of abused children. He explained that families in which children were neglected and abused were "worlds apart from other people in their ideas of good behavior and moral standards."[21]

After school that day, in a desolate section of the town of Riga, very close to the Riga/Chili border south of the village of Churchville, two boys were out joyriding on a motorcycle. They were Jim Gillen, 13 years old, and his friend Mark Allen, who was 15.[22] It was a great day for it, sunny and mild, temperature in the low sixties—light jacket weather.

The boys were in eighth and tenth grades respectively. Though they lived close to one another, they were in different school districts. Jim attended Caledonia-Mumford Central School while Mark went to Churchville-Chili. Still, they were very close—so much so that Jim's mom often referred to Mark as her "other son."

Despite being too young to drive, Mark had a motorcycle, an 80cc Suzuki, which he rode up and down the area's all-but-deserted roads. The odds of seeing another motor vehicle were slim. The odds of running into a patrolling sheriff's car were even slimmer.

Mark drove the motorcycle while Jim sat behind him and held on. They had a circuit they ran, involving Griffin and Stearns roads, a route that, because the area was so sparsely populated, only passed a couple of farm houses.

They were on their third time around the circuit and heading south on Stearns Road when Jim first realized that something was wrong. He felt Mark's body go rigid. Mark had been talkative, but stopped talking and slowed the bike. Something had gotten his attention.

"Hang on," Mark said, as he made a quick U-turn.

"What's wrong?" Jim asked.

"I don't know what I just saw," Mark said. "I've got to check this out. Something in the ditch. I don't know what it was. I hope it was a doll."

Jim didn't like the sound of that.

Mark rode tentatively back to the spot, about 700 feet south of Griffin Road, and the boys together looked down into the deep ditch that ran along the side of the road.

"Woah," they said in unison.

They wished it was only a doll, but there was something about it that was clearly not doll. There was a sadness, the queasy melancholy of a life wasted, emanating from the motionless figure, a little girl without pants or underwear, prepubescent, head toward the south, feet toward the north. No bloating. The boys were no experts in decomposition, of course, but they had the idea that the body hadn't been there long.

The head was against a large rock, police called it a boulder, and the boys got the impression that the body had been placed at that spot, rather than merely rolled down the incline. The body was so light in weight that a man would've had no trouble getting down there while carrying it.

For a moment the boys didn't know what to do. Jim remembered feeling very alone at that moment, suddenly aware of how desolate that stretch of road was, a newly sinister desolation that, for him, would never go away.

What they did was go to Jim's house. They parked the motorcycle in the garage and told Jim's dad what they'd seen. Mr. Gillen, Jim Sr., called the sheriff's office. Then he and the boys got into his car together and rode back to the spot, where a large redheaded deputy soon joined them. He took a quick look and made a call from his car. Many cars showed up after that, one of them containing Sheriff Al Skinner himself.[23]

The boys were put in the back of a sheriff's vehicle and told to wait, someone would be asking them questions. Jim remembered getting bored with the wait. It got dark and still they sat, trying to come to grips with what they'd seen and what it meant.

Who would want to do that to a little girl? It didn't make sense.

When they were finally questioned, the boys told the absolute truth about everything, except for their mode of transportation. They said they'd been riding bicycles.

Sheriff Skinner told reporters he believed the girl had been slain elsewhere and then transported by car to the dumpsite. Carmen was found wearing only a purple sweater, blue socks and white sneakers. (The initial BOLO for the missing girl had stated that she'd been wearing a red and black sweater, and dark blue sneakers, but this turned out to be wrong.[24]) She had been wearing a full-length coat and slacks when she disappeared but those items were missing.

(The coat was found the following day by Sheriff's Deputy William Yotter in a culvert about 100 yards from the body. The pants and undergarments remained missing.)

The entire body had been scratched by fingernails—perhaps an indication that a woman was involved in this crime—and there was bruising near her throat. The Medical Examiner determined that she'd been dead for "at least 24 hours." She'd been strangled from the front—face-to-face.

Justiano Colon—despite the fact that he'd never had a romantic relationship with Carmen's mother and had impregnated her when she was a child—took a patriarch's stance with the press. He told a reporter, "[Carmen] was friendly, friendly to everybody. That is probably what happened. A guy has to be crazy to do what he did."

Carmen's grandmother added, "Why? Why did they do that? Why an innocent girl?"

Jim and Mark, the boys who discovered Carmen's body, were in for a rude shock when they got on the school bus on Friday morning. Their names had appeared in that morning's *Democrat and Chronicle*, and the kids teased them about their horrifying evening.

"He's coming for you. He knows who you are now and he's coming for you!" they said.

The kids might've been goofing around, but Jim took it seriously for a day or two. Then he realized he was in no danger. Why would the killer be mad at him? Because he found the body? If the guy didn't want the body found he would have done a better job of hiding it.

Many years later, Jim and Mark were driving in Mark's Catalina through the city of Rochester and near an overpass saw a man lying in the middle of the road. They both thought the same thing: "Oh no, not again." But it turned out the guy was just drunk.

The Lend-A-Hand Fund of the Gannett Rochester Newspapers announced on Friday, November 19, that they had donated $200 to the Colon family for purchase of food and clothing "during the mourning period." By the weekend, a $2,500 reward had been established by the same organization.[25] Both of Rochester's daily papers—the *Democrat and Chronicle* in the morning and *Times-*

Union in the afternoon—were Gannett papers.

Callers could remain anonymous and would be assigned an ID number that allowed those providing information leading to an arrest to collect the reward money. Other rewards had been set up as well: $1,000 from Michael J. Macaluso Jr.'s Citizens for a Decent Community (CDC), and $500 from the Ibero-American Action League, Inc.

Edward Morrell, owner of Morrell's Cigar Store, said he knew Carmen, that she used to come into his store and buy candy, said he would *personally* give $100 to anyone with important info.

At 3:00 p.m. on Saturday afternoon police were called to the Sibley, Lindsay and Curr department store at 228 Main Street East—a store known to Rochesterians as Sibley's—because of a disturbing piece of recently discovered graffiti.

On a wooden door leading into a sixth-floor men's room, someone had written in pencil: "I killed a 10-year-old girl—who will be next?" The door was dusted for fingerprints and photographs were taken. The incident was never publically mentioned again.

What *was* mentioned and often was the incident along the Western Expressway. Editorials screamed shame at the motorists who didn't stop, but investigators found those eyewitnesses potentially valuable and urged them to come forward. For a fleeting instant, they'd all seen the killer's car, and perhaps, just maybe, the killer. About a dozen of the Western Expressway motorists described for authorities what they saw. Many more chose to remain silent.

Sheriff's Chief of Detectives Michael Cerretto had it figured that Carmen knew her killer. The Bull's Head area had been canvassed and canvassed again and no one had seen a struggle. "That leads us to believe it was probably some one known to her," Cerretto said.[26]

Sheriff Skinner reported that during the first 24 hours of the murder investigation eight men had been questioned, but no solid suspects had emerged.

As the weekend following the murder wound down, investigators kept hitting it hard, telling reporters that they were "intensifying" their search for the killer.[27] Carmen's neighborhood was canvassed a second time, as was the area around the Jax Drugs where Carmen was last seen.

"Somebody must've seen something," said Sheriff's Detective Sgt. Donald Clark. "We've got a lot of people to talk to."

Witnesses to other elements of the crime were non-existent. Only 13 calls had been received on the newspaper hotline, a disappointing number. These reported suspicious cars (two of them abandoned) and suspicious men, but nothing that could be directly tied to the murder.

Carmen's funeral services were held on Monday, November 22, at 8:30 a.m. at Guillermina's home on Romeyn Street, and at 9:00 a.m. at Sts. Peter and Paul's Roman Catholic Church on Main Street West. Carmen was buried in Holy Sepulchre Cemetery. Approximately 200 persons attended the services.[28] The funeral Mass was said in Spanish.

Carmen's grandmother seemed in damage-control mode as she expressed her dislike of the neighborhood where Carmen lived, but they were poor and it was the best they could afford. She reiterated emphatically that Carmen walking alone the two blocks to the drug store was not a regular occurrence, that Carmen was seldom allowed to leave her grandparents' fenced-in front yard.

Carmen's murder reminded some officials of 12-year-old Mayran Hacenliyan, a child of a Turkish tailors who was raped and strangled in her Martin Street apartment home in Rochester on June 6, 1969 by a home invader who was waiting for a neighborhood porn theater to open.

Mayran was a seventh-grader at Benjamin Franklin High School and had been home alone that day waiting for a sewing machine to be delivered. The family had only been in the U.S. for nine months. John S. Kinne, 60 years old, had been released from Attica only three days earlier after serving three years for attempted incest. (He was arrested along with a son in his twenties regarding a series of incidents involving one of his daughters who was then 12. The incidents took place in Steuben County.) He was arrested three days after Mayran's murder, convicted, and sentenced to another 25 years.

Life went on in Carmen's neighborhood, but under a cloud of what the Rochester *Democrat and Chronicle (D&C)* called "silent fear."[29] The reporter, Sandy Flickner, spotted a six-year-old girl walking down Brown Street by herself. "Hi," she said as she passed. How could a parent let a girl that age go out alone after what happened? It was unfathomable.

The reporter visited Padilla's Market, Cruppe's Dry Cleaners, and Morrell's Cigar Store, and found that the mood was heavy in the neighborhood with suspicion allowed to fester because of the area's multi-lingual composition. People spoke Italian, Greek, Spanish, or English.

Ramon Padilla lived on Maple Street, had six children and recalled a time when a guy tried to get one of his daughters into his car. Was that the guy? The police kept an eye on her for five days, but the guy didn't try it again. But that was a while back, long before Carmen.

One woman admitted that she had called the police earlier in the week to report a man she had seen in a car talking to a little girl, but she didn't want to talk about it.

Morrell, the guy in the cigar store, said that police came in and showed him a bunch of photos, asked if any of them looked familiar. None did. Now, every time someone came in for a cigar, he tried to remember those photos. Was this guy one of them?

"It is the same reaction all over Bull's Head—everybody's looking, looking," Morrell said.

Douglas Murray, who lived on Carmen's block, said that he had lived in the neighborhood for 42 years and had seen it grow more dangerous. He'd taken to listening to a police radio at home to keep track of what was happening.

"All my grandchildren play in the backyard when they're here. I don't let them out. Never did. But there's more fear now," Murray said.

For two weeks, investigators focused their attention on Bull's Head. Detective Cerretto said, "We feel everything lies right here at Bull's Head. Somebody had to see something. We'll keep right on plugging, running everything down and hope the pieces tie together someday."[30]

For the portion of Monroe County outside the city of Rochester, the jurisdiction of the sheriff's office, Carmen's murder was the first unsolved homicide in five years, since the 1966 Genesee Junction murders.[31] Before that, the last unsolved case was the double homicide of Shari Smoyer and Jack King in Pittsford during the summer of 1963.

At first there was only a strong circumstantial case that it was Carmen who was seen running down the shoulder of the Western Expressway. The girl had looked like Carmen. She'd been described as naked from the waist down and the body was found in that condition.[32] The ID of Carmen as the girl running away became official on November 29 when Carmen's missing size-ten green pants were found.[33] Crumpled and frozen they were in a field in the town of Riga, 200 feet from the Western Expressway, near a barren rest area about a mile east of the Churchville exit.[34] The location was only "a few hundred feet" from the spot where motorists had seen Carmen. The finding also confirmed it was the killer's car that was seen backing up alongside Route 490 on the late afternoon of November 16.

Cerretto said that Carmen was apparently raped and killed near the expressway, most likely at a rest stop not far from the spot where Carmen had temporarily gotten away, a rest stop that had a reputation for illicit sexual activity. The killer then, Cerretto said, took her body to the dumpsite two miles away on the little-used Stearns Road.

There was much psychoanalysis of the motorist witnesses. *D&C* reporter Thom Akeman talked to University of Buffalo social psychologist Dr. Victor Harris, who said the commuters who passed Carmen may have been unaware of exactly what it was that they were seeing.

"There's a real question of whether, in fact, people even notice there's an emergency. They may see something going on. But an emergency is a rare occurrence to most people and they may not know how to cope with it," Dr. Harris explained.

After that, the case moved to the newspapers' back pages, with "news" limited to the growing numbers of "tips" being called in to various hot lines and the steadily growing reward money.

A letter to the editor in the *Times-Union* on November 30 by a former Rochesterian put words to a feeling had by many. The letter was entitled by the paper as "Girl's Death Shame of Rochester." The writer said she usually bragged about coming from Rochester but now her head was bowed in shame as she read of the dead little girl and the hundreds of Rochesterians who had an opportunity to save her and couldn't bother to take the time. She concluded, "I pray to God that your children and mine will never be in such need and encounter only those who refuse to help."[35]

Angel Luis Colon, Carmen's first cousin, and Justiano Colon, her biological father, wrote a letter to the *D&C* that ran on December 2. The letter thanked all of those who had sent money, and in an apparent attempt to ameliorate the family's public relations, "corrected" the comment in the November 28 issue of the paper that Carmen wasn't liked by some members of her family.

"The family loved her very much, especially her uncles and aunts," the letter read. "She was a nice little girl and respected everyone. She was always happy and was always smiling." More damage control. There would be no more mentions of screaming in the night.

On December 21, the Monroe County Sheriff's Office (MCSO) gave Carmen's case to three detectives. The Rochester Police Department (RPD) pulled the last of their detectives off the investigation.[36] The three remaining men would be retracing the steps of previous investigators.

Nary a word was ever heard from Guillermina.

In February 1972, the anti-porn, anti-abortion contingent known as Citizens for a Decent Community, put up five billboards in the approaches to the Bull's Head and Western Expressway sections of Rochester[37], where Carmen was abducted and seen trying to escape her abductor. These featured an eight-foot-high photo of Carmen Colon and read,

"...DO YOU KNOW
WHO KILLED CARMEN COLON?
PLEASE HELP BEFORE IT HAPPENS AGAIN
REWARDS for INFORMATION TOTAL $6,000.00
BE A **SECRET WITNESS**. NO CLUE IS TOO SMALL
PHONE: SECRET WITNESS LINE 436-2213
OR WRITE CITIZENS FOR A DECENT COMMUNITY
Box 9796 ROCHESTER N.Y. 14623
YOUR IDENTITY WILL BE KEPT **SECRET**"[38]

About the billboards, Macaluso said, "Out of all the means of communication, this was one of the few that hadn't been used to locate someone who may know something about the crime."

Macaluso noted that his organization, the CDC, did not have to rent the billboards. They had been donated for one month by the Rochester Outdoor Advertising Company.

Sheriff's Sgt. Nicholas DeRosa, on the case, since Day One, said the billboards had given the investigation a surge of new life. "We're getting calls and letters again," he said, and thanked the CDC.

"Who will be next?" said the Sibley's graffito.

"Before it happens again," said the billboards.

There were tiny indicators that this was, just maybe, the beginning of a series of events. When Kathy Bernhard and George-Ann Formicola were murdered in the town of Chili on June 25, 1966, no one asked who would be next. No one wrote "Stop me before I do it again." It was treated as an isolated incident—a one-off. But Carmen Colon's murder was something else. There was a feeling in the air that this was *start* of something.

In March, the Carmen Colon case received national coverage in a two-page photo story in *Life* magazine. The *Life* photographer came to Rochester and met with Macaluso, who said that the response to the billboards had been so tremendous that he was thinking of putting up billboards regarding other unsolved area homicides such as "the sex slaying of [George-Ann Formicola and Kathy Bernhard] in 1966."

"It's a shame that these things have to go unsolved, not because of poor police work, but because it is difficult to get people to come forward," Macaluso said.[39] He said it was his idea to put up the billboards.

In college, Macaluso worked at an outdoor advertising firm. "I saw [billboards'] effectiveness. I could see how they worked." The most important part of the billboard, he said, was the photo of Carmen smiling. "This town shouldn't sleep until her killer is caught."

In the middle of March 1972, District Attorney Jack B. Lazarus and two Sheriff's detectives (Clark and DeRosa) boarded a plane at the Rochester-Monroe County Airport and moved the front line of the Carmen Colon investigation to Puerto Rico.[40]

At first details were few, but it was known that a specific suspect was being targeted. We later learned that it was Carmen Colon's uncle, Miguel Colon, her mom's boyfriend, but at the time all we knew was that he was a man who'd lived in Rochester, had a long criminal record, and had only recently traveled to Puerto Rico.

The suspect was said to have left Rochester soon after the murder. The investigation of the suspect had taken investigators to New York City and Syracuse. One witness said that he had spoken with Miguel, and heard the uncle say that he needed to get away pronto because "he'd done something wrong in Rochester."

The new phase of the investigation was being conducted with the full cooperation of the San Juan police department. A five-man contingent arrived in Puerto Rico on the afternoon of March 15.

A San Juan reporter said the police team interviewed several persons, and that the target of the investigation was made known to investigators through a telephoned tip to Macaluso's CDC hotline from a New York City informant.[41] The informant had heard about the case in a Spanish-language newspaper sold in New York City. The team of investigators included District Attorney Lazarus, detectives Clark and DeRosa, a Spanish interpreter borrowed from Family Court named Emilio Serrano, and Thomas Lauricella, a stenographer from the D.A.'s office.

The Puerto Rican investigation hit a simple snag. They couldn't find their suspect.[42] He was, according to MCSO Investigator Patrick Crough, "hiding in the jungle."[43] It wasn't until two days later that the suspects "whereabouts were pinpointed."

Miguel Colon was said to have gone into hiding when it was reported in the San Juan newspaper that a team of investigators had traveled to the island in search of him.[44]

The suspect, however, had "not yet been found"—so a certain amount of semantics were involved in the optimistic report. The investigators were "moving in on him," and were now comfortable revealing details of the phone tip the CDC had received, that the suspect was reported to have said that he had done a "terrible thing" and mentioned Carmen Colon by name.

On March 22 it was reported that all of that pinpointing had been for naught, and that the suspect was now considered to be "armed and on the run."[45] The Rochester investigators blamed the *San Juan Star* for announcing their arrival, thus giving the suspect the heads-up that they were hot on his trail. The suspect, it was reported, had left his restaurant job without picking up his pay after reading that he was being sought. The trail went cold and after six days on the island the team returned to Rochester without their man.

The District Attorney blamed the media[46] for the failure: "We always seemed to be a day or two behind this individual," he said. "There is no question in my mind that the *San Juan Star* hindered our location of the individual. I feel we would have had him in custody Friday night if not for the article. The suspect didn't return to where he was staying Friday and didn't return to his job Friday night, even though he had five days' pay coming. The D.A. said the *Democrat and Chronicle* was also to blame because they had contacted the *San Juan Star* in an attempt to locate Lazarus, thus alerting the Puerto Rican English-language newspaper that a suspect in the case was being sought there.

The Rochester paper didn't take the accusation lightly. Stuart A. Dunham, executive editor of the *D&C*, said Lazarus should look in the mirror before he started doling out blame: "Apparently Mr. Lazarus knew of the presence of the suspect in Puerto Rico for several weeks. When he finally decided to lead a contingent to Puerto Rico, word of the trip leaked and became widely known in Rochester. In spite of a desire to cover the investigation in a normal way, the Rochester newspapers chose to refrain for two days from publishing news of Mr. Lazarus' trip. Finally, on Thursday, after Mr. Lazarus had arrived in Puerto Rico, the *D&C*, along with the radio and TV media, published the fact that the investigation had moved in that direction. Mr. Lazarus did not discuss publication of the story with the *D&C* editors nor was there ever any agreement between the district attorney's office and Gannett newspapers to withhold publication. Television reports to this effect were erroneous. We suspect that an attempt is being made here to blame the media unfairly for the failure of an investigation."

The *San Juan Star* also defended itself. Its managing editor said, "It would seem that Mr. Lazarus talks too much and, at the same time, not enough. He apparently let it become common knowledge in Rochester that he intended to go to Puerto Rico to seek the suspect in the Carmen Colon killing. Having thus alerted the Rochester news media of his impending trip, he failed to impress upon them the need for absolute secrecy in the case. Certainly he failed to impress upon the *San Juan Star* the need for secrecy—because he never talked to this newspaper, despite our repeated attempts to reach him. If we had been informed that the suspect's capture depended on non-publication of the story we would have been most happy to cooperate with the police. We have cooperated in similar cases many times in the past by refraining from publishing such news. We're afraid Mr. Lazarus has only himself to blame for the inept way the case was handled."

Just when it looked like the D.A. had botched it but good, the investigation caught a break. In fact, it caught what seemed at the time like *the* break. Still the subject of a manhunt by the FBI and Puerto Rican authorities, the suspect—who was said to have been in Puerto Rico since November 20, 1971, two days after Carmen's body was found—turned himself in during the early evening of March 26 to a police drug and narcotics unit in Guaynabo about six miles outside San Juan.

This happy accident read more like police subterfuge when it was revealed decades later that police had told Miguel that they had his mother (Carmen's grandmother) in custody and were going to keep her incarcerated until he turned himself in. The ploy worked like a charm.

The narcotics unit took the man to the detective division of the Commonwealth Police Department in San Juan. They learned when he first got to Puerto Rico back in November, he'd lived in the San Juan suburb of Puerta de Tierra, but during the time he was being sought, he moved to at least two other towns, Carolina and Guaynabo.

The MCSO was contacted by telephone. Detective DeRosa flew to San Juan, and took custody of the man. The suspect was promptly—and willingly—put on a plane and flown to Rochester, arriving at the airport at 9:00 p.m. on the evening of March 27.[47] He was taken to the sheriff's office in the Civic Center Plaza where interrogation began.

Imagine the falling faces as their number-one suspect not only didn't confess but also vigorously proclaimed his innocence. The first thing he did was make clear was that he had not been running away from anyone.

Why had he left his job without picking up his pay in Puerto Rico when he knew he was being sought?

He didn't know he was being sought, he said. He left to visit a sick aunt. When he learned he was being sought he turned himself in. Then he demanded a lie detector test,[48] which he passed.

Despite Uncle Miguel's denials, D.A. Jack Lazarus "felt strongly" that he was his niece's murderer. The only thing preventing Lazarus from prosecuting Miguel Colon was his belief that there wasn't enough evidence to secure a conviction.[49]

In June 1972, Carmen's grandparents and an aunt and uncle moved from their Brown Street home to a house on Grand Avenue, less than a block from Webster Avenue,[50] a neighborhood that would become very important later in our story.

Tips in the case dried up. By November of 1972, Detective Clark's optimism was audibly fading. He was saying things like, "With the help of God and a guilty conscience on the part of the murderer, we'll solve the case."[51]

The file on the case had swollen dramatically to fill four two-inch-thick volumes. Each volume held several hundred reports, mostly anonymous tips regarding possible sexual deviates.

Clark said, "This is probably the most difficult type of murder case to handle because there was no definite description of the car, no clues on the body to identify the perpetrator, no physical evidence of any type."

MCSO Detective Nicholas DeRosa was one of the men who traveled to Puerto Rico to look for Miguel Colon. Years later DeRosa said that he was "disappointed that they never threw it into the grand jury, to see if Colon would be indicted."

Almost 20 years later, a violent incident occurred that solidified for many Miguel Colon's status as premier suspect. At 12:45 p.m. on February 18, 1991, in their house on Radio Street in Rochester, Miguel Colon, now 43-years old, shot his wife Guillermina in the neck, arm, and hand. He also shot her younger brother Juan Melendez in the chest when he tried to intervene.[52] Melendez fell, hit his head, and also received a concussion. When policeman Clarence D. Fitch, a 20-year veteran of the RPD, responded to the shooting, Miguel stood in the doorway to his home and begged the cop to shoot him. When Fitch refused to do so, Uncle

Miguel placed his own gun to his head and killed himself. Miguel was apparently jealous and was having financial difficulties. Guillermina was taken to Rochester General and Juan to Strong Memorial Hospital. Both fully recovered. With Miguel dead, police talked to the Colon family and asked if Miguel had ever admitted killing Carmen. He reportedly had not. On the contrary, the family members all tried to impress on police how much they believed Miguel was innocent.[53] Some investigators however, like Crough, still believed that Miguel was Carmen's killer.

It was not until 1995 that Guillermina made a public statement regarding the murder of her daughter.[54] It took her 24 years. She told Jack Jones of the *D&C* that she had lived her entire life in poverty but if she could have only one thing before she died, it wouldn't be riches, but rather a solution to the mystery of who killed Carmen. She spoke in Spanish, her words translated for the reporter by her daughter Luz—the girl with the earache on that dark day. "I feel that I could die knowing who did this to my Carmencita. I could die more peacefully than I have lived. It is the only thing I want in my life, to know that this person had to pay for the terrible things he did to my little girl. That pain has not stopped. Carmen would be 34 this year. I still feel that pain of my daughter gone. If the person who did this could have any compassion, he would see the pain and the suffering that the families of these little girls have gone through for all this time. Maybe this person could have compassion or the guts to turn himself in, or at least write a letter."

In November 2001, the Discovery Channel produced a documentary about Carmen Colon's murder that was broadcast as part of their *Cold Case, New Evidence* series. The show came to the conclusion that her Uncle Miguel killed Carmen.

The show got itself into big trouble when, while discussing Carmen's uncle and his theoretic guilt, they showed a photo of the wrong Miguel Colon. The photo they showed was of a 67-year-old retiree, unrelated to this case. The photo used on TV was his 1967 pistol permit photograph, which had been turned over to the TV show by the MCSO who said they got it from the RPD. So there was plenty of blame to go around.

Colon, the man in the photo, sued for $15 million in damages.[55] He sued the City of Rochester, the RPD, the MCSO, Discovery

Channel, and Film Garden Entertainment, Inc.[56] The Honorable Andrew V. Siracuse, New York State Supreme Court, Monroe County, presided over the case.[57] The suit was dismissed by the trial court, which found that since the plaintiff's friends and acquaintances knew him to be alive, it would have been clear that the Miguel Colon referred to in the TV show was not he.

However, lawyers for Colon pointed out, it was the reaction of strangers that resulted in damages, those who didn't know Colon, but would now associate his face with the murder of a little girl.

The judge in the case wrote, "The allegation that the Miguel Colon in the photograph is the likely murderer of Carmen Colon is of course actionable, *per se*, and the Court hesitates to hold as a matter of law that the program could not be interpreted as so suggesting. This would appear to be a question of fact rather than of law." In appellate court, the defamation causes of action were dismissed.

Carmen's murder led the local newscasts for months. There followed a lull—1972 came and went and all little girls in Rochester were safe from sex killers. But come the spring of 1973, just as Mike Macaluso's billboard and the pencil-wielding Sibley's graffiti-artist had predicted, *it happened again.*

The Two-Fisted Redhead

On April 2, 1973[58], a rainy Monday, the day after trout-fishing season started, someone was driving the streets of Rochester's inner city fishing for little girls. That was the day when eleven-year-old Wanda Lee Walkowicz, a blue-eyed, orange-haired, freckle-faced special-education student at Rochester's School 8, disappeared while running an errand for her mother, the pretty redheaded widow, Mrs. Joyce Elaine Walkowicz.[59]

Wanda was born on August 4, 1961, stood four-foot seven-inches tall, and weighed 77 pounds. The family lived in an upstairs apartment in a brown clapboard house at 132 Avenue D in the Conkey Avenue neighborhood of Rochester's east side.

Folks had varying opinions of the job Joyce was doing as a mother. Some criticized her because she sometimes visited neighborhood taverns. Others lauded her because when she went to a bar she sometimes took her kids with her. Better than leaving them home alone to play with matches, was the thinking.

On the other hand, one neighbor described Joyce as being "drunk all the time." The same, it was said, was true of her live-in boyfriend "Junior."

Joyce came from a dysfunctional family, and now was doing her best to keep her own family functioning. It was an ongoing battle, made more difficult by the fact that she had no guidelines to go by.

Joyce's sister Joann remembered the heartbreak of their upbringing. Their mom, Wanda's grandmother, had been so heavily into alcohol and men that she lost the kids. Joyce and her sister were raised in a series of foster homes, sometimes together, but mostly separated. Joyce, in some unfortunate ways, took after their mom: she was wild as a kid with a reputation as a fun girl—but maybe one who lacked sufficient self-respect. To her credit, once Joyce wed, she settled down as a married woman and young mother. But she was widowed while still in her twenties, and her sobriety crumbled. She imitated her mom and enveloped herself in a carapace of booze and boys.

She returned to "her wild ways." There was "a parade" of men coming in and out of Joyce's home. Joann's impression was that many of them were nice guys, but that "Joyce treated them nasty."[60]

And what of little Wanda?

Aunt Joann said, "She was just a sweetheart, but because Joyce was the way she was, Wanda—more than other little girls her age—had many responsibilities in the home."

Although it was not uncommon to see Wanda outside playing when the weather was nice, on the rainy late afternoon of her disappearance, Wanda was worrying over a coloring book in her room when she heard that her mother needed groceries for dinner.

Wanda asked and was allowed to go by herself the three blocks to the Hillside Deli at the southwest corner of Avenue A and Conkey Avenue. She was wearing a blue-and-white dress, white socks and sneakers, and a red-and-green checked coat.

As was true in the Colon case, it was late afternoon, about five o'clock. Wanda encountered two friends on the street on the way there, and made it to the store without incident. She purchased $8.52 worth of groceries for that evening's dinner.

Several witnesses came forward to say they saw Wanda leave the deli with her bag. The girl and the bag seemed about the same size. Observing were the deli clerks, two male customers in the store, and a person on the street.

The deli clerks were William Van Orden and Richard Checchi. Van Orden bagged Wanda's groceries, everything into one bag so she could carry it home. Wanda, they recalled, had bounced into the deli as bright as day.

"She told me to hurry up because she was in a hurry," Van Orden said.

Van Orden remembered exactly what items Wanda had asked for because he wrote it down in a little book with the Walkowicz charge account. It contained dog food, cat food, tuna fish, two quarts of milk, bread, cupcakes, soup, and Pampers for Wanda's two-year-old half-sister Michelle.

Checchi said he also remembered the girl saying she was in a hurry. "She often says that," he commented. "I didn't think anything of it. Everything was normal."

Wanda carried with her a little brown charge book. Checchi wrote the eight-dollar-plus charge in her book and handed it back to her. Struggling a bit with the size of the bag she was carrying,

Wanda left the store and turned left, northward, toward home. Several people saw her struggling with her bag. When she was last seen, she was standing in front of a barbershop on Conkey, just north of Avenue B.[61]

There were three youngsters, playmates of Wanda, who saw Wanda bracing the bag against the school fence so she could get a better grip. They weren't sure, in fact they were pretty vague, but there might've been a brown car passing just then. They looked away, looked back, and she was gone.

* * *

About 90 minutes later, Wanda's ten-year-old sister Ruth Marie (pseudonym) came into the deli, accompanied by her friend and neighbor, twelve-year-old Francine Eiskamp, looking for Wanda. Ruth said tomorrow was her birthday, and bought more groceries. None of this struck the clerk as unusual as it was common for the girls to come in and do the shopping. When Joyce came in it was usually to pay the bill.

Ruth and Franciene also stopped at the houses of a couple of Wanda's friends to see if she was there.

Joyce first called the RPD at 7:47 p.m., but they said she should give a quick look around the neighborhood and call back. At 8:00 a distraught Joyce appeared at the deli to look for Wanda. She called the police a second time at 8:15, and this time they took Joyce's report. Police swooped in and within minutes a full search of the neighborhood was underway—but Wanda and all traces of her large bag of groceries were gone.

Police wondered: was the weather a factor? It had rained that evening, but had there been a sudden pentateuchal deluge as Wanda returned from the deli with her big bag? Perhaps she knew what rain did to a paper bag and was frantic for shelter. The theory didn't help that much if she got into a car, but if she ran into one of the houses she passed on her way home, this offered a finite set of possibilities that investigators could methodically cover.

There were investigators who didn't believe Wanda got into a car because it was daylight and the neighborhood was bustling such that someone would have seen her abduction—it was assumed that she would have struggled and drawn attention to herself if her abductor were a stranger—and as far as they could tell no one saw anything that registered alarm.

Investigators were almost certain that Wanda was not carrying any money on her, none changed hands in the deli, and she was an unlikely victim for a robbery anyway. She also was not considered a good candidate for running away.

There was a report in the press, printed once and never followed up on, that Secret Service agents had visited the apartment building where Wanda lived on the afternoon of her disappearance. The agents, the report said, were there to interview someone in another apartment, and while there reported hearing "a disturbance somewhere in the building."[62]

Police asked Joyce if she was aware that Wanda and a friend had been followed by a stranger on the previous Saturday night, 10:00 p.m., March 31, as the girls walked in the dark.

Joyce said she was aware of the stalking incident, and became so distraught at the memory and fear that Wanda was gone for good that she had to be treated for shock at Rochester General Hospital.[63]

Although it is hard to imagine, Joyce's shock may have been even worse but for the fact that she had neither heard of Carmen Colon nor her fate and had no idea that Wanda's disappearance was possibly a repeating pattern.

The stalking incident[64] now took on new significance. Wanda's friend's mom had filed a report with police on Saturday night. Police came but found no sign of the man.

The girls reported that they hadn't gotten a good look at his face because he hid behind a bush when they spotted him. The only detail that the girls noticed was that he had "a buckle on his shoe." The girls said that the man had chased them.[65]

The evening newspaper also reported the stalking incident, although the revised story changed the location. The morning paper said the girls had been walking along the railroad tracks that ran parallel to Conkey Avenue, returning from the Avenue D Recreation Center. The evening paper said that the man chased the girls along Avenue D. Both versions agreed that the man had jumped out of the bushes and had buckles on his shoes.[66]

On April 3, detectives canvassed the neighborhood, showing people along Conkey Avenue a photo of a known sex offender, described as having big ears and a big nose, and asking if anyone

The Double-Initial Murders

had seen him around. No one had.

Ten miles east of Conkey Avenue, at 10:15 a.m. on the morning of April 3, just west of the Irondequoit Bay Bridge, on a hillside next to a Route 104 access road in the town of Webster, State Trooper Thomas Zimmer spotted something white on the hillside and went to investigate.

The thing that caught his eye turned out to be Wanda's dress. Heartbreakingly, as he got closer he could see that she was in it. The small body was face down.

About 17 hours had passed since Wanda's disappearance. Of the double-initial victims, Wanda's remains were found the quickest. Indeed, her body was discovered before the press had an opportunity to report she was missing.

The exact location of the body, according to the RPD, was "on a hill 75 yards from Route 104 and about 25 feet from the rest area."[67] The body had been thrown over a railing and allowed to roll down an embankment.

Near Wanda's body crime-scene investigators found feces. The stool was analyzed at the crime lab, verified as human and found to contain Seconal, a barbiturate that was popularly taken in pill form ("reds") as a recreational drug during the 1970s. This fact was not made public.[68]

Monroe County Medical Examiner Dr. John F. Edland performed the autopsy and verified that the girl had been raped and strangled, "possibly with a belt."

Dr. Edland discovered custard in the girl's stomach, but it was mystery where she had gotten it. She hadn't gotten it from home and the assumption was that her killer must have given her the food.

The surgeon said that the girl's clothes were found intact: "I imagine she was raped and killed somewhere else and the killer then put her clothes back on. It looks like she was tossed out of the car as the killer drove by."

Wanda had been strangled from behind, while Carmen Colon had been strangled face-to-face. This represented a significant difference. Either there were two killers or one with a split personality.

He added that there were marks on the neck and elsewhere on the body indicating that there had been a struggle. "She was such a tiny little thing. I don't think she was capable of putting up much of a struggle."[69]

On the day Wanda's body was discovered, the *D&C* announced a special "Secret Witness" line and a $2,500 reward fund established by Gannett Newspapers. They gave the number to call and noted that the line was not attached to the newspaper's switchboard. Callers would not necessarily have to identify themselves. There was also an address given for those who preferred to give their tips by mail. Callers would be assigned a six-digit number. Writers were instructed to include any six-digit number in their own handwriting in the upper right-hand corner of their letter.

A second address was given for those who wanted to contribute to the Wanda fund: c/o John Pratt, Central Trust Company, 45 Exchange St., Rochester.[70]

The paper asked neighbors about the little redhead. Chuck Stechma, who worked at the Avenue D Playground-Recreation Center ("just on the other side of the railroad tracks") told reporter Bill O'Brien that even though Wanda was smaller and perhaps younger than some of her friends, she was a leader. He knew Wanda, her mother Joyce, and Joyce's boyfriend "Junior." The adults had been Stechma's drinking buddies at a local saloon called Shenanigans Tavern, which had since closed. Stechma was asked when he had last seen Wanda and he had to admit it had been a while, maybe not since Christmas when they came in to see Santa Claus at the rec center. During the summer, though, he'd seen her almost every day. "She was a happy little girl. Very smart. Mature. And athletic. She played kickball—all the games where she could run a lot. She was the kind of little girl you just wanted to be around and see her when she grew up."

"She was a scrapper, a tough little redhead," said State Police Investigator Harry S. Crosier. "She'd take on 12- or 13-year-old boys in fights at school and beat the hell out of them."

One of the first suspects questioned was an old man who in 1971, according to Junior, had offered Wanda and a friend a "dime for kisses."[71] The man was advised by authorities to try to be less creepy.

Although Wanda was considered a bright child, her life was marred by chaos. Dad died at age 30, mom was on welfare. Visitors to her apartment described it as "worn."

O'Brien talked to another rec center worker, Bernie Conversi, who said that, although he couldn't be absolutely sure, he thought he saw someone who looked like Wanda at about 7:00 p.m. on Monday night. O'Brien thought it unlikely.

Hillside Deli clerk, Richard Checchi, wasn't afraid of bold conclusions. He said Wanda came into the deli almost every night and sometime twice after school. "She seemed like a fairly intelligent girl and not the type to get into a car with any stranger," Checchi said.

The reporter talked to Virginia Soules, Wanda's aunt (sister of Wanda's dad). "We were afraid something like this would happen," Aunt Virginia said. She didn't explain what she meant by this. Because it was a bad neighborhood? Because Wanda was frequently unsupervised? Because Wanda had been stalked 48 hours before she disappeared? If it was a concern, why allow her to walk around by herself? Questions unasked and unanswered.

What Aunt Virginia did say was that she had warned the girls not to go out at night. She'd warned them not to go by the railroad tracks. When sister-in-law Joyce needed to be hospitalized, Wanda's sister Ruth came to stay with Virginia.

Virginia's sister Susan Walkowicz worked at Kodak. She didn't speak with reporters but co-workers recalled her coming to work with swollen eyes from crying.

The reporter followed up on the notion that there were concerns about safety in the neighborhood. Wanda's friend Franciene Eiskamp, the same little girl who had accompanied Ruth Marie on the initial search for Wanda, said that she and Wanda had gone to Maplewood Park on the Sunday before she disappeared, the day after the stalking incident, but she personally would never go by the railroad tracks.

Another neighbor said that she didn't allow her kids to go out alone anymore, that she tried to keep her kids in front of the house where she could keep her eyes on them.

The neighborhood had gone downhill, said Henry J. Pape, who had a business next to the playground. The area was once elegant but now the stretch from the railroad tracks to St. Paul Street had deteriorated. The large two-story homes had been divided into apartments and occupied by transients.

Edward DuPlessi of Avenue D said he remembered Wanda and

Ruth very fondly. They used to make money by cleaning his house and he never had to worry about them touching things. They were good girls.

Captain Andrew Sparacino noted that the similarities in the murders of Carmen Colon and Wanda Walkowicz were obvious: age of the victims, alone on the street, week day, after school, performing errands for their mothers. He didn't mention anything about initials.

On the other side of the family, Aunt Joann Spock was both sad and angry. Angry because police never talked to her or her husband—she lived only a little more than a mile away from Joyce, on Mark Street. But she and her husband weren't considered worthy of a police interview—and because of that she'd had to learn that Wanda was dead from watching the TV news.

Joann's son John, Wanda's first cousin, was ten at the time, but remembered being pulled out of school to "help the family search the woods," although he couldn't recall which woods they were. He remembered Wanda being a quiet kid and very observant. "She would stay outside the group and watch." As for his Aunt Joyce, after Wanda's death she "was never the same. It completely destroyed her inside."

Aunt Joann did give one of the first newspaper interviews after Wanda's body was found. Today she doesn't remember what she said, but she was quoted in the *Times-Union* as noting it was Ruth's birthday, that Wanda's father was dead, that Wanda had a sister who was two and named Michelle, that Wanda was a normal little girl who enjoyed being helpful for her mother, and that *she loved animals*.

The same reporter spoke with Wanda's grandmother, Lena Chatterton of Mark Street, the woman who'd lost her children due to alcohol and men. She said that Wanda was "quite interested in just about everything." It is unknown how well Rena knew her grandchildren.

Wanda attended a special class (non-graded) at school 8, where one of her teachers was Joseph Hillmon. He described her as "a real good student, well-liked by her classmates. She was a shy type girl, but not to the extent that she couldn't make friends easily."

What did he mean by "shy"?

"She wasn't the first to volunteer answers to questions but she would respond when asked. When there was an oral report to be given, she always wanted to go last," he said. "She is an avid student and does a lot of independent type work because her class is ungraded."

In his last written comments in Wanda's permanent record, Mr. Hilmon wrote, "Wanda is a steady, diligent worker. She completes most assignments. Her work is always neat." He had given her two plusses for "outstanding behavior."

Truancy was an issue, he admitted. In the past 181-day school year—when she attended School 22, which was then on Zimbrich Street—Wanda had been absent 54 days. The teacher was asked if she had a health problem and he said he felt the problem was that "she had a lot of responsibilities at home."

He offered a synopsis of the things Wanda was learning in her last week. She had a list of spelling words she was struggling with, but was having better luck learning how to start sentences with clauses for who, when, and where.

In social studies the children were learning about Mexico. In science, she was learning about insects, how they grew and the names of their various body parts.

Mary Gras, Wanda's math teacher, said that Wanda was likeable, capable, and conscientious when it came to doing her work.

Why, then, was Wanda in special class?

It was Gras's understanding that Wanda was a slow reader, and that was why she was in the ungraded class. Today we might recognize this as a kid with dyslexia, but those were different times.

Another factor, no doubt, was all of the school she missed. She had been unable to keep up with her class and had moved to a special class in a new school *much* closer to home.

By the morning of April 5, city, county, and state police were working around the clock. As RPD Lieutenant Anthony Fantigrossi put it, they were "establishing the link between the victim and the killer."

Fantigrossi and Sparacino headed up the investigation for the city, and Captain Richard Boland for the state police.[72] The case was frustrating: As far as they could tell, no one saw Wanda get into a car, and no one saw her between her disappearance and when her body was dumped in Webster. The investigation had to this point focused on Wanda's neighbors and known sex offenders. All were asked to provide an alibi.

During the first 24 hours of the city newspaper's secret-witness phone line, 72 calls were received, mostly describing vehicles seen in the vicinity of the Hillside Deli when Wanda was last seen, and incidents involving other neighborhood children.

Speculation was rampant. What was the monster like? Was he a sturdy man who would appear normal, even superior, unless caught in the act? Or was he someone shadowy and inchoate, a specter, clearly incomplete and inadequate?

People liked to believe that they could tell a monster if they saw one, but history tells us that monsters, like wolves in sheep's clothing, are not what they seem. They can offer a seamless imitation of humanity.

The CDC was back. On Thursday, the *D&C* offered a new method for potential witnesses to input their information, listing the phone number and post office box number for Michael Macaluso's Citizens for a Decent Community hotline, which had established its own $1,000 reward.[73] Each lead would be checked out thoroughly no matter how inconsequential it might seem. That had to be the case—although authorities were aware they were giving countless spiteful citizens an open invitation to harass their enemies.

Some tips were interesting, however. One said that on Saturday night at the corner of Driving Park Avenue and Archer Street (just on the other side of the Genesee River from Wanda's neighborhood) a man in a 1971 Ford LTD tried to lure two ten-year-old girls into his car. The man was described as about 30 years old, five feet ten inches tall, and wearing a long black coat. He had a black beard and a mole on his forehead. The car was described as having a black top and a white bottom.

Police questioned a friend of the Walkowicz family who'd played cards with Wanda for a few hours on Sunday night at her home. Someone in the Walkowicz apartment, possibly Junior, reported the man, but it turned out he had a "solid" alibi.

On Wednesday, roadblocks were set up on Conkey Avenue, and drivers were asked if they normally drove through the neighborhood, and if so, had they seen anything unusual at the time of Wanda's disappearance. Special interest was given to any car that turned to evade the roadblock.

There was brief interest in a tip from a grocery store stock boy, miles from Conkey Avenue, who said "a weird looking man" in his mid-twenties came into the store and asked for directions to Route 104, near to which Wanda's body was found.

Asked directly if they thought there was a link between the murders of Carmen and Wanda, police said no.[74] But, just in case one did develop, Sheriff's Sergeant Donald Clark, who had been assigned to the Colon case, was put on the Walkowicz team.

Sgt. Clark said that the Colon investigation was still wide open, although generally inactive after 18 months. There had been a new lead only a few weeks earlier, a young man in California arrested for a similar rape-murder of a little girl. "We were notified because when the police arrested him they found a newspaper clipping of the Carmen Colon case in his wallet. But he wasn't our man because it was proved beyond a shadow of a doubt that he was in the service and stationed in Vietnam at the time of the murder. There's been nothing since then," Sgt. Clark said.

It was raining again in Rochester and the forecast for the next day wasn't good. Despite this, a police photographer went up in a helicopter and took aerial photos of the areas between the Conkey Avenue neighborhood and the dumpsite in Webster.

The idea was to determine the most probable path taken to get from one location to the other, and to determine where in between the rape and murder might have taken place. Because of the weather, the photos didn't come out well, and plans were made to make another attempt at a future date. In the meantime, looking at a map would have to do.

In that Wednesday afternoon's paper, a forensic psychiatrist offered his analysis of the killer, based on the little that was known about his behavior. He was a pedophile, drove a car, and had at least some weekday afternoons free. He had some knowledge of the road map both in the city and the county.

Dr. David Barry of the University of Rochester said the killer might "tend to be a loner with considerable difficulties establishing sexual or personal relationships with adults. The need for human contact with someone who won't rebuff them will impel them initially to approach a youngster. Girls in their pre-teens are very appealing, because they're unguarded, not cynical, and very pleasant."[75] Of course, things get out of hand rapidly, and then there was a situation that the guy needed to control. These men, Dr. Barry said, often had mental handicaps and poor social skills. "They don't react appropriately to the kinds of cues we're always receiving in social situations. They have an inability to back off, to know what goes and what doesn't go in the situation. They see the initial acceptance from the victim and that's all they see. They build it up in their minds to total acceptance." The next thing they know, they'd raped a child and that realization was "a psychological catastrophe for the man who does it. Because he is still thinking on a primitive level, he may think only of doing away with the evidence so no one will ever know what he's done." Such crimes, he said, were usually impulsive and came about when the urge coincided with an opportunity. He said that the killer would most likely have a history of "showing sexual interest in young girls."

When the urge coincided with the opportunity. Remember Dr. Barry's name. He would soon become very important to our story.

By Thursday night, police said they had narrowed the investigation to "a few promising leads."[76] Still, they had no suspects. They were leaning toward the theory that Wanda knew her killer, but this was largely based on the common feeling among those who knew her that she was too smart to get into a car with a stranger.

But what if, some said, the man grabbed the bag of groceries away from Wanda? What if somehow the man had convinced her it was a bad idea to scream her lungs out?

She would have known that she was physically unable to get the groceries back and would be forced to abandon the groceries in order to get away from him. She might follow him and do as she was told. He could take her to his car, put the groceries in his trunk. What would she do then?

Sparacino also pointed out, "If she were being forced into a car with a bag of groceries in her hand, I can't see how some of the groceries didn't fall on the street in the struggle and no one saw anything. The sex pervert does not plan that much ahead. He has an immediate need that must be satisfied. The fact that the girl had to walk by her school is important because schools tend to draw these kinds of people. We've eliminated many, many people but the trail is by no means cold." Somewhat nonsensically but desperately optimistic, he added, "The momentum is just beginning because the bulk of the work is out of the way."

Investigators went into Jimmy's Tavern on Conkey between A and B, looking for witnesses. Beggars couldn't be choosers and in real life sometimes the best witnesses have had a snootful. Sure enough, they ran into one of their best witnesses yet.

She may have been rosy-cheeked with drink, but she knew what she saw: she saw Wanda emerge from the deli, struggling with the bag and walking from left to right, passing right by on the other side of the two-lane street.

Wanda was a block and a half to her right and walking away when the witness stopped watching her. Investigators now concentrated on the occupants of those homes north of where the bar witness saw Wanda last.

Although the investigation concentrated on Conkey Avenue, there were 50 detectives working, and they scoured the northeast side of the city, knocking on doors and asking questions. Men who were interrogated after Carmen Colon's murder were hauled in and questioned again.

Police received a tip that a black and yellow car was seen at 6:00 p.m. on Monday on Harris Street near Avenue A. That would be one block west of where Wanda was last seen.

This witness saw a little girl getting into or leaving the car. Police said it was unlikely that the car was connected with Wanda's murder. The incident wasn't on the route the girl would have used to walk home. (This sighting might have been of Wanda's friend Linda, who lived on Harris street and also had red hair.)

A mom on Avenue D called the police and reported that a man had offered money to her eleven-year-old daughter. All she had to do was go for a ride with him. The girl was taken to a police station and asked to look at mug shots of sex offenders to see if any looked familiar. None did.[77]

Police were looking forward to interviewing Joyce Walkowicz, who was still too tranquilized to talk. Stories of the "parade of men" going through Joyce's house must have made the investigators anxious.

Several men of interest were brought in for questioning, including one who seemed especially promising, having just gotten out of prison for sexually attacking a young girl, but he had an alibi that checked out.

Michael Macaluso's CDC acquired another billboard, this one with Wanda's photo on it. Carmen's murder *had* been the start of something and the CDC predicted it on their first billboard, a premonition, apparently, worthy of the lead.

Wanda's billboard read:

> It Happened Again!
> WHO KILLED WANDA WALKOWICZ
> REWARDS for INFORMATION TOTAL $10,000.00
> SECRET WITNESS — NO CLUE IS TOO SMALL
> SECRET WITNESS LINE: 436-2213
> WRITE CITIZENS FOR A DECENT COMMUNITY
> PO BOX 9796 ROCHESTER N.Y. 14623
> YOUR IDENTITY WILL BE KEPT SECRET

By Friday, April 6, more than 200 leads had been called in to the newspaper secret-witness line. One of them in particular had gotten the investigators' attention. The anonymous caller claimed to have seen a white man of medium height forcing a red-haired girl into a light-colored Dodge Dart at Avenue D and Conkey Avenue between 5:30 and 6:00 on Monday evening. The man, the caller said, was armed with a sharp instrument, possibly a knife.[78] Despite pleas in the papers, the "witness" never called back.

The info was made more intriguing by the fact that a second caller, with no known connection to the first, described a similar car near the Webster dumpsite. In response to the calls, the sheriff's office, the RPD, and Webster and Irondequoit police all issued a be-on-the-lookout for a light-colored Dodge Dart wanted in connection with the murder.

Det. Lt. Fantigrossi admitted that he didn't think anyone saw Wanda's abduction. The reason was the crime was "too hideous. It makes everyone's blood run cold. I can't believe anyone would cover up for someone like this."

Police complained that too many of the phone "tips" were not tips at all but uninformed theories. Actual information was being coordinated between law enforcement agencies by a "command post" located behind Spacacino's office on the fourth floor of the Public Safety Building. On the walls of the command post were aerial photos of the known crime scenes and surrounding areas, as well as an over-sized map depicting the route Wanda took on the evening of her disappearance.

The Friday morning newspaper contained Wanda's obituary. She was survived by her mother, Mrs. Joyce Walkowicz; two sisters, Ruth Marie and Michele; her paternal grandmother, Mrs. Carl (Wanda) Kabelac; her maternal grandmother, Mrs. Lee Chatterton; aunts, uncles, and cousins.

Friends of the family were invited to call at the Richard L. Ferleski Funeral Home on Hudson Ave. A prayer service would be held Friday morning April 6, 1973 at 8:30 followed by Mass of the Resurrection at 9 o'clock at St. Michael's Church on North Clinton Avenue. Interment would be at Holy Sepulchre Cemetery."

Funeral rites for Wanda were observed on April 6, 1973 under a soaking rain. At the mass in the lofty Gothic church, church pastor Rev. Benedict Ehmann said, referring to the rain, "It's as if nature herself is in sympathy with what has been done to our little child."

Wanda's casket was heartbreakingly small, white and gold and sprinkled with flowers.[79] Joyce and Ruth led the mourners. They had their arms wrapped around each other as they followed the casket in and out of the church. Joyce could be seen whispering to her daughter and both fought to hold back tears.

At the mass, the reading was from Lamentations: "Widows and strangers they slay and they say the Lord sees not…"

Father Ehmann added, "But we know our little friend is with God. She has returned to her Heavenly Father and to her earthly father. She has left her mother to go to her father."

With that Joyce broke down and sobbed loudly.

The priest continued: "She was the Temple of the Holy Spirit and that temple was violated. We pray that the yoke of fear be lifted from our neighborhood. We pray that the courts deal swiftly and effectively with justice and that the criminal and pervert turn from their ways and be cured."

In attendance at the mass, sitting in the front pew, were 25 of

Wanda's classmates from School 8. Hanging from the pulpit was a hand-made paper-and-burlap Lenten sign that read, "Penance is Love."

The St. Bernard's Seminary Choir sang, "Around and Around," "Gelineau Psalms," "I am the Bread of Life," and concluded with "Amazing Grace." The procession from the church to the cemetery featured the hearse and approximately 25 other cars carrying about a hundred people.

As that was going on, Sparacino and Boland were telling the *D&C* that "things are looking a lot brighter," although it was difficult to fathom what they could have meant, as they followed up that optimism by pointing out that despite "promising leads" they were no closer to finding a suspect.

That, Sparacino explained, was why they were partaking in activities that could potentially produce their own leads, such as setting up roadblocks.

Investigators had been given a composite drawing of a suspect, but Boland refused to tell reporter David Medina from which witness's information the composite was derived. "What drawing?" was Boland's only comment.

What *was* known was that the drawing had been prepared by Sgt. Robert Tacito on Friday morning, and had been compared with composite drawings that had been used on the Carmen Colon investigation. None of these composites, if they existed, were ever released to the public.

There was a rumor going around that a witness who claimed to have seen Wanda's body being dumped in Webster was being questioned by authorities, but Sparacino and Boland denied that this was true.[80]

Getting back to the generic optimism, the leaders of the investigation jotted down the home phone numbers of reporters covering the story, just in case they needed to be notified about an arrest over the weekend.

By Sunday morning, almost a week after Wanda's murder, all optimism had dissolved.[81] It was revealed for the first time that a suspect had been taken into custody on Friday and interrogated for ten hours, through Saturday.

Police thought they had their man, until the suspect offered them "a solid alibi" and passed a lie-detector test. The man was, however, charged with endangering the welfare of a child regarding a 1972 incident unrelated to Wanda's murder.

Sparacino was philosophical: "When it's not the guy, it's just not the guy. There's not too much more we can do in that direction." Unfortunately, he revealed, that had been the "only real lead" in the case. Now they were back to square one. There was nothing to do but regroup and start in again. "All of the fellows will have to get together early Monday and rehash things. Sometimes the second time around you pick up something you missed before."

A reporter asked, "What about the report involving the light-colored Dodge Dart and the armed man who was seen struggling with a red-headed girl?"

Sparacino said, "That report appears to be without basis."

Repeated attempts to get that tipster to call back with further details were in vain.

"Did the bad weather have an effect?"

Sparacino said, "Yes, problematic. If it had been a clear day, there might have been a better chance that someone would have seen something. It's hard to believe that at that time of day someone could have forced her into a car without anyone seeing."

Over the weekend, Joyce Walkowicz consented to an interview with the newspaper and spoke to reporter Chuck Freadhoff.[82] Forty-eight hours had passed since Wanda's funeral. Joyce was dry-eyed and sedate.

The interview was predictably heartbreaking. Joyce was eager to show off Wanda's final report card, which was her best ever. "I'm going to frame it," Joyce said. "She was excellent in spelling. Just the other day she was reading a science book and said, 'Mommy, I feel like doing an experiment.' She liked math and loved art. She always wanted to be a leader. She always had to be the little boss. She'd fight with anyone; she'd beat anybody up. She was very mature for her age. She would go out and buy her clothes. She'd do little things around the house to earn money. Each cleaning job was worth so much money and she was earning about $11 a month. The place was spotless. She was more grown-up than I really realized. She was fussy about the way she looked, always fixing her hair. She wasn't prejudiced. It didn't matter to her what color her friends were."

Joyce said that she couldn't stand to stay in the neighborhood now that Wanda was gone.

"I want to move away from here. I can't even go to that store. I have to worry about my other daughter. She can't go anyplace and play. I know it could happen in any neighborhood, but if Ruth is going out, she's not going alone. She's not going to the store alone."

After a pause she continued, "The memories...just to look down the street and know...If I get the money together I'll move soon. She wouldn't have accepted a ride with anyone she didn't know. A friend of ours, who she knew, offered her a ride once, when it was raining and she refused. She just wouldn't get in the car. Maybe somehow she passed a house, and someone...I mean if the grocery bag was breaking...I don't know. I can't figure it out. Maybe because it was raining. If it was a stranger she wouldn't have gone into their house...unless maybe a lady. She wouldn't have gotten in a car unless she was forced. But there was the custard. She couldn't have eaten with a stranger. She was a nervous girl and would have gotten a stomachache. She couldn't have eaten it. She didn't get it here and she didn't buy any. I don't know..."

Wanda's neighborhood was on a nervous edge. All strangers were suspicious. There was a killer among them. It could be anyone.[83] Police noticed the difference. A call or two per day reporting suspicious activity was normal for the neighborhood, but since the murder that number had increased to more than a dozen per day.

On Sunday night an elderly man walked into a store to buy something and winked at a little girl. The clerk called the police.

Wanda's neighborhood, which didn't have a name, was considered to be bordered by Norton Street to the north, St. Paul St. to the west, Clifford Avenue to the south and North Clinton Avenue to the east. It was a largely residential area, with the strip of shops along Conkey Avenue, where Wanda was last seen, being the hub of commercial activity.

Police received a tip that someone in a brown car had abducted a red-haired girl in the vicinity of Conkey Avenue. Nothing further came of this. There had been published reports of a brown car immediately following the abduction. The caller offered no new detail.

Though it wasn't heavily reported, Wanda's murder was the second unsolved homicide in that area in six months. The other victim was 60-year-old Jose Bas, shot in the face during a holdup of his store on Conkey Ave. across the street from School 8, about 50 feet from where Wanda was last seen. People stopped going to that store after the murder, and had just started to come back when Wanda disappeared. Bas's son, who took over the store, was like Joyce Walkowicz looking to get out.

A new week began and the investigation bogged down. Everyone with a lead to share had already reported it. There was no news.[84] Investigators were resorting to re-checking old leads, just to make certain nothing had been overlooked. That was it for the daily coverage in the newspaper. Like the Carmen Colon case, the trail gradually revealed itself to be cold all along.

Two weeks after Wanda's murder, a gas-station attendant contacted police and said he'd seen a crying girl trying to get out of a green Pinto hatchback. The driver was a fortyish man with a tattoo on his right forearm. Police put a plea in the papers. If that was you in that Pinto, and you are innocent, give us a call and an explanation and we'll cross you off our to-do list. No one called.

The case was next mentioned in the D&C on April 20, and then in an article about something else. It was an interview with CDC head-honcho and billboard master Michael Macaluso. The interview was not about the murders, however, but rather about Macaluso's other favorite subject: pornography.[85]

It was Macaluso's contention that the popularity and availability of porn was causing the murders of little girls in the Rochester area. He made it clear that he was against the showing of all X-Rated movies, such as "Last Tango in Paris" and "The Devil in Miss Jones," which were then showing in local theaters, but R-rated movies as well.

Macaluso said, "Each film has something new and different. They are escalating."

A recent anti-dirty-movie meeting drew only a dozen supporters, which must have been a disappointment. Macaluso said that local disc jockeys were "dragged" into promoting dirty movies by playing their theme songs on air.[86] The CDC had another target, however, and that was the newspapers that ran explicit ads for the movies, papers like the D&C, and were planning a campaign to "persuade newspapers to change their policy."

"If Gannett [the D&C's parent company] is going to persist, we're going to see more Carmen Colons and Wanda Walkowiczes. You've read the advertising movie copy. It's designed to appeal to the curiosity," Macaluso said.

CDC supporters said at the meeting that they blamed a "corrupting influence" that had crept into classrooms, and "the loss of leadership from the church." The CDC briefed the supporters on their continuing efforts to find Wanda Walkowicz's killer and announced plans to support an anti-porn bill before the State legislature.

In June, a plan to build a low-income housing project in Wanda's neighborhood was slammed because it would "increase fear" on those streets. Because it was the area where Wanda disappeared, elderly persons were "afraid to walk the streets at night."[87]

In July, the paper ran a front-page follow-up feature on Joyce Walkowicz, where it shared space with the growing Watergate scandal. How had the mom been getting along in the weeks since her daughter's murder?[88] Mostly what Joyce had been doing was chain-smoking. She was up to three packs a day.

"It's hard for it to be like before," she said. She'd lost twelve pounds since the murder, unable to eat, and she took pills to get to sleep at night. She was afraid to sleep, because sleep brought nightmares that had her waking up screaming.

"It haunts me, even at the strangest times. I'll be watching TV and it'll pop into my head. I'll see him *doing it* to her. I'll try to picture him strangling her. I'm suspicious of everyone now. The autopsy showed she died two hours after her last meal. I know Wanda. She could not eat if she was upset. She had a nervous stomach. If she knew her killer, I'm sure I know him, too. Whenever I walk down Avenue D, I look at the men and wonder, could it be him? Could it be him? Even with my friends I am suspicious. I look at them and wonder. It turns my stomach to think he could have passed by my house and looked me square in the face."

She shifted gears to thank everyone who had been so helpful in her time of need, to emphasize that the most important thing was for her to take care of Wanda's sisters, and to do that she would need to find a job. At the moment they were living on the $376 a month she was supposed to receive in child-support from her husband's social security benefits. Wanda's death, however, caused a mix up at the social security office.

"I can't be sure I'll receive any money at all. At one point I had to apply for emergency welfare funds."

She said that job-hunting was complicated by the fact that people recognized her name. Once employers figured out who she was, they questioned if she was "emotionally ready" to work.

Joyce told her interviewer that she was used to life's hard knocks, that she had been "the black sheep of her family," that her parents had divorced when she was a baby and that she and her siblings were shuttled between foster homes, so many she'd lost count of them.

She remembered one family however, one that had refused to take her in after they had a look at her. "I was too fat, they said." For a time she lived at the Hillside Children's Center and once planned to run away to New York City but she didn't get very far. A night watchman caught her climbing down the fire escape.

She met Wanda's father, Richard F. Walkowicz, when she was 19, but he died in 1967. During his life, Wanda's dad had made the newspapers a handful of times, first when he was eleven and cut himself on barbed wire when trying to sneak into Red Wing Stadium on Norton Street for an exhibition game between the Wings and the Baltimore Orioles, and again when he was 21 (January 1959) when he and a friend Raymond L. Pratt, were caught stealing radiators from the Veterans Auto Parts lot on Lee Road in Gates. In 1959, he lived on Weyl Street, in the home of his mother, Mrs. Wanda McManus. He appeared on the society page when he became engaged to Miss Joyce Chatterton, daughter of Mr. and Mrs. Edward Neubauer of Ariel Park (only about 200 yards southwest of Conkey and Avenue A) in May 1959. They originally planned an August wedding, but that was moved up to early March.

Richard and Joyce were photographed together on Leap Year Day 1960 as they applied for a marriage license, a cute photo in which an eager Joyce tugged a seemingly reluctant Richard through a door marked "Marriage License." The newspaper noted in its caption that Richard's apparent reluctance was put on for the photographer's benefit.

Since Richard's death, for Joyce then there had been affairs, an abortion, and another baby to feed.

To rub salt in the wound, three months after Wanda's murder, Joyce's boyfriend "Junior" left her.[89]

Five days after the Joyce Walkowicz interview, Michael Macaluso put the case back in the headlines. He announced that, in addition to the billboard already up, the CDC was postering utility poles and store windows all around Wanda's neighborhood, and that the posters would be bi-lingual.[90]

Macaluso said, "We feel there may be someone in the Spanish-speaking community who has information about Wanda but doesn't read the newspapers or watch television and isn't aware of the reward fund." That fund was up to $10,000.

The posters asked, "Did you see anything which might be a clue? Did you see a girl carrying a shopping bag the afternoon of April 2?"

In September, Rochester TV station WOKR, Channel 13, announced production of a police case documentary series (the true-crime genre didn't yet exist), focusing on local unsolved cases. Each show would feature a filmed re-enactment of the crime, followed by a panel of officials, the district attorney and police investigators, discussing the crime, and soliciting phone calls from potential witnesses who might be watching.[91]

Newsman Andy Anderson would host the show and producer Alvin White would also function as the reporter taking viewers on a tour of the crime scene. The first 30-minute episode, to be shown at 10:30 p.m. on Sunday, October 21, would focus on Wanda's murder. The show was subsequently entitled "Eyewitness Crime".[92]

In Wanda's episode, news footage was used to show the recovery of her body and scenes of her funeral. Displayed for viewers who might have been witnesses, were the items in Wanda's grocery bag (in hopes that someone might have found them and not realized their significance), and the plaid coat Wanda had worn when abducted. Viewers were asked to call in on a hot line number, their anonymity guaranteed. The plea for info was broadcasted in English, Spanish, and in sign language for the deaf. WOKR station manager and weatherman Jerry Carr (who doubled as Chiller, host of

Chiller Theater, the weekly monster movie show) said the idea for the show came from an article in the *New York Times* discussing a similar program in Germany. The program resulted in 200 phone calls,[93] but no useful leads.

Fear grew to panic on November 26, 1973[94] when a third little girl vanished, this time in the Marketview section of Rochester.[95]

The Friendless Girl

It was a dark Monday afternoon after school, November 26, 1973, three days after Thanksgiving. As ten-year-old Michelle Maenza was walking home from school all by herself, she was stolen away.[96] But this time was different. There were *witnesses*. First and foremost among those who saw Michelle's abduction was another young child who was quickly overwhelmed by the implications of what she'd seen. She knew Michelle and she saw Michelle in the car. She saw the man's face, and the man was a very bad man. We're calling that young witness Cynthia Nicoletti.

But let's first take a look at poor Michelle, who was chubby and slow and lived on a crooked little dead-end street called Webster Crescent. At home for Michelle things were good. True, she lived in a broken home. Dad lived on Hall Street, about a mile away. Mom Carolyn had custody of Michelle and her two sisters, eight-year-old Marie, and Christine, who was an infant. Dad Christopher took the couple's two sons, Angel, 14, and Stephen, 13.[97] The house was a whole bunch emptier and quieter than it used to be.

But it was safe. The tight cul-de-sac of Webster Crescent was an enclave of security, a private place for Michelle, a small sanctuary in a big painful world.

Michelle had been a special-education pupil at School 33 on Webster Avenue since September and before that Corpus Christi School on Main Street East. At school the humiliations were compounded daily, and it was pure hell.

The girl with the hazel eyes and shoulder-length brown hair, felt like she existed just to absorb punishment. She was a weeping never-ending target of verbal tortures. Her cheeks were always wet and her face was always hot. It was worst of all when she was with her family. Her abusers were brazen, and her mom and sister shared her humiliation.

Her name was Michelle. But everyone called her Stinky.

By the time anyone bothered to comment on Michelle she was important for a sad reason and the verbiage dripped kindness. Her School 33 teacher, Sheldon Sherry, protectively described her as an "average" student.

"She was a friendly girl," Sherry said. On Michelle's last day there, he recalled, "She got in line with the rest and went out."

By all other accounts, Michelle's last day of school had been a rough one. She'd been teased relentlessly during recess—baby, baby, baby, baby—so severely that she had to leave her classroom and spent most of the afternoon crying in the nurse's office.

To make matters worse, she and her primary tormentor had been made to stay after school, so when Carolyn arrived to pick up Michelle and her sister, Michelle wasn't released. She did *not* get in line with the rest and go out. Mom walked the sister home and left Michelle to fend for herself.

Walking home alone was okay with Michelle. After her very, very bad day, Michelle left school somewhere between 3:20 and 3:30 p.m., walking southwest. She made it at least to the intersection of Webster Avenue and Ackerman Street. That was where she took a detour.

Cynthia Nicoletti saw her in that spot. Michelle was on foot, not heading home but visiting the Goodman Plaza of stores. Her Uncle Phil saw her near the stores and asked her if he could give her a lift home. Michelle said no thanks. It had been a tough day and perhaps being alone was working for her.

Michelle was wearing a three-quarter-length purple-hooded coat with silver trim, purple slacks with a zigzag pattern, and knee-high black boots. Cynthia left and came back to that same corner, Webster and Ackerman, and saw Michelle in a car driven by a man. The man drove wildly, cut the corner, and she had to jump back to avoid being run over..

She could see the man's face through the windshield. The car screamed out of Ackerman Street and turned recklessly left onto Webster Avenue, so wild that a second car had to slam on the brakes to prevent an accident. The car with Michelle in it never slowed down and in a flash it was gone.

*   *   *

Cynthia Nicoletti didn't tell her mother right away what she'd seen. She hid in a closet huddled with a bag containing her mother's wedding dress.

Carolyn Maenza called the RPD to report Michelle's disappearance at 5:40 p.m. She called from a neighbor's house and was reportedly so upset that she could hardly talk.[98]

There were people at Michelle's school that thought, when they heard she was missing, that she had run away, fed up with the torments she had suffered during recess.

Carolyn knew better—and police shared her grim realization. Sure they canvassed the neighborhood, searched backyards, any potential hiding places. Nearby parks, parking lots, and deserted areas were scrutinized.[99]

But the whole time, even though police didn't want to say so, they were also looking at potential dumpsites, eyes peeled for lifeless remains. "Everywhere I went," said one detective, "cop cars were slow-driving along the shoulders of roads looking into ditches."

The process held a horrible sense of déjà vu.

Michelle's uncle Philip Maenza worked in a gas station at the corner of Webster Avenue and Melville Street, two blocks south of Ackerman but a half block north of Michelle's block.

Investigators asked, "You see Michelle?"

Uncle Phil said, "She didn't pass my gas station."

This was technically true, except he eventually admitted that seeing Michelle at the Goodman Plaza while in his car.

"I offered her a ride home and that she refused.

"Why didn't you tell us that earlier?" police asked.

"I was afraid people would blame me.[100] I could have brought her home safely. I should've…" He became emotional.

After such a bad day, Michelle might have been attracted to anyone she considered nice, yet she didn't want to get in a car with Uncle Philip.[101] Years later, Michelle's brother Stephen said that his late Uncle Philip never stopped being upset by the memory.[102]

Cousin Geanine Maenza recalled, "My father told Stephen that he saw her and offered her a ride but she declined. I am 100% sure there is no misinformation and suspects on this side of the Maenza family."[103]

Geanine's older sister remembered coming home from school and seeing cop cars all over—around the house on Webster Crescent and in the plaza where Michelle was said to have been picked up. She remembered their Italian grandmother (Christopher's mom), who came to America at 14. When she heard of Michelle's disappearance, she wailed, "He took her, he took her. I know he did it, he took her." Grandma was referring to the same man who had killed Carmen and Wanda.

Michelle's disappearance sent a spell of gloom over the city. Initial "witnesses" painted a confusing picture. Michelle was seen in various parts of the city: on the other side of the river, Burrows Street off of vice-ridden Lyell Avenue at 5:30. A female motorist reported seeing a frightened girl riding in a dark green pick-up truck on Browncroft Boulevard at about 5:40. The leads "didn't check out," police said.

"We're not too encouraged," said Captain Andrew Sparacino on the day of Michelle's disappearance. "The longer she remains missing the more concerned we are. But all we know now is that she's missing."[104]

The RPD was joined in the search by the MCSO, as well as all of the area town police forces, and just about anywhere there was a secluded or wooded area, there was a cop searching. They examined vacant structures close to Michelle's home, along Webster Avenue, Bay Street, side streets like Grand and Parcells avenues, and in dark-blue swarms around Goodman Plaza.

At first, police tried really hard to separate Maenza from Colon and Walkowicz. Despite a horrible feeling in their bones, they didn't know enough to assume a connection.

But for the Maenzas and their neighbors along the crescent, everyone assumed the worst. They didn't even have to say their fears aloud. This was *just* like Carmen and Wanda.

Carolyn Maenza spoke to reporters sparingly and was prone to polite answers. She said the little girl had no problems at home or at school. There was no reason for her to run away. Someone had snatched her.[105]

A reporter visited the cul-de-sac and found neighbors eager to get their two cents in. The little bent street was great for kids. Was. With no through traffic, children played in the street. All summer, neighbors sat on porches, feet propped on porch railings. Neighbors visited each other all year round. No more. Everyone stayed in, watching TV. Waiting for news.

Neighbor Mrs. Walter Murphy said Carolyn was a good mother, the type of woman who always knew where her kids were. Mrs. Murphy said Carolyn usually walked Michelle home from school but didn't on this day because she had made her own journey to the Goodman Plaza in search of a missing purse she'd lost over the weekend. There was an early theory that Michelle may have been going to the plaza in search of her mother's purse, but no one knew for sure what was going through the little girl's mind.

Mrs. Murphy frequently saw Carolyn and her three daughters going together to the grocery store, or the Laundromat, or just to visit neighbors. Sometimes Mrs. Maenza would drive in the afternoons to School 33 where she would pick up Michelle and her sister. Michelle was shy and often played with younger children because kids her age derided her. She didn't think Michelle would accept a ride from a stranger but, on the other hand, she couldn't imagine her out there hiding somewhere.

Next-door neighbor Mrs. June Grelik said she received a visit from Carolyn on Tuesday morning but she was so upset she could barely spit out her words. She didn't mention Carmen or Wanda, but she gave the impression she was thinking the worst. She was punishing herself because Michelle wasn't supposed to walk home alone. She was supposed to escort her daughter home, but things got mixed up and this time it didn't happen. Carolyn wished so hard that she could go back in time and wait for her daughter to get out of school rather than abandoning her there. Carolyn said that she woke up on Tuesday morning and when she realized that Michelle was still not home she felt a panicky feeling in her chest. Mrs. Grelik was so concerned about Carolyn that she called an ambulance. Carolyn was taken to Strong Memorial Hospital, where she was administered a strong sedative and released. She did not return to her home, and her whereabouts were kept private.

Mrs. Heeman from across the street agreed that Michelle was "not the type" to run away, and was keeping her own grandchild out of School 33 out of fear there was a predator there.

Storeowner Nicholas Finocchio remembered the Maenzas coming into his store for candy. It was always a bit of a production, Carolyn pushing a baby carriage, Michelle holding the door for her.

Dad Christopher said, "She wants to be friends with everybody. She is easily swayed. That's what I am worried about."

Michelle's fully clothed and lifeless body was found two days after her disappearance, at 10:30 a.m. on November 28, in a ditch about eight feet from the north shoulder of Eddy Road in the town of Macedon in Wayne County.[106]

The body was found laying partially on its side and front. The killer had dropped the body at the top of the incline at the side of the road and rolled it down. The silver-trimmed three-quarter-length coat that Michelle had reportedly been wearing when she was abducted was missing. The location was 70 yards east of Mill Road and about three-tenths of a mile west of Walworth-Palmyra Road. As was true of Carmen and Wanda's dump sites, this was an unusually deserted stretch of road. Eddy Road was two miles long and in 1973 there were only ten houses on it.

Fire Chief of the Walworth Volunteer Fire Department, Gene VanDeWalle, was enjoying that new-car smell. The department had just purchased a new fire van and he was on his way to show it to fire fighter Richard Stalker on Eddy Road. Stalker wasn't home yet so VanDeWalle cruised the area for a while.[107]

He crossed the invisible border between Walworth and Macedon, heading south on Eddy when he saw something. He felt butterflies in the pit of his stomach, before his mind fully registered what he had seen. It was off the other side of the road, so he stopped and turned around. By then there was no denying it. It was a body. He didn't even get out of the truck. He was in an official car, and could've used the two-way radio to report his sad discovery. But he decided against it.

"I didn't want it to go out over the air," VanDeWalle said years later.

So he drove to the nearest phone and told Wayne County Sheriff's Office that he'd found a body, possibly that little girl.

"Meet me at the post office," a deputy said.

VanDeWalle remembers that it felt like hours waiting at the post office, his heart thumping—although he realizes it was probably only a few minutes. The deputy arrived. VanDeWalle wanted to escort the deputy in his van to the scene, but the deputy had other ideas.

"You come with me. We go together," the deputy said, and VanDeWalle climbed into his car.

For a few anxious minutes, VanDeWalle had difficulty finding the spot. It wasn't where he thought it was. He fought back panic—

"Oh, no! Somebody snatched it!"—but it turned out to be just a little further down the road.

The deputy got out of the car, went to the edge of the road's shoulder, looked down at the body, and then returned to the car to call for back-up.

"At that point, a stream of cars arrived, cars all the way up and down the road," VanDeWalle recalled. "They kept me there all day. Made me tell the same story ten times."

He never got too close of a look at the body, but he did see it in some detail. The thing that got to him was the exposure. He could tell it had been there all night. There's been rain the night before and her hair was all wet.

Richard Pisciotti, who would later become Wayne County sheriff, said there were "brown bits of dry foliage in Michelle's cold grasping fingers."[108]

Detective Fantigrossi said Michelle had "obviously" been strangled. "There were bruises all over her neck," he said.[109]

Michelle's three-quarter length coat was discovered at 1:00 p.m. that afternoon by a Wayne County sheriff's deputy, also in a ditch on Eddy Road, about a half-mile west of the body. The coat's location, near but not at the dumpsite, was seen as significant. Fantigrossi theorized that the killer may have discovered that the coat was still in the car after leaving the dumpsite, and simply threw it out of the car.

As was true of Wanda, Michelle appeared to have been *stripped and redressed* by her killer. Some of the snaps on her shirt had been damaged during the violence.

The location was so remote that "canvassing the neighborhood" was over in a snap. Three neighbors had potentially useful information. One reported seeing a light-colored 1966 Chevy parked on the Eddy Road shoulder facing the wrong way at 5:30 p.m.[110] Another said that she heard a bang and dogs barking at one o'clock on Wednesday morning. A third reported she saw a car driving by slowly about 10:30 Tuesday night.

The body was moved from the dumpsite to the Newark State School in Newark, N.Y. At 2:55 p.m., Michelle's dad Christopher, accompanied by Uncle Philip, arrived and positively identified the body.

"Why did they have to do this to her?" her father sobbed softly.

When Carolyn Maenza heard the news she had to be taken to Genesee Hospital for sedation.

Wayne County acting coroner Dr. William Welch performed the autopsy with Dr. Edland assisting. It was made official that the girl had been raped and strangled.

Because Edland had conducted the post-mortem procedures on Carmen and Wanda, he was selected to attend this autopsy to look for similarities between the cases. Richard Pisciotti took photographs. Everyone privy to the Wanda and Michelle crime scenes guarantee that they had the same killer. Fantigrossi said Michelle's crime scene was "an exact duplicate" of Wanda's scene.

The pattern remained the same. Late afternoon on a school day, picked up urban, dumped rural. Strangled. Raped. Michelle had marks on her face, neck, and one arm. She appeared as if she had been strangled by both a belt and hands. From behind. Like Wanda. Everything was like Wanda.

Dr. Edland went futuristic state-of-the-art and tried to find fingerprints on the body using a technique involving iodine and silver. On Michelle's neck he found something. An impression was made by blowing iodine vapor across the neck, which lodged on the fats and oils left there by a sweaty wrist. A silver-plated piece of metal was pressed onto the area, and the iodine etched a copy of the print into the metal. The impression was promptly photographed with a New York State Police fingerprint camera, as it would deteriorate rapidly on the silver-coated plate.[111]

Best guess was that a wrist and a small portion of palm had made the print. Although the print had some crucial detail, it was nonetheless impossible to determine if it was a right or left wrist. Partial prints were also found on Michelle's boots and coat, but these turned out to be unhelpful.

Some autopsy results were made public immediately. Importantly, it was reported that, according to Dr. Edland, what appeared to be the remains of a cheeseburger ("remnants of cheese, meat, and onions") were in Michelle's stomach. The food was largely undigested. She'd eaten the burger approximately an hour and a half before she died. It was definitely not lunch. Michelle had not eaten the burger between the time she left school and when she was abducted, so she must have been with her killer when she ate her final meal. With the morning paper everyone knew about the cheeseburger.

This, too, tied Maenza with the Walkowicz case. Wanda was found to have eaten custard shortly before her death, a meal fed to her by her killer. The contents of Carmen Colon's stomach, on the other hand, indicated that her final meal had been consumed at home.

Dr. Edland said Michelle was raped before she was strangled, choked perhaps with a belt or rope. It was impossible to determine the precise time of death but it was theorized, because of changes in the body, that death had come on Monday, the same day that Michelle disappeared. There were bruises on the face and upper arms and shoulders. She'd been beaten. Semen was recovered.

Dr. Edland chose his words carefully. They had three semen samples, there was semen from each victim, and they all had something in common, not a blood type, but rather a blood group. The semen revealed something about the killer, but not his blood type. In those pre-DNA days this probably means the killer had been determined to be either a secretor or a non-secretor.

A secretor is a person who secretes their blood type antigens into their body fluids, such as saliva or semen. Non-secretors do not. If evidence came from a secretor and a person of interest was a non-secretor—or vice versa—the suspect could be eliminated.

Dr. Edland said that it was easy to think of one killer out there responsible for the three hideous crimes, but urged everyone to keep "an open mind" to the notion of multiple killers: "Cases like this can bring on others who want to get into the act. There may be an imitator," the medical examiner explained.

So, Wanda and Michelle, most definitely the same guy. Carmen, maybe not.

RPD Captain Andrew Sparacino met with Paul Byork, chief deputy of the Wayne County Sheriff's Department, on the night of the 28th to discuss strategy, where to canvass, and who would need to be interviewed first. A huge task force was assigned to this case. More than 800 suspects would be questioned, none arrested.

The award for first public mention of the double-initials angle goes to D&C writer Bob Minzesheimer, who wrote in the November 29, 1973 edition, "And oddly, each had the same initials in her first and last name—CC, WW and MM."[112]

Minzesheimer asked Detective Fantigrossi about the initials and the similarities in the girls' backgrounds—Catholic, dad not around, mom on welfare.

Fantigrossi said the difficult part from an investigatory viewpoint was to distinguish between what was a connection and what was coincidence.[113] The initials were coincidences without significance when it came to solving the crimes. Police were not "wasting time" by working with theories based on letter combinations.[114] The clues that mattered were time of day, girls all alone, all found alongside rural roads. It didn't matter how they spelled their names.

"I don't think the guy is familiar with the girls," Fantigrossi said. "This type of crime is not a planned crime. This person has a mental problem and when he gets the sex urge, he moves. There's no planning. I am operating under the theory that the girls got into their killer's car because they were enticed, not because they knew or trusted the person.

"The type of person who commits a crime like this is an introvert. We're checking persons with sex-offender backgrounds. We had a strong suspect in the Wanda Walkowicz case but he was cleared. We'll talk to the same suspects in this investigation. We talked to two suspects on Wednesday but both were cleared."

Fantigrossi reminded the public that real-life monsters do not look like monsters in horror movies. The guy could be living next-door to you and you wouldn't know.

"It's not like these guys walk around with a sign around their neck," he said.

A list of school employees was compiled in hopes that police might find someone who'd had contact with all three girls. Welfare workers who might have had contact with the families were also checked.

A neighbor of the Maenzas' was interviewed thoroughly after she reported a man who had tried to "become friendly" with her niece. Due to journalistic euphemisms, it was difficult to determine what the man had done.

The Rochester Telephone Company placed a half-page ad in the morning paper asking for tips. It read, in all caps, *"HELP IF YOU CAN! THERE IS A KILLER LOOSE IN ROCHESTER."* The civilian assumption that one man was responsible for all three killings was absolute.

New hotlines were set up. New rewards were offered, not just by the Gannett Newspapers, but also from the Northeast Kiwanis Club ($1,000), and the Italian-American Civil Rights League.

The *Times-Union* printed photos of the three girls side by side with their first names only underneath. The caption under "CARMEN" made it clear that her body had been discovered in the town of Riga.[115]

A list of school employees was compiled in hopes that police might find someone who knew all three girls. Welfare workers who'd had contact with the families were also checked.

A thousand calls came in per day at first, but the great bulk of the callers had nothing concrete to offer. Many reported their enemies as the killer—with wives most frequently reporting their husbands or ex-husbands. In those days, before caller I.D., crank phone calls were an epidemic. Some used the hotlines as an excuse to demonstrate their unique unpleasantness—like the guy who said he knew something, but he wasn't going to say anything until the reward money matched his price.

The problem was investigators couldn't afford to completely ignore any of them.

Some tips were promising. On Friday, November 30, police first interviewed Cynthia Nicoletti, the child witness who saw Michelle in the front seat of a tan two-door with a dent on its left side. The car was speeding down Ackerman Street and around the corner onto Webster, almost hitting another car that was turning onto Ackerman.

Cynthia's statements were lent considerable credibility by the fact that she had gone home and, after a stint snuggling with her mother's wedding dress, told her story to her mother before Michelle was reported missing.[116]

Fantigrossi told Jack Marsh of the *Times-Union* that he questioned the child witness's accuracy, and was hesitant to focus the investigation based on her observations alone.[117]

That attitude would change, however. She had clearly seen what she had seen. How else would she know about the near accident at the corner of Ackerman and Webster Ave., cars screeching on the brakes as the car containing Michelle entered

Webster Avenue without looking? The driver of the car turning onto Ackerman would soon corroborate that incident, at which point police took Cynthia's story more seriously.

The corroborating witness, a woman driver, said she was turning left from Webster onto Ackerman and the other car was speeding out of Ackerman into Webster—exactly as Cynthia had seen it. The woman reported that at least two other vehicles were forced to stop abruptly because of the near collision.[118]

That news brought a call from a woman who began to tell the Gannett Rochester Newspapers "Secret Witness Line" operator that she too was one of the motorists forced to stop because of the near collision at Ackerman and Webster, but she turned out to be skittish and hung up before completing her message.[119] The second woman began to give information about the car Michelle was reportedly seen riding in but became fearful that she wasn't speaking to someone directly involved in the investigation. She said she would make no further comments until her identification number was printed in the paper. The *D&C* printed her number in its December 3 edition (1202-66), in hopes that she would call back with her potentially important information.

On November 30, an anonymous caller reported that a witness told a cashier in the Goodman Plaza vicinity that she had seen a man at the plaza's coin laundry offer Michelle a ride home, and that she accepted. The man and the girl, whom she believed to be Michelle, left together.[120] This sounded like a key clue, except for one thing. The caller was not the witness, but a Goodman Plaza cashier that had spoken to the witness, would recognize her if she saw her again, but did not know her name. Police pleaded for the witness herself to come forward or call one of the tip lines, but she did not. So the coin laundry incident dropped out of the investigation's timeline completely.

A witness came forward saying he'd read about the abduction and slaying in the papers, and that knowledge added importance to something he'd seen and even at the time been disturbed by. The man saw a light-colored car parked beside a lonely Wayne County road at dusk with the trunk up. The location was on Route 350, near the intersection of Eddy Road, very close to the spot where Michelle's coat was found in an overgrown swamp, and about three-quarters of a mile from where Michelle's body was found.[121]

Being a Good Samaritan, he assumed the guy was having mechanical problems, perhaps a flat tire or something in the engine and stopped to offer his assistance. He didn't notice the make of the car or the license plate number. What he did notice as he approached on foot, was that a chubby young girl was in the car.[122]

The man "grabbed the girl and pushed her behind his back." The witness had a confrontation with the driver of the car: he offered his assistance and was told gruffly and with raised fists that no assistance was required.

"How close did you get to him?" a reporter later asked the witness.

"Pretty close. Three or four feet."

"What was he wearing?"

"Jeans, light blue jacket."

"What type of jacket?"

"Snowmobile or skiing jacket, zipped up the front, quilted like, came down to his hips. Plaid shirt, one collar hanging outside the jacket, one tucked in."

"Would you recognize him if you saw him again?"

"I believe I would. I got a pretty good look at him. He was dirty, disheveled. Unshaven. What else…? Oh yeah, he had long fingernails."

The fingernail comment made investigators think back to 1971 and the many fingernail scratch marks on Carmen Colon's body.

The witness described the guy as six-feet or taller, maybe 170 pounds, dark curly hair, medium complexion. He could see the guy in his mind: clear skin, hair down on his forehead.

At the request of the police, the witness was called into the offices of Gannett Newspapers where he sat with sketch artist Richard Roberts. Getting a drawing of the suspect turned out to be a difficult process. The witness spent a day constructing the composite sketch using a police identification kit. When a face was finally completed, the witness said he wasn't satisfied with it.

Trying another tact, the witness was shown an array of mug shots to see if he could find the suspect's picture. Finally, after a downright grueling process, authorities were able to get a likeness that satisfied the witness.

Police said they were withholding details regarding the witness because they didn't want to discourage others who might want to come forward, but did say that the sketch was based on solid info.

Four-hundred mourners, friends and strangers alike, called for two hours in the afternoon and two hours during the evening on Friday, November 30, at the Profetta-Nanna Funeral Home on North Goodman Street.

The funeral mass was celebrated at Corpus Christi Church at 9:00 a.m. on Saturday, presided over by Msgr. John E. Maney. Approximately 60 people attended. The brown casket was carried by five men into the church, followed by the weeping mom on buckling knees, helped down the aisle to her front pew by two men who sometimes physically supported her to keep her upright.[123]

There was an open casket. Michelle's body wore a black dress and white top. After the mass, as people tried to console Carolyn, a nurse sat beside the grieving mom, holding her hand.

Michelle's father Christopher was last to leave the church. He sat and stared off into space. When nudged and told it was time to go to the cemetery, he said, "She was a sweet little girl. She didn't fight much."

Mourners left the church angry. One woman said that she looked forward to a day when the public would be allowed to torture the guy who did this to Michelle, to pull out each of his fingernails one at a time, to kill him slowly because a quick death was too good for him.

Another man felt like he had to lash out at something, but without so much as a suspect in the case, there was nothing at which to lash out. "It's like groping in the dark," he said.

A rumor ran like a virus through the gathering. A strange man had been parked out in front of the church, just watching, observing. Someone called the cops but the guy left before they arrived.

Chances are good that the "strange man" was himself a police officer, trying in vain to be inconspicuous as he observed the crowd, hoping the curious killer would make an appearance. Undercover detectives were admittedly on the scene.

Michelle was—like Carmen and Wanda—buried in Holy Sepulchre Cemetery. According to cousin Geanine, Michelle's mom eventually met someone and moved.

On the afternoon of December 3, the *Times-Union* published Richard Roberts' drawing based on the Good Samaritan's description. It sent a chill up and down Monroe County's collective spine. The drawing—distributed by police to newspapers, TV stations, and police agencies throughout the northeast—did nothing to soothe the fears of the community. It showed a creepy countenance and coiffure, hair combed down over the forehead, forming a point at the bridge of his nose. Very odd. It depicted the killer both from the front and side, like a mug shot. He had sideburns down to his earlobes, was unshaven, and wore a collared shirt. Both his nose and chin were thin and pointy, a frightening image, yet one that could change to unrecognizable with a simple sweep of a comb. Despite the downright weirdness of the sketch, it lit up the hotlines. It seemed everyone knew someone who looked like the guy in the sketch. More bad dads and ex-husbands were reported.

The Good Samaritan encounter was publicized without key details—although it was subsequently revealed that it occurred after sunset and in diminished light. What authorities would say on the record was that the sketch was based on solid information, as the witness had stood close to the suspect.

And so the killer had been spotted a few times during his time with Michelle Maenza, first as he drove his car out of Michelle's neighborhood seconds after the abduction, then again as he either had, or was pretending to have, a flat tire.

The publication of the sketch produced so many leads that the investigation team had to be expanded. At its peak, there were 50 investigators working Michelle's murder. The City of Rochester, Monroe and Wayne Counties, and the State all contributed as much manpower as they could spare.[124]

And the eyewitnesses kept coming…

The drawing of the suspect brought forward 61-year-old Gilbert E. Cole, a Gannett Rochester Newspapers security guard who said that the man in the sketch had approached him on Saturday, December 1, and asked if there were any new developments in the case. The guard took note of the man because he seemed nervous, shifty, and glanced around before asking the question. Cole had another interesting observation. The curious man also *stuttered badly* when he said the word "M-M-Michelle."

The guard asked the man to wait while he checked the most recent paper for developments, but the man flared with impatience and started to walk out. Cole asked him to stop but the man picked up his step and "bolted" out the door. The guard kept his eye on him and watched as he climbed into a light-brown Ford Pinto and drove away on Exchange Street.

Cole described the man as about 30, five-seven, or five-eight, with a light-brown collar-length hair and sideburns that extended onto his cheek. He wore a blue waist-length jacket. He appeared to have a bit more beard that was shown in the sketch, and the guard had the impression that he was starting to grow a moustache.

The description offered by the security guard and that offered by the Good Samaritan were different in one aspect, the man's height. To explain this, police theorized that Cole's station was an elevated booth that enabled him to look down on even tall men.

On December 5, twenty-seven community organizations held a meeting at Rochester's East High School for a seminar on how to keep children safe—attendance 160.

That afternoon, the *Times-Union* printed "Open Letter to Slayer: Turn Yourself In." The piece gave a calm and itemized argument for the killer to give up. First of all, if he gave himself to the police he would never have to worry about being turned over to an angry mob. Instead, despite the horrific nature of his crimes, he would be given the safeguards due all American citizens. He would receive medical care, physical and psychiatric; he would be given a fair trial—elsewhere if it turned out no fair jury could be assembled in Monroe or Wayne counties. Even though the cops, hard-working and honorable men, didn't feel the killer would give up, the paper said it thought there was a chance.

"If you do not surrender, what then?" the paper concluded. "You must know that the search for you will never end. How many nights will you lie awake, waiting and worrying? How much longer will you be able to face your family or your friends? How many doors can you hide behind?"[125]

That same day, police interviewed a woman who said she'd pulled into the parking lot of a Carrols Drive-In, a fast-food restaurant, at the Panorama Plaza in Penfield about an hour after

Michelle's abduction.[126] She hadn't gotten out of her car right away because there was a song on the radio that she liked, and she waited for the song to finish. That gave her an opportunity to gaze around her surroundings. Unlike the Good Samaritan witness, this woman saw what she saw in the daylight.

She said she pulled into the Panorama Plaza parking lot and parked alongside a light-colored—possibly beige—Plymouth Duster, either 1971 or 1972, with a young girl in it. She tried to get the young girl's attention because she had a round face and looked cute. When the witness's favorite song ended, she got out and walked toward the restaurant. At that moment, exiting the restaurant was a man holding a paper bag of food and a cup. He got into the car with the little girl and drove off.[127]

The witness helped an artist sketch the man she saw. She said he'd been wearing a blue quilted jacket, plaid shirt, and blue jeans that were tucked into the tops of his cowboy boots. She said the boots had a buckle at the top. (Was this the same buckle seen on the shoes of the man who stalked Wanda Walkowicz and her friend two days before Wanda's murder?)

Detective Fantigrossi said, regarding the Penfield sighting, "If this person is innocent, he'll come forward and say he was out there for a legitimate reason." The same thing went for the guy with the flat tire. If everything was hunky-dory, just call us and let us know. But Fantigrossi didn't think that would happen. He thought the killer had screwed up, and allowed himself to be repeatedly seen.

Police, Fantigrossi said, were planning to use a photograph of a policeman with a similar build to the suspect, and dressed like the suspect, with the suspect's sketch superimposed atop the body. "Maybe that picture will impress on someone's mind what he was wearing."

The Wayne County Sheriff's Office mapped out the most likely routes between the fast-food restaurant, the scene of the flat tire, and the dumpsite, and picked up debris from alongside the road, enough to fill a couple of pickup trucks, in hopes of finding some discarded something that might be linked to Michelle's murder—but nothing panned out.

The new full-body photo of the man in the boots with a superimposed composite sketch covering the head brought a fresh surge of tips reporting men who looked like the sketch, but none of those tips bore results.[128]

The number of new callers dwindled as Rochester headed into its third holiday season with "a killer on the loose." Interestingly, looking back with hindsight, there still had only been *a handful of published references* to the similarity in the victims' names, and authorities always proclaimed the similarity insignificant. The double-initial angle, which would become the case's trademark, was still just a footnote, just one of those weird things.

Times-Union reporter Jack Marsh spent a day with Detectives Joseph Perticone and Joseph Gangemi to get a feel for what the investigators went through during an average day on the Michelle Maenza investigation.[129]

One of the first things Marsh learned was just how the great majority of the tips coming into the various hotlines started out promising and dwindled rapidly into vagueness and, upon further scrutiny, nothing at all.

"I know who killed Michelle Maenza," one started. "I don't know his name but I saw him in Nick Tahou's (a downtown restaurant) last week."

On this day, one new tip needed checking, and that was added to a list of nine suspects the detectives were already scheduled to investigate that day, a process that began immediately following roll call.

The new tip was from a guy who worked with someone who was into little girls and looked like the drawing. Turned out to be nothing, but at least there was a physical body for them to look at and question.

"You've got to check every one because the way his luck is running, the one name we didn't check would turn out to be him," said Perticone. "Chances are we've already heard this guy's name but just haven't gotten to him yet. I tell you we've got to get this guy or there's no question he'll hit again. The more we eliminate, the closer we get."

Gangemi added, "You don't want to take a day off because something may pop and you want to be there. In the meantime, this is all we can do. Check every name, every lookalike right down to the wire."

Over the next six hours, Marsh reported, the detectives put more than a hundred miles on their unmarked sedan. They knocked on about 20 doors and spoke to maybe 40 people. It was a frustrating day and they only located one suspect, a guy named David, a known sex offender with 15 addresses, the most recent in a ramshackle apartment house near Monroe High School.

There was nobody home at David's apartment so the cops visited those listed as his last three employers. Only one of them recalled David, and said he hadn't seen him in years.

They did run into a customer at one of the places of work who remembered David, saying, "He was a goofy type. You'd be talking to him and all of a sudden he'd blow his stack." The guy put two and two together and figured out why the questions. "When I saw that sketch in the paper, it looked just like him, but I didn't want to blow him in."

A visit to the post office revealed that David had left a forwarding address from the last address on their list. They went to the new address and found an abandoned house with a "For Sale" sign on it. While there, they spoke to a neighbor who remembered David and his friends living in the abandoned house. "They got busted for drugs over the summer and the landlord evicted them," the neighbor offered.

The detectives made a note to contact the narcotics division about David and moved to the second name on the list. A guy named Timothy with a skin-crawlingly long and varied record of sex offenses. At Timothy's house they saw a woman peeking out the window and asked her where he was. She said he left, looking for work, took the bus, she didn't know where. Bus? Yeah, Timothy didn't know how to drive. Next.

They headed south to visit Joseph, a guy who looked like the newspaper sketch but had no priors. Joseph's mom met the detectives at the door, and she was plenty pissed off.

"What's this all about? Investigators were here just yesterday," she yelled. "My son is asleep upstairs." The detectives showed the mother the sketch and she failed to see the resemblance. "He doesn't look anything like that evil, creepy guy in the paper."

Next up was Rick, an alcoholic with a long-in-the-tooth attempted rape charge on his record. Guys age-out as sex criminals, so this didn't look good. But things perked up when a light-colored sedan was parked out front, registered to a woman.

A man answered the downstairs door, never heard of Rick. Nobody answered the upstairs door. As they pulled away from that address, they received a call on their radio.

A man resembling the sketch had been spotted on a city bus and was being held by a patrolman on Main Street West at Bull's Head, practically on top of the spot where Carmen Colon was snatched.

The detectives threw on the siren and ran red lights to get there. They found the frightened suspect sitting in the back of a patrol car while a gathering of curious pedestrians gawked. There was immediate disappointment. The guy was too young, and his hair was too light.

They made sure the patrolmen got the guy's name and info, then returned to their car. Next on their list was Stanley, a factory worker from a neighboring county who'd once tried to lure a girl into his car. They found him right away.

"Do you remember what shift you worked on November 26?" Perticone asked.

"Remember well," Stanley said. "It was the day that little girl disappeared. I got off at four and was home by five." That checked with his boss. Michelle was abducted before that.

They were looking for a lanky man with light-colored car and Stanley was short and heavy and drove a dark car. Cross Stanley off the list. And that concluded Perticone and Gangemi's very frustrating day.

On December 11, the Good Samaritan witness came forward a second time and muddied what had been believed to be clear waters. He said that he had seen that same man again and this time he'd had an opportunity to write down his license plate number.[130] There was much optimism the next morning as investigators from the RPD and the Wayne County Sheriff's Department traveled to the town of Lyons, 40 miles east of Rochester on Route 31, to interview a suspect.[131] The WCSD picked the guy up so he was waiting for Sparacino and Fantigrossi when they arrived. Wayne County Sheriff Richard Kise dealt with the press, saying that he could not comment on the questioning, or confirm that a suspect was in custody. He could however confirm that *someone* was being questioned.

Sure enough, the suspect was in his twenties and greatly resembled the sketches. He was questioned for nine hours.[132] The interrogation went on for so long primarily because it got off to such a bad start.

They asked the guy what he'd been doing on November 26 and he said he had no idea. Didn't remember. Couldn't remember anything about that day. They asked him if they could search his home. He said sure, he didn't have anything to hide.

The subsequent search revealed nothing of significance. He was taken to State Police Troop E headquarters in Farmington, Ontario County, where he was administered, and passed, a polygraph examination. He was cleared outright when phone records revealed that he was out of Rochester when the killings occurred.

He had made phone calls from his home phone at 2:13 and 3:25 p.m. on November 26, so he couldn't have abducted Michelle at the Goodman Plaza at 3:30. Wayne County deputies drove the suspect home and let him go.

Sparacino remarked about the man's resemblance to the sketch: "He looked pretty darn good. If you saw the person I saw, he resembled the sketch pretty good." The Lyons man was unemployed, once married but divorced. He had a criminal record, although not one that included sex offenses.

Michelle Maenza's murder soaked into the fabric of other cases—such as that against Linn Smeal, the operator of the Monroe Theater, a run-down Rochester cinema that showed dirty movies. The three movies on trial were "Meatball," "Midnite," and "Fire Down Below."[133] Smeal was eventually convicted on obscenity charges, and that December, his lawyer, Thomas G. Presutti, asked State Supreme Court Justice George D. Ogden to overturn the verdict because the jurors were influenced by news of the Maenza slaying.

The timing couldn't have been worse, Presutti said. The jury had been sworn in on the day Michelle disappeared. The lawyer's argument was based on a story by James A. Sykes that ran in the December 5 edition of the *Times-Union*, saying that two jurors in the obscenity case had said that Michelle Maenza's murder was discussed in the jury room during deliberations.

In his argument, the lawyer said, "When the jury went outside the evidence and considered not a football game, not a baseball game, but a tremendous tragedy that affects the whole community, the defendants...were deprived of a constitutional right. The jury did not render a fair impartial unbiased verdict on the evidence."

Assistant District Attorney Herbert J. Lewis offered the counter-argument, "A jury cannot impeach its own verdict. If they did talk about the Maenza case it was within the scope of their deliberations and was not an outside influence. You cannot divorce yourself from what goes on in life."

The *Times-Union* story quoted one juror as saying that, regarding the Maenza case, "By and large we tried to talk it down. Some jurors feared an explicit film might cause someone to practice what he saw on just anyone he came to."

A week later the judge decided that jurors discussing Michele's murder during deliberation was not a reason to set aside the verdict.[134]

On December 14, Fantigrossi said that he was still optimistic. The numerous reliable eyewitness reports in the Maenza case were still encouraging. It was a lot more than they'd had to go on in either of the previous two murders.

"I think we are going to get him," he concluded.

Fantigrossi said that he was as experienced as they come, 24 years on the job, yet this triple homicide was brand new to him. The term serial killer didn't yet exist, so police in a large sense struggled with the vocabulary to explain what exactly they were looking for, but it was a man who had pressure building up inside of him, and when the pressure built up to a certain point, he had to go out and commit another murder. Now they had three eyewitnesses who had all seen the man, clearly the same man. The man had no doubt changed his clothes since that day, especially after he knew he could be identified through his blue jacket, plaid shirt, and buckled cowboy boots. But, other than that, Fantigrossi theorized, he doubted that the killer had changed his lifestyle much.

"He's going about his normal business, even though he is running scared," Fantigrossi concluded.[135]

Calls to the police hotline became infrequent so the hotline was discontinued and potential tipsters were instructed to call the regular police phone number. Four days before Christmas, a suspect was questioned for an hour before being released, again brought in based solely on the fact that he resembled the sketch.[136]

By January of 1974 the investigatory team working the case had shrunk from 50 to 15.[137] Although most of the activity involved legwork, running down the fewer and fewer leads that came in, crime-scene investigation was still taking place. Michelle's jacket and soil confiscated from beneath the spot where her body lay had been sent to the FBI for analysis. It was hoped that there would be something, perhaps something microscopic—a hair, a fiber from a car seat—that would point the investigation to a specific individual. Unfortunately, the jacket yielded nothing of value. All the scientists in Washington could find was Michelle's own blood.

On New Year's Day, 1974, an 18-year-old woman was walking to work on Ashwood Drive near Lyceum Street, in the northeastern section of Rochester. A man following her in a car got out, grabbed her left arm, and led her at gunpoint into a nearby garage.[138]

A neighbor who saw the armed abduction called police. RPD Sergeant Ernest Morf happened to be nearby in a patrol car and rapidly reported to the scene. By the time the sergeant arrived, the man had forced the woman to undress.

Hearing the cop's approach the man bolted out of the garage and through adjoining backyards. Because of a light snow that had fallen during the night, Morf, now joined by Patrolman Lynde Johnston, was easily able to follow the fleeing man's tracks, and the chase ended a block and a half later outside a home on Fieldwood Drive where the man locked himself inside a parked car.

The policemen approached the man but stopped when they saw he had a gun. Morf called for backup on a portable radio, and while waiting for other officers to arrive heard a gunshot from inside the car.

When backup arrived, the car was forced open and the man was found slumped over the steering wheel, dead of a self-inflicted gunshot wound to the right temple from a .45 automatic pistol.

The man was identified as a city firefighter, 25-year-old Dennis S. Termini, of Bock Street, about a half mile south of where the abduction occurred. Termini's obituary noted that his parents and a sister survived him. He was buried in Holy Sepulchre Cemetery (as were all three of the murder victims).

Crime scene investigators found things in Termini's car that would heat him up as a double-initials suspect, but they didn't realize it at first. He had white cat hairs. His car resembled the one seen by the Good Samaritan in Macedon. They also found hair that would late be described as "similar" to Michelle Maenza's hair.

Termini turned out to be Rochester's "Garage Rapist" who had been active during the double-initials era, raping 14 teenagers and women between 1971 and 1973.

Investigation revealed that Termini had been hired as a city firefighter despite an unfavorable psychiatric report, citing several complaints of sexual offenses in Termini's background, although he had never been charged with a crime.[139]

In 1972, the Monroe County Civil Service Commission rejected Termini's application because of an unfavorable report. Fire Commissioner John F. Hurley interceded however, and Termini was approved.

Following Termini's suicide, Hurley said he didn't recall appearing before the commission on Termini's behalf. Reviewing the case, Hurley said that, if he did argue on Termini's behalf it was probably because his father was a lieutenant in the city fire department.

Was Termini the killer? Joyce Walkowicz was convinced he was the one. Many investigators agreed with Joyce. He had been known to abduct victims urban and rape them rural. And he had been known to stalk the same neighborhoods from which the double-initial girls had disappeared. Plus, he drove a car similar in appearance (same color, same dent) to the one seen by Cynthia Nicoletti.

The evidence that one guy killed all three girls began and ended with cat hairs. White cat hairs, found on all three bodies. Termini had white cat hairs in his car.

Bingo—and it got better.

According to Patrick Crough, "Remarkably, detectives were able to place Termini in the area where Michelle was walking home when she disappeared."[140] He kept his firefighter's clothes in his car and could dress as an authority figure, and in his car police found a map of Wayne County.

Wouldn't a little girl forget the don't-talk-to-strangers rule if a fireman told her that her house was on fire?

There were things not to like about Termini as the killer, too. No evidence for example that he was a pedophile.

(In 2007, the fireman's body was disinterred from Holy Sepulchre Cemetery for reasons of DNA comparison. Monroe County Medical Examiner Dr. Caroline Dignan and her chief investigator Robert Zerby conducted the exhumation and autopsy. The process was done efficiently. In attendance were Rochester Police Investigator Mark Mariano and MCSO Investigator Patrick Crough. According to Crough, "Only an hour passed between the back hoe entering the soil and the casket being placed in the Medical Examiner's truck."[141] The casket was taken to the M.E.'s office where it was unsealed and opened. This process broke the casket. Everyone attending the autopsy had to wear masks to prevent inhalation of the potentially deadly spores that inhabit aged human remains. The remains were identified as those of Termini, bone and tissue samples were taken, and the remains were placed in a new casket for re-burial the next morning. Subsequent testing of the bone and tissue samples revealed that Termini's DNA did not match that found at one of the double-initial crime scenes[142]. According to Mariano, the body was very well preserved. You could still see the wax cork the mortician had used to plug the bullet hole in Termini's temple.[143])

In a broad stroke sense, the double-initial victims had much in common. All were on welfare, all Catholic, all in special education classes, and all from a broken home. But when it came down to details, they had nothing in common at all. They never shared a common location, not even two out of the three.

Investigators noticed leaflets in each girl's home from the Gates Baptist Temple on Buffalo Road. Urban missionaries from the suburb of Gates would go door to door in the poorer sections of the city and try to recruit kids to come to their church.

If you signed up, a school bus would pick up your kids, take them for Sunday school, and return them after. The missionaries were questioned, and told investigators that it wasn't that big of a coincidence, as they had been quite thorough in their canvassing of the inner city. According to the victims' families, none of the girls had ever taken the bus to Gates.[144]

It was the infancy of criminal profiling, and in February 1974 the Maenza investigators met with a psychiatrist seeking insight into what sort of monster would be capable of kidnapping, raping, and murdering little girls.[145]

The psychiatrist was 37-year-old Dr. David J. Barry, the Monroe County director of mental health for court and probation and an assistant professor of psychiatry at the University of Rochester.

Dr. Barry had discussed the murders in the newspaper following Wanda's murder as well, but now that there were three he had a fantastic theory. He might not have been aware of it, but he was myth-building, and the things he said in the paper largely outlined the manner in which the killer was thought of from then on.

His method, Dr. Barry explained, was to "start from the clues" and then "expand in a number of different directions" to formulate "possible pictures" of "people [the police] might search for.[146]

Barry's analysis was that the killer had a chaotic childhood, and had been abused by his parents. The guy would have a record in Family Court for delinquency and would now be in his twenties or early thirties.

It was possible of course, he said, that the killer, though abused as a child, had no record for delinquent or criminal behavior. Perhaps he'd been lucky and was never caught. It might not be a guy who was obviously sick, or a known child molester. Perhaps the guy was "canny," and able to present himself in public as a normal fellow.

Folks prone to outrageous behavior, he said, "become pretty adept at an early age in covering up the kind of behavior that brings outrage."[147]

The doctor hoped the guy would have a fit of guilty conscience. It wasn't a given that he had no conscience. Maybe he struggled with his demons; maybe his life was a constant effort to supress the cruel trick nature had cursed him with, the relentless desire for forbidden sex.

Maybe the guy wanted to be caught.

Maybe he needed to self-punish.

But now it didn't appear that that was the case. Perhaps the killer didn't feel shame at all. Perhaps now he felt pride. The whole community was afraid of him—and in that mass effect he might feel a sick sense of empowerment.

Dr. Barry warned that it was oversimplification and perhaps misleading to say that a fresh examination of the clues might yield a type of person or a type of personality that would enable law enforcement to predict the perpetrator's future behavior. Such pigeonholing, he said, flew in the face of thorough investigation. Force-feeding clues into a pattern might result in excluding potentially enlightening leads that were incongruent with the direction of previous clues.

He said he was impressed by, and had spoken to police of, the killer's orderliness, how he dressed his victims after taking their lives. He left few clues at the crime scenes, and made an orderly and unhurried exit.

The killer had strategic and tactical skills. He could think ahead and execute a plan. He was orderly. It was hard to say if the killer was emotional, but Dr. Barry sensed that he would *appear* unemotional. That seemingly simple fact made the killer much cagier than the average criminal.

The doctor felt that it wasn't what witnesses saw that was important as opposed to what they didn't see. No one had seen any of the victims getting into the killer's car. Yet the abductions happened in highly traveled public areas. This indicated that the killer had previous rapport with the victims, and that he wasn't just grabbing them and dragging them into his car.

Dr. Barry said he'd been asked by a detective, how likely was it that the killer had had three urges, acted on those urges, and three times, from his POV, gotten the job done. Not likely at all. Such a project required scouting. Who knew how many hours he spent lurking, seeking out the perfect victims—"suitable prospects," Dr. Barry called them. This was part of the killer's "work of courtship."

The guy must be in his car a lot, cruising around all the time, keeping his eyes open. Before the crime, there must be occasions when he encounters the prospects, and establishes a familiarity and trust of some kind.

Was the killer smart? Not necessarily, Dr. Barry said. Methodical, yes. Clever, difficult to say. The killer was *careful*. He considered consequences when he devised his plans. Many criminals thought only in terms of the present, adrenaline junkies in search of kicks. This killer wasn't like that. He was weighing risks versus rewards all the time.

Some felt it was impossible for a man smart enough to devise such a plan, to terrorize a community in this way, to also be deviate enough to want sex from children. Ludicrous. Two completely different parts of the psyche, the doctor said, part of the mental makeup that no doubt made the killer unique.

The *D&C* interviewer made reference to the downright weirdness of the double initials in the girls' names. Was the killer trying to leave clues that would help police catch him? Or, was the whole thing a pile of coincidences, with as many as three different killers at work here?

Most unlikely, Dr. Barry replied. The same man killed Wanda and Michelle. A certainty. The M.O. was identical. Carmen was different but not that different. Darned close. His feeling was that it was one guy. And not just any guy—a filthy perverted murderer who was simultaneously laying out the most esoteric of clues, just to match wits with the police, perhaps because deep down inside he wanted to be apprehended.

Dr. Barry admitted that he wasn't married to the "wants to be caught" theory. Those guys were usually overcome with guilt following a crime and sometimes left a clue on purpose to help police, yet that guilt was not strong enough for them to turn themselves in and save law enforcement the work.

"If we look at the possible significances—the double initials, the towns of the same initials in which or near which the bodies were found[148], and the fact that the double initials occupy the numbers in the alphabet of 3, 13, and 23—if we look at that as possible coincidence, we hear from the statisticians that such a series of connections as found here might be coincidence is absolutely remote," Dr. Barry said.

That led Dr. Barry to his profile: the killer was a diabolically clever Zodiac-type who was carefully plotting these crimes in advance as a way of carrying out some complex and largely unconscious scheme for getting revenge on the world.

What Dr. Barry didn't have was an acknowledgement from the killer himself that the initials pattern was real and had meaning. Killers like the Zodiac Killer in Northern California, the Son of Sam in New York, BTK in Wichita, Kansas, and possibly even Jack the Ripper himself in Whitechapel, London, couldn't resist communicating directly with the police, and the press, to let them know that the game existed and so everyone could better enjoy watching it played. From the "Double Initials Killer" we heard nothing.

Dr. Barry theorized that perhaps the killer was married, engaged, or had a girlfriend—and that his deviant urges could be satisfied with just three murders in two years. It is often an erroneous assumption to think a sex killer has a strong sex drive. Not necessarily so. It might be the lack of drive compelling the killer to seek out increasingly aberrant sexual activity.

If caught, could the killer be helped?

Dr. Barry had no answer. Without meeting the fellow, how could he know if there was hope? Medicine might help. There were those who could help—at university-affiliated hospitals, for example—but Dr. Barry doubted that this was the sort of facility in which the killer would end up. Nobody at, say, Attica could help him.

Dr. Barry said that there was certainly a chance the killer would strike again and the only positive was that he attacked infrequently, as compared to other violent sexual offenders.

Also, he said, the aging process and hormonal changes might make the killer a decreasing risk over time. Like hard narcotics addicts, sex killers tended to mature out of their condition. Deviant urges gradually declined at the same rate as the male sex drive with advancing years, not that that offered immediate hope.

Dr. Barry said there were three groups the killer might fit into: 1) Men in their late teens, sexually inexperienced and afraid women will reject them. 2) Men in their early thirties with some degree of marital and professional success but who have had recent failures that left them depressed. And 3) older men, sometimes impotent, who drank heavily and feared sexual failure with mature women.[149]

And there it was: Birth of the Double Initial Killer (DIK). He was a criminal mastermind killing girls with the same first and last initial and dumping their bodies in a town that also started with that letter.

If one believed in the numerology of the case, if the victims represented the 3rd, 13th, and 23rd letters of the alphabet, the next victim's initials would be GG, and her body would be dumped in the towns of Gates or Greece.

All of the victims attended a numbered school. Carmen

attended School No. 5, Wanda 8, and Michelle 33. 5/8/33. Could be a birthdate?

The terror spawned by Dr. Barry's theory became so strong that anything contrary to the double-initials theory went unheard. Rochesterians forgot that Carmen Colon was found in Riga. It was close to the village of Churchville. Close to the town of Chili, for that matter, too. Maybe the killer got confused and didn't realize that he'd crossed the border. The theory played by horseshoe rules. Close enough.

On September 22, 1974, the morning paper ran a huge story: "The Double-Initials Murders," and that is what they were called from then on. It was here that the public first learned about the white cat hairs. Young girls—and a lot of women, too—with alliterative names, looked at the map to see where their bodies would be dumped.

The dissenting point of view was buried deep into the article. State Police Investigator Michael Iaculli said, "We decided long ago that the initials had nothing to do with it. If it *was* the initials, the individual would have to stake out the place and wait for the girl…and you can't watch her for too long or someone will notice. Who knew Wanda was going to the store?" He pointed out the "key differences" between Carmen's murder and the other two.

Iaculli said that the murders, unfortunately, did not make Rochester special. "Almost every metropolitan area has had the same type of crime: New Jersey. Long Island. Connecticut. Pennsylvania. They have all had crimes like this where nobody has been apprehended." Iaculli blamed the Miranda Act. "We could have picked up the killer and had to release him because we were not able to properly question the individual."

Medical examiner Dr. Edland offered his own criminal profile: there was a chance that the killer led a normal life, although he was probably sexually immature and terrified of females because of rejection. "He has a psychopathic fear of rejection by women. What we see is an abbreviated courtship, a date. He picks them up, buys them food, rapes them, kills them…he kills them so nobody else can have them." Or maybe he killed them to remove from the world the only witness to his crime. Dr. Edland said that, contrary to police sources, he did not think that the victims were chosen at random, or that there was more than one killer involved. "I really think it is one guy," he said, a man who acts when "an irresistible impulse comes over him." He noted that Carmen was found nude while the others had been clumsily redressed. This was not necessarily a difference in M.O., because we know Carmen lost her pants in the frenzied activity alongside the Western Expressway.

When it came to the double-initial angle, Dr. Edland was all in: "I believe he selects his victims. It could be a person who has access to public records, someone who works in the social services department...I think this guy is much more clever than the police give him credit for. And there's the contempt part of it: if he had wanted to, it would have been easy in Monroe County to hide the body so that it wouldn't be found for a while...but here they're all found within a day or two of abduction, right off obvious roads."

Dr. Edland admitted that he was fascinated by unusual murder cases and like many others was intrigued by the notion that the girls' initials *meant* something. "We don't have that many sophisticated and unusual cases here," he said. "I like playing the devil's advocate, and it's smart to throw in a new idea in a case like this." Since all victims were Catholic, people with "religious backgrounds" should be scrutinized, he said.

As fear amped up, the investigation grew chillier than ever. A week after the Termini incident, the only Wayne County Sheriff's investigator working full-time on the Maenza case, Investigator Richard J. Pisciotti, was reassigned because the sheriff's department was shorthanded. Michelle's case was now officially cold in Wayne County.[150]

Theodore F. Given, Jr.

At 1:30 p.m., Saturday, August 3, 1974—a little bit more than eight months after Michelle Maenza's murder—a man approached two nine-year-old girls in Lions Park at the end of Kentucky Avenue off Long Pond Road in the Rochester suburb of Gates.[151] He lured the girls, neither of whom had the same first and last initial, by telling them he was going to show them baby bunnies in the trunk of his car. He then forced the girls into the trunk, slammed the lid, and drove off. The drive, the girls estimated, lasted about ten minutes. The girls were extremely frightened because the man threatened them not to talk.

The kidnapper drove the girls to what they described as a "large gray" vacated house, tied up one of them in the basement and sexually attacked the other. The girls endured a three-hour ordeal. The man then drove the girls back to where he'd snatched them, and there let them go. Adults in Lions Park witnessed the girls' release at 4:30 p.m. Police were called 45 minutes later by one of the girls' parents. The upstairs girl was taken by her parents to Strong Memorial Hospital and her friend was brought by her parents to the Gates Town Hall.

Police interviewed both girls on Sunday at the Gates Police Department (GPD). Based on the statements of the victims and park witnesses, the GPD released a description and composite drawing of the suspect. The man was said to be six-foot, 175 pounds, and approximately 30 years old. He had brown hair, long sideburns, and a beard and moustache.

Police searched 20 vacant houses on the west side of Monroe County but failed to locate the crime scene.

At a press conference, 27-year-old Gates Police Chief Thomas Roche was asked if he thought they were seeking the DIK. Chief Roche said no. He didn't think the rape case was connected to the murders. The reason was simple, these victims didn't have the same first and last initial and the guy didn't kill them when he was finished.[152]

Chief Roche said that the key to the investigation was the suspect's automobile, which was described as a 1968 or 1969 compact, possibly a Ford Falcon, with some kind of "pin striping" on the driver's side. A suspect was questioned on Sunday, but was released that afternoon.

At 10:30 p.m. on August 5, the Monday following the crime, GPD Investigator Edwin Wilcox received a call from an unknown white male.[153] The caller wanted to know if there was a reward for information on the suspect in the Lions Park rape case. He was told there was not, and responded saying he wanted to do the right thing anyway. He said that he knew the location of the car used in that crime, which was always parked on the street but was now parked—hidden, if you will—behind a nearby building. The hood of the car, the caller said, had been removed.

"When was the last time you saw the car parked on the street?" Wilcox asked.

"Saturday night," the caller replied. He said he was going to hang up and call back the next day, worried that the car's owner would know that it was he who'd called police.

Wilcox, however, kept the man on the line for another ten minutes, until he eventually gave the address of a house on Child Street, in the Dutchtown section of Rochester, not far from Bull's Head.[154]

"Who owns the car?"

"Fella named Ted Given."

After discussing the call with Chief Roche, Wilcox and another Gates officer went to the Child Street address. They examined the car, found it a "direct hit," and called for back-up. The front and rear of the house were secured.

When back-up arrived, Wilcox knocked on the house's north side (back) door. A man answered, not Given, and instructed police to try the front door. After "much knocking" at the front, a blonde woman, about 20 years old, answered and unlocked the door, allowing the police to enter the building. At first the woman maintained that no one was home except her, but eventually conceded that Given was there. Wilcox and "Clay" searched the attic and the main floor but found nothing.

The written report just said "Clay". This most likely referred to Sheriff's Deputy Clayton Berardi, who worked Gates now and again and was a friend of Wilcox's, thus apt to show up as "Clay" in a written report.

Years later, Lieutenant Michael Wilcox recalled that Clay

could at that time have been a plainclothes investigator, and for this level crime may have been assigned to slip into Given's neighborhood without arousing suspicion.

Wilcox then returned to the attic with RPD officer Albert Brunette. The ceiling consisted of bed sheets that had been tacked to the roof beams. They found Given Jr. hiding in the rafters on the street end of the attic.

"Okay, come on down," Wilcox said.

Years later Wilcox said Given came down all right, tumbling down, from rafters to the floor, face down splat, taking a few bed sheets with him.[155] Brunette immediately jumped on Given's back, pointed a pistol at his head, and looped his left forearm around Given's neck.

According to Wilcox's written report, Given was "taken without incident and I cuffed him, staying with him until he was placed in the rear of (car) 402. Weapons were on the suspect until cuffed." It was verified that he was 27-year-old Theodore F. Given, Jr. He was charged with kidnapping and rape.

Following the apprehension of the suspect, Wilcox went to Wynne Auto Spring to look for the "deck lid," i.e. the missing hood of Given's car. He didn't find it, and then returned to the Child Street house with police photographer Tony Yasbeck where he confiscated Given's clothes and the scene was photographed. The hoodless car was a gold 1965 Plymouth Valiant.

(In the *Rochester Daily Record* dated July 3, 1974, a Theodore F. Given [Sr.] was listed as living at 60 Parsells Avenue, a location about 200 yards as the crow flies from the Maenza home on Webster Crescent. Givens' home was kitty-corner on Parsells from the Jungle Trader Pet Shop at Parsells and Webster Avenue. On April 2, 1973, the morning before Wanda Walkowicz's disappearance, that very pet shop was written up in the morning paper as the city's largest supplier of baby bunnies during the weeks before Easter, and adult bunnies to meat companies later in the year.[156] The proprietor at the pet shop was the double-initialed Joseph Jorgen.[157] Our witness to Michelle Maenza's abduction, Cynthia Nicoletti, said that she remembered the pet shop at the corner of Parsells and Webster.[158] She didn't remember the name of it, but it was an exotic place near Carl's convenience store. She went in there once with her family and found that the guy who ran the place was the brother of Sister Rita Jorgen, one of her teachers at Corpus Christie, the school where Michelle Maenza had attended the year before she switched to School 33. Given Jr. later admitted that he was living with his dad on Parsells, sleeping on his couch at the time of Michelle's murder, and he claimed he'd been questioned by police in the days after Michelle's murder because he drove a car that resembled their suspect's car. Not that anyone publically noticed, but he also greatly resembled the sketch of the man seen with Michelle Maenza eight months earlier.)

Given was ordered by Gates Town Judge (and former Sheriff's Chief of Detectives) Michael Cerretto to be held without bail in the Monroe County jail and to be given a mental exam.[159] A background check revealed that Given had been incarcerated at the time of the Colon murder, but out in time for Walkowicz and Maenza.

Given first made the papers in 1966 when, on May 4 at age 19 while living on Beach Ave., he was caught burglarizing Ace Cleaners & Launderers Inc. on Dewey Avenue. He was sentenced to a five-year prison term, scheduled to expire November 11, 1971.

He was released in 1968 and put on parole. While on parole he was arrested in Florida in a stolen car that he'd driven across state lines, convicted and sentenced to three years. He was released from a federal prison in March 29, 1971 and re-arrested in April on parole violation charges and sent to Attica where he remained until September 12, 1972. He was free until July 17, 1973 when fresh parole violations—traffic violations, crossing the county line, lying to a parole officer, buying a car without approval, breaking curfew, and possessing weapons—put him briefly back behind bars.

Asked to explain himself, Given said he knew he wasn't supposed to leave Monroe County but he didn't know Albion was past the county line. The lying was just because he put his fiancée's address down as his own, and the weapons were a paint-scraping knife and a Boy Scout knife he used in his work. All of his violations, he argued, were toward a goal of a stable life: a steady relationship and work.

The timeline offered by the D&C's 1973 article[160] indicated that Given was in for Colon and out for Walkowicz and Maenza. Since the predominant thinking at the time was that all three little girls had been killed by the same man, Given's timeline raised no red flags.

Only days after Given's arrest, one of his nine-year-old victims appeared in court, testifying at a preliminary hearing to determine if there was enough evidence to send the case to the Grand Jury.

In her testimony, the small victim recounted how it all happened, how she and her friend were in Lions Park at about 1:30 p.m. when a strange man came up and asked them if they'd seen any snakes. The girls said they had not.

She testified, "Then we asked him if we could help him look for snakes." They found a few snakes together, and then the man asked them if they would like a guinea pig or a rabbit. The man left them for a few minutes and returned with his car. "We said we didn't want a guinea pig, but we wanted to see one. The man opened his trunk and then picked me up by surprise and put me in the car trunk. Then he put [my friend] in." She testified that they were driven to a strange house and she was tied to a post in the basement while the man took her friend upstairs. She could hear her friend crying and saying, "Stop, you are hurting me."

The man came downstairs and tied a man's shirt around her head as a blindfold and then used a knife to cut the ropes that were holding her to the basement pole. She asked him if he was going to hurt her and he said no.

He put both girls in the backseat of his car and drove around for a while. Then he stopped the car, removed their blindfolds and dropped them off back where they started in Lions Park.

"Do you see the man in this courtroom?" asked Assistant District Attorney Vincent P. Mitrano.

"No," she said.

He asked her to look around carefully but she again shook her head no, she didn't see the man.

Despite this prosecutorial setback, Cerretto refused to dismiss the charges, and referred the case to the Monroe County Grand Jury based on a statement from Sheriff's Chief of Detectives William Mahoney that he heard Given confess to the crimes soon after his arrest.[161]

The girl left the courtroom and waited out in the hall with her mother as Mahoney testified that, after arresting Given at his home, the suspect was taken to the Monroe County Public Safety Building, read his rights and then asked about the kidnapping and rape. Given, Mahoney testified, began to cry and said, "Yes, I am involved." Mahoney asked Given why he did it, and Given responded, "I had a sudden urge."

Public defenders representing Given said that he appeared badly battered when they first saw him, making them wonder under what conditions he confessed.

Asked how he got the lacerations and bruises, Given said he was beaten and "almost castrated" by Chief Mahoney.

Mahoney responded, "I never laid a hand on him. There was no physical contact with him at all." Mahoney said Given had agreed to sign a written statement, but then changed his mind when the written statement was handed to him.

The story of the victim's inability to identify Given shared the front page of the paper with a huge banner headline announcing the resignation of President Nixon.

On August 13, 1974, public defender Peter L. Yellin filed a writ of habeas corpus in Monroe County court for Given's release. The writ argued that Given had been "illegally detained" because of a coerced confession and a lack of identification by the victim.

The FBI was investigating the charges that Given had been roughed up before confessing back on August 5, and made note of an August 6 doctor exam in which Given was found to have a burn on his right forearm and other injuries. Given explained the injury by saying that Mahoney burned him with a cigarette.[162]

On August 16, both sides argued their case before Monroe County Judge Hyman T. Maas, who ruled in favor of the police, that Given was being legally detained at the time of his confession, and ordered that he remain in jail.[163] The judge however made it clear that he was not ruling on the police brutality charges, merely on the writ to release the suspect due to illegal detainment. The judge said that his refusal to release Given was based on a decision that proper procedures were followed in a Town of Gates preliminary hearing after which Given was ordered held without bail to await Grand Jury action. On August 30, a Monroe County Grand Jury indicted Given on one charge of rape and two counts of kidnapping.[164]

In January, courts took up the matter of the alleged police

brutality.[165] The star witness at that hearing was WHAM radio newsman Edward M. Hasbrouck, who said before Monroe County Judge Donald J. Mark that he was sitting in the detective division's office on the night of Given's arrest, as Given was brought to the Monroe County Sheriff's detective division. Hasbrouck said the suspect had scratch marks on the left side of his chest and stomach and had two bruises on the left side of his neck. The reporter could see the marks on the suspect's upper body because he was clad only in slacks and socks. Given was asked to remove his shirt in court so the witness could better describe the location of the marks.

Gates Police Chief Roche and Officer Wilcox testified that they saw Given at the time of his arrest and during his interrogation and saw no marks on his body. Wilcox did admit that he later noticed a quarter-sized bruise on Given's neck during the arraignment in Gates Town Court, about eight hours after his arrest.

RPD officer Albert Brunette testified as to the violent details of Given's arrest, that he fell from the rafters hard to the floor, an incident that could easily have left marks on his face, neck and body. Roche recalled for the court how Given had cried during questioning, and again during his arraignment.

On January 21, Mahoney testified that he "never touched" Given. The following day, Given testified on his own behalf, telling the court that he only confessed to stop Mahoney's savage beating.[166] The attack began, he said, when he refused to sign a statement that Mahoney had prepared.

Given testified that his response was, "No, I won't sign it because it's not true. I didn't tell you what you've got in the statement." That started the violence. "He slapped me in the back of the head, hard enough to knock me off the sofa. He started grabbing my hair and yanking my head back. He bounced me up and down on the floor, kicked me. And tried to slam my head into a desk. He started getting very, very obscene with his language, really bad, calling me all sorts of names. I told him I was in Albion on the day of the crime but he didn't believe me. Mahoney lighted a cigarette and threatened to burn me if I didn't sign the statement and when I refused he burned my right arm."

At that point, according to Given's testimony, Undersheriff John Kinnicutt, who was also in the room, told Mahoney to stop for a while. Mahoney then threatened to shoot him and claim that he'd done it while Given was attempting escape.

When Given still refused, Mahoney allegedly said, "Get this degenerate bastard out of here."

Asked about the fall he took during his arrest, Given admitted that he had been hiding in the rafters but said that he climbed down slowly and didn't fall as the arresting officer said he had.

Photos were introduced at the hearing, taken by Philip Knight, an investigator for the public defender's office, that showed the burn on Given's arm, welts on his chest and the back of his neck, and a black right eye. Knight said that Given was actually in worse shape than the photos showed. Given's ears were discolored and bleeding, and he had suffered an injury to his scrotum.

"The next day Given was taken to Strong Memorial Hospital," Knight testified.

Others to testify were an unnamed jail inmate who saw no marks on Given when he partook in a line-up with the suspect, and Channel 13 cameraman Thomas Cannon who filmed Given as he walked to the line-up, a film that showed no injuries.

On January 23, 1975, Dr. Alfred Angrist, an expert in medical and legal aspects of traumatic injuries from New York City, told the court that in his opinion Given received a "sophisticated beating" at the hands of the police.[167]

"The nature and location of the injuries are such to preclude any other explanation," Dr. Angrist testified.

He said that the guy who beat up Given knew what he was doing because "injuries in these locations produce very little evidence of trauma."

Following Dr. Angrist's testimony, there was argument that it should be thrown out on the grounds that Dr. Angrist had never actually examined Given.

In response, the defense put another doctor on the stand, one that had seen Given in person. He was Dr. W. Bradford Patterson, who examined the suspect at Strong and said that his injuries were "consistent" with his story that he had been beaten.

Dr. Patterson said Given had a "severe wound" to his scrotum, and that there were bruises under Given's arms that suggested that he had been grabbed there violently by an "external force." The doctor didn't believe that the injuries could have been self-induced or that they could have been caused by a fall.

During the examination, Dr. Patterson testified, the suspect did not seem angry, but rather frightened, and came close to tears as he described the details of the beating to the physician.

On January 24, 1975, Given read his written confession aloud in a courtroom and then denied he had ever made that statement.

Two days later Lieutenant Anthony Gombatto, the jail's security supervisor testified that he'd seen scratches on Given when he was first jailed, and was concerned enough to contact jail superintendent Robert Stanwick and ask that an incident report be made out.[168] That request was not carried out and Gombatto had to fill out a report on his own a few days later.

On January 29, Judge Mark reserved decision on whether Given's confession would be admissible at Given's trial. The decision he eventually came to, in the middle of February, was that yes, Given was injured while in police custody, and yes, his confession is admissible because it was voluntary and not the product of physical coercion. In other words: *"Sorry Ted. Sure, cops beat you, yanked your nuts, but that doesn't mean you get away with child rape, you degenerate bastard."*

The case limped along in the courts with motions and countermotions, adjournments and delays, until July when the parents of the now ten-year-old Gates victim, who was scheduled to testify as to what happened to her, complained, requesting that the girl's portion of the proceedings be completed before the end of summer vacation so the girl could begin the difficult process of forgetting what happened to her.

The mother complained that the previous spring the girl's schoolwork had suffered because court proceedings dragged and newspapers carried "frequent reminders of the rape-kidnapping."[169]

The parents went to the courthouse to talk to Judge Mark but had to settle for an hour-long chat with an assistant D.A. The meeting had its effect however, and Judge Mark publically stated that he hoped to have the trial over "before the girls return to school in the fall."

He scheduled the trial to start August 21, but it never came to be as Given pleaded guilty to reduced charges (attempted rape) on August 15.

Mahoney was a happy guy. He felt vindicated. Given *was* a child-rapist and a liar.

The parents of the victims were angered in September when Judge Marks sentenced Given to a minimum sentence of 7 ½ to 15 years. One mom said, "They made him seem like a saint or something."

The father of the other girl said, "I wish everyone would get involved in a court situation. It's the only way you know how grossly unjust and screwed up the system is. I don't understand how a system like that could run for years and years and years."

The D.A. said it was the best he could do, as he would never have been able to convict on the rape charge because he couldn't prove penetration. Monroe County Sheriff William Lombard called it a "travesty of justice." [170]

The matter caused quite a controversy and became a sticking point in Judge Mark's re-election bid. In 1976 a Grand Jury cleared the Gates police of all police brutality charges in the case. Given served ten years in prison and returned to Monroe County, at which time he continued his perverted ways.[171]

A look into Given's background revealed that he had been in trouble, and subsequently institutionalized, for almost all of his adult life. When we first see him, he is in the Newark State School[172] for delinquents, the facility that would one day be the site of Michelle Maenza's autopsy. It was a hellish "school" in a dank building previously known as the Newark Custodial Institution for Developmentally Disabled, Childbearing Children; State Custodial Asylum for Feeble-Minded Women, and, after admitting boys, the Newark State School for Mental Defectives. Closed since 1991, the building, now scarred with graffiti, still stands like a haunting monument to the horrors it once hid.

Given escaped from Newark State and, while on the run, forced entry into 22 cottages along Seneca Lake.[173] Deputy Sheriffs said Given and another youthful escapee had stolen rifles, ammunition, food, and sleeping bags. The burglaries took place between Shannon's Corners and Glenora Point. The teens were caught in a small shack near the town of Glenora.[174] Given was caught, and arraigned on the morning of November 23, 1963, the day after President Kennedy was assassinated. Given had been taking advantage of the fact that everyone was glued to their TV sets to break into summer homes. Given waived examination and was ordered by Peace Justice Ralph Hart to be held for grand jury action on burglary third degree, petit larceny, malicious mischief, and conspiracy charges. Until then he would be staying at the Yates County Jail.[175]

We next hear from Given on May 26, 1966. Given, now 19 and living in Rochester[176] was charged with burglary and petit larceny in connection with stealing keys and other items from Ace Cleaners & Launderers Inc. on Dewey Ave. The crime took place on May 4.

In the years following Given's arrest, law enforcement in the Monroe County area were kept busy because of a full-fledged mafia war in the area. The first wave of arrests resulted in countercharges that evidence against the gangsters had been manufactured. While the arrested hoods were released, Mahoney, the guy who allegedly gave Given bad nads, ended up himself going to prison.

In the meantime, Monroe County's double-initial kids were going through hell. The amped up mythology and the resulting terror affected everyone, of course, but most deeply the girls of appropriate age with alliterative names.

One such victim of the double-initial *craze* was a girl we'll call Debbie DiFranco, a pretty brunette who was 13 in 1973 and lived in a town only a few miles outside of Rochester. Years later Debbie could still feel that fear.[177]

She recalled feeling so much like a target that one time she became paralyzed by fear when walking along railroad tracks behind her house with a friend and unexpectedly encountering a hunter.

Part of the problem was she'd been a target before. Debbie knew she could be subjected to sick stuff. When she was really little she had her picture in the paper at Easter wearing a babushka and holding a bunny. The paper printed her name and address. Three days later she received an envelope full of obscene pictures, which she was still trying to puzzle out when her older sister pulled them away and gave them to mom who called the cops.

Kenneth Bianchi

From a murder-mystery point of view, one of the most interesting men living in Monroe County from 1971-73 was Kenneth Alessio Bianchi, born May 22, 1951. He lived in the nearby town of Gates and later became one of the Hillside Stranglers, killer of ten girls and women in the Los Angeles, California area in 1977-78, and two more in the state of Washington before his arrest in January of 1979.[178]

Kenny Bianchi and I went to the same school for one year. For the 1961-62 school year, Bianchi was in the fifth grade and I was in kindergarten at Holy Family School, at the corner of Jay and Ames.[179]

Bianchi moved from Dutchtown to Gates about the time I moved to Chili, one town to the south. His biological mother was an alcoholic sex worker who gave birth to Kenny when she was 17. He was put up for adoption and adopted as the only child of the Bianchis. Dad worked at the American Brake-Shoe Factory.

According to his adopted mother, Kenneth was a compulsive liar from the time he could speak. He had anger management issues and a petit mall syndrome that had him unpredictably zoning out into trances.

When he was five he fell off a jungle gym onto his face. He may have suffered a brain injury. At age seven he went to a doctor for "urinary dribbling" and a year later was treated in a Rochester psychiatric center.

He was twice kicked out of grammar school, all the time wearing a sanitary napkin because of his urinary difficulties. His Dad died when he was 13, but Kenneth showed no emotion. He went to Gates-Chili High, joined a motorcycle club, and began proposing to women. Some turned him down (a woman named Susan, twice, because he didn't have a good job) and some accepted resulting in brief marriages: the double-initialed Brenda Beck for several months, and a second wife for eight months.

When he was 18 he reportedly wrote a letter to a girlfriend in which he said he had killed a man and was a suspect in the double-initial cases. After high school he attended Monroe Community College to learn to be a police officer. Bianchi twice applied for a job at the MCSO, first as a road patrol deputy, then as a jail guard, but was rejected.[180]

He took a series of guard jobs at Rochester department stores. Some ended when he was caught stealing. He was briefly an ambulance driver and technician. He worked for the Bareham Security Agency from October 1973 until he quit in March 1974.

At 9:50 p.m. on April 24, 1975, while working as a guard for Rochester Central Alarms, he received an alarm from the Rob Ray Liquor Store on Herman Street, and upon arrival found the basement door forced open. He walked down the stairs and said in his command voice, "Hands up, up against the wall." The robbers, a pair of 17-year-olds, did as he said. Ken held them at gunpoint until cops came and arrested them. It was the highlight of his career in security.[181]

At age 25 he headed west, and was twice more rejected by law enforcement agencies. He wanted to have a job with a cop-like uniform, so he could use it for off-hour scams. In L.A., he teamed up with his older cousin Angelo Buono and they became the killing duo known as the Hillside Stranglers.

Although Buono and Bianchi killed mostly grown women, often abducting them under the guise of being undercover police officers who just needed to ask a few questions. But two of their victims were 12 and 14, so tender years didn't necessarily discourage them.

Bianchi's name was first mentioned in connection with the double-initial cases in January 1979, soon after his Washington arrest, when he was still just a suspect in the Hillside Strangler cases, being held on $150,000 bail in Bellingham, Washington, on a charge of possession of stolen property belonging to two Western Washington University co-eds who had been found strangled.

A local boy had become a famous serial killer. That got Rochesterians to thinking. Bianchi's history was scrutinized. Harry Bareham, Bianchi's one-time employer, said Bianchi was well-mannered but "expected too much, too fast. He got a little authority and went haywire."

Gates cop John R. Arend knew Bianchi for eight years and once gave him a reference. Upon hearing of his arrest, Arend said, "He's a very, very quiet boy. Not moody, but quiet. Not the loner type. He liked girls, but wasn't overly crazy about them. He said he wanted to be a police officer because he wanted to help people."

Detective Anthony Fantigrossi said that Bianchi's name "never came up" in the double-initials investigation. If Bianchi had been questioned at all, it might have been during a blanket screening of those driving a certain kind of car. And yet Bianchi said he was chased out of town by the interview about his car. Many people were interviewed because they drove Cadillacs. As far as we know, Bianchi was the only one to use it as an excuse to switch coasts. Still, it was an exaggeration to say he fled. He was questioned about his car sometime between 1971-74, and didn't go to L.A. until 1976.

It was easy to view a Hillside Strangler as a solid double-initials suspect. Sex crimes, similar method of killing and disposing. At the time of Carmen's murder Bianchi drove a black and white Caddy, much like the car on the shoulder of the Western Expressway. The DIK had a blood characteristic found in only 20 percent of people—and Bianchi had it, too. Bianchi and his cousin Buono used fake badges to force women into Buono's car. The victims were driven to Buono's home, raped, tortured, and killed, and their remains were later dumped down hillsides usually at the side of the road. The victims all died of strangulation. The Hillside Strangler killings began during the autumn of 1977, and continued in quick intervals until February of 1978.

The victims were:

Yolanda Washington, 19 years old, October 17, 1977. Body found naked on a slope in Forest Lawn Cemetery, posed lasciviously.

Judith Lynn Miller, 15 years old, October 31, 1977, Halloween. A diminutive woman, 90 pounds, Miller's body was found naked on a hillside close to the road in La Cresenta. Her neck, wrists and ankles bore rope marks.

Elissa Teresa Kastin, age 21, November 6, 1977. A waitress at Healthfaire Restaurant near Hollywood and Vine. Her body was found naked near Chevy Chase Drive in Glendale, near a country club. Because there was a high guardrail at the side of the road, some investigators theorized that it must've taken two men to lift the sturdy body up and over.

Jill Barcomb, 19 years old, November 9, 1977. Knew previous victim Judith Miller. Lived in Hollywood. January 1977, prostitution conviction in Syracuse, N.Y. Body found naked, beaten, and strangled in Franklin Canyon, north of Beverly Hills.

Jane Evelyn King, age 28, November 10, 1977. Body found off a southbound off-ramp of the Golden State Freeway. Not found for two weeks.

Dolores "Dolly" Cepeda, age 12, and Sonja Johnson, 14 years old, both November 13, 1977. Sonja was from Eagle Rock and went to St. Ignatius School in Highland Park. They were friends and had gone shopping together. A witness saw the girls get off a bus and subsequently talk to two men in a large two-tone sedan. Their bodies were found by two little boys in Elysian Park.

Kristina Weckler, age 20, November 20, 1977. Honor student at the Pasadena Art Center of Design, resided in apartment house on East Garfield Avenue. Body found nude, in a desolate location in the hills between Glendale and Eagle Rock.

Lauren Wagner, age 18, November 29, 1977. Recent graduate of Monroe High School in the San Fernando Valley. Her abduction was witnessed by a neighbor who said that Lauren was driving and pulled over to the curb at 9:00 p.m. A car containing two men pulled up alongside her. There appeared to be a disagreement of some sort, but Lauren ended up climbing into the men's car. Her body was found off Cliff Drive in the hills of Mount Washington.

Kimberly Martin, age 17, December 9, 1977. Tall blonde, call girl. Her final client called her to apartment 114 at 1950 Tamarind, which turned out to be vacant. The killer, investigation revealed, called her from a pay phone in the lobby of the Ivar Street branch of the Hollywood Public Library.

Some time during the 1977 murder spree the pair picked up a woman named Catharine Lorre, with the intention of killing her. But, when they found out she was the daughter of actor Peter Lorre—star of movies such as *M*, *Casablanca*, and *The Maltese Falcon*—they let her go.

Cindy Lee Hudspeth, age 20, February 16, 1978. Her body, raped and strangled, locked in the trunk of her own car, a Datsun, and pushed over a cliff along the Angeles Crest Highway. She was last seen at her apartment building on East Garfield Avenue, and was "probably" headed to her job answering phones at Glendale Community College. Cindy had once lived across the street from victim Kristina Weckler, although there was no evidence that the two women knew each other.

An eleventh murder attempt in 1978 was botched. Bianchi

revealed to Buono that he had been talking to police about the murders and had even participated in a ride-along. Buono threatened to kill Bianchi and Bianchi split for the northwest.

That was the end of Bianchi and Buono's career as the Hillside Stranglers. Bianchi killed two more women on his own:

Karen Mandic, age 22 and Diane Wilder, age 27, both January 11, 1979 in Bellingham, Washington, students at Western Washington University. Bianchi was working as a security guard and lured the women into a house he was guarding. Without Buono, the double homicide was poorly conceived and Bianchi was under arrest within hours.

That's a dozen victims in all, and interestingly not a single one had the same first and last initial.

At trial, Bianchi claimed he was not guilty because of insanity. His claim, which was demonstrably phony, was that he had a split personality, and "Steven Walker" who lived inside Kenny's body was the actual killer. Doctors who examined Bianchi came to the conclusion that there was nothing split about his personality. The problem with Kenny was that he had an antisocial personality disorder and was a sexual sadist.

The case for the defense at Kenny's 1980 trial was a riot. One character witness was a woman named Virginia Compton who met Kenny while he was in prison. She testified that she hoped to buy a mortuary one day for the purpose of necrophilia, and, oh yeah, by the way, Kenny told her all about the murders and it was all Buono, Kenny had nothing to do with it.

Compton was later arrested after trying to strangle a woman to death in a motel room, an attempt, she explained, to get authorities to think Kenny couldn't be the Hillside Strangler because the Hillside Strangler was still on the loose.

Bianchi gave Compton a sample of his semen during one of her visits to plant on the victim and make it look like a man had committed the attack. Obviously, these were the days before DNA. Bianchi never considered that someday science would be able to connect a semen sample to its source just like a fingerprint.

Still, the notion that Bianchi thought of faking a crime scene using planted semen was interesting.

Bianchi is in prison for the rest of his life, a resident of the Washington State Penitentiary in Walla Walla. He testified against his cousin at Buono's trial. He tried to make his testimony confusing, but the jury convicted Buono anyway.

By July 1981, double-initials investigators were referring to Bianchi as a "serious suspect"[182]—serious enough so that Bianchi's palm print, taken in jail, was compared to the mark lifted from Michelle Maenza's neck with the iodine and silver technique.

Those who hoped the comparison would be quick and definitive were disappointed. A Toronto expert was assigned comparison duty. John F. Hinds of the Ontario Provincial police forensic lab, said to expect weeks of analysis—and it might even take longer than usual because of an ongoing Canadian postal strike.[183]

The difficulty, Hinds explained, was that the Maenza print, a copy of which he'd been in possession of for a couple of years, was mostly wrist and only a small portion of palm. The print had detail but it was impossible to determine if it was a left or right wrist.

Reaction was mixed. Of course, most prayed that the prints would match and a case against Bianchi built. But Wayne County Sheriff Pisciotti seemed a tad peeved. He'd learned about the impending comparison in the newspaper. Since Maenza was his case, the girl had been found in Wayne County, he felt like he should have been closer to the front lines.

"Apparently there was a lapse in communication," the sheriff said. He didn't care who solved the case, as long as it was solved; he just wanted to be kept in the loop.

On July 17, 1981 Monroe County District Attorney Donald O. Chesworth and Wayne County D.A. Stephen R. Sirkin said they had plans to have a meeting and "pool knowledge" regarding Bianchi.

Later that summer, the Canadian print expert must've come to the conclusion that Bianchi's palm print and the print lifted from Maenza's neck had such little overlap (if any) that no conclusion was possible.

On August 20, Superior Court Judge Ronald George in Los Angeles ordered Bianchi to submit a wrist prints to Rochester police. The prints arrived in Toronto on September 30. A month later, John Hinds said he was at the halfway point in his comparison. By January 21, 1982, he still wasn't done. "It's complicated work," he explained.

On March 3, he announced that he could not establish a match.

"I'm not saying the print isn't his, we were just unable to match it." Sheriff Pisciotti said the testing did not eliminate Bianchi as a suspect. Turned out, not only weren't they sure if the mark on Maenza's neck was made by a right or left wrist, they weren't sure if it was a wrist at all.

"It might've been another part of the arm," Pisciotti admitted.

For the rest of that year and most of the next, Rochester area authorities wanted badly to interrogate Bianchi regarding the double-initial killings, but he still had legal duties in L.A., as he was the key witness in his cousin's trial. When that case was finished, L.A. authorities said, the folks from back east could have a crack at him.

In the meantime, there was a joint Monroe and Wayne County investigation seeking elements that might tend to link Bianchi with the double-initial victims. It yielded nothing. By the end of 1983, they were still expressing interest in doing further print tests on parts of Bianchi's body, and talking to him about his love of the alphabet, but they had stopped referring to him as a serious suspect.

By 1993 the cloud of suspicion was getting on Bianchi's nerves. He didn't like the fact that it was occasionally printed in the paper that he might've raped and killed little girls. It was bad for his reputation and that could be rough in prison. No one wanted to be pegged as "short eyes", i.e. a child molester. Sometimes guys like that get their just desserts.

So he wrote a letter to Monroe County D.A. Howard R. Relin: "There is no physical trace evidence, witnesses, or admissions by me concerning those three murders. I did not commit those three murders. I respectfully request a final determination on this. Drop me as a suspect or charge me. This indefinite status must end."[184]

Relin said it was "bizarre" getting a letter from Bianchi "out of the blue." The timing was puzzling as there was nothing going on in the double-initials cases and hadn't been for some time. He wondered what prompted Bianchi to write.

By the time DNA technology was available, in Monroe County only the sample from the Wanda Walkowicz crime scene was viable for comparison, so when Bianchi's DNA did not match he was cleared of that murder only—and even then there was a chance he could've been involved. Bianchi was not eliminated at all as a Carmen Colon suspect, and his car did resemble one seen on the shoulder of the Western Expressway.[185]

By December of 2008, Bianchi was more sick and tired of being a DIK suspect than ever. In a precise print/script hybrid that resembled a font, Bianchi penned a letter to a member of Rochester media, explaining his innocence, and offering up some theories as to why his protestations of innocence were slow to take.

Bianchi couldn't believe his name still popped up in connection with the three murders, that he understood that the extreme emotions that were unleashed by a child's murder were difficult to quell and produced desperation for a solution, a frenzy that could easily send an investigation awry.

Bianchi emphasized that he had a job-related alibi for one of the murders, and since the murders were connected, that cleared him of all three. Then there was the wrist print. A court order had been unnecessarily acquired (they could've just asked him) for his wrist prints and there was no match. So he was officially cleared of Walkowicz and Maenza. Bianchi pointed out that his DNA profile was in a database both in California and Washington. He suspected that police in New York had tried to match it to the Walkowicz evidence. Therefore, he was not a suspect in any way, shape, or form, and there was no reason to interview him, on videotape or otherwise.

"I am as innocent of those 'Double Initial' killings as you are," Bianchi wrote. "What the hell is wrong with you? Witch hunts like this lead to innocent people being put in prison."

He wrote that modern reporters didn't rock the boat. Journalists were like cattle, being led by the nose to the news they were supposed to see. They tended to lean one way or another on the political spectrum, never neutral as he was certain they taught in journalism schools. There was no objectivity. They were too afraid to offend their advertisers. Bianchi urged his reader to wake up, to leave the pack and report the truth. One day Bianchi would be proven innocent and here was an opportunity for a career-altering scoop." He signed "Sincerely, Kenneth Bianchi."

Shelley

On April 11, 1976, almost two-and-a-half years after the murder of Michelle Maenza, the strangled body of six-year-old Michelle McMurray was discovered on a grassy area next to the driveway to a building near the corner of Jay and Orchard streets in Rochester, next door to the building in which she lived in a walkup apartment above a grocery store. The discovery was made at 4:00 a.m., just an hour after she had been reported missing. Police said that the little girl had been raped twice, and strangled. They had no strong suspects.

Detective Anthony Fantigrossi said that other than the fact that she was young, raped, and killed, and that she had the same first and last initial, there was *nothing* to connect this case to the three previous murders.

The girl's 22-year-old mother, Deborah Ruggles, a single mom, said that she had last seen her daughter at about two o'clock on the morning of the murder. She told police that she left the child alone to go out and buy cigarettes at a neighborhood bar (the Princess Restaurant on Lake Avenue).

The door to the apartment was locked from the outside but not chained closed from the inside, so the woman could let herself in when she returned. She told police that she returned to her apartment an hour later, accompanied by a man she had met in the bar, and discovered the child to be missing. She quickly searched the apartment for her daughter and called police immediately.

The little girl's body was found wearing a tee-shirt and panties. Police said that they were working under the assumption that the killer was someone the mother and daughter knew, noting that he entered the home through the front door and "simulated a break-in." A fire escape ladder leading to an open door of the second-floor apartment had been pulled down, but police believed the killer did this on his way out, rather than in. Robbery was ruled out as a motive as nothing other than the child was taken.

Two men were questioned during the first 24 hours of the investigation, and both were released. Eventually 65 men would be interrogated. Police said that they didn't think more than one man was involved in the murder despite the fact that the victim had been raped at least twice. Neither the police nor the medical examiner would comment on how the girl had been strangled.[186] (Although it later came out that the killer used his hands.)

The mother apparently agreed that her daughter's killer was someone she knew. "I think they meant it for me," she reportedly told a friend. Ruggles and her daughter had lived in the building since January, and were recipients of welfare.

The little girl wasn't well cared for, neighbors said. Whereas other little girls had to be inside by dusk, little Shelley (as Michelle McMurray was called) stayed outside alone until 9 or 9:30. Shelley had told a young friend that her mother often wasn't around and that there was a key in the mailbox so she could let herself into the apartment.

On the Saturday night before the murder a man named Robert Niesen stopped by the apartment. He was a bus-driver and Sunday school teacher for the Gates Baptist Temple. (That's the same evangelical church whose leaflets were found in the homes of Carmen, Wanda, and Michelle Maenza.) The man wanted to find out if Shelley needed a ride to church the next morning and found her alone in the apartment. Five hours later, Shelley was still home alone when she was attacked.[187]

One reason that Rochester police were not quick to consider this the work of a serial killer was that they had used that tact in the past and it had gotten them nowhere. The emphasis would be on finding Shelley's murderer, and if he happened to be the guy for the others, all the better.

There were key differences between this and the other murders. Shelley was younger. The abduction and dump were completely different. There was even something about the sexual attack, authorities didn't elaborate, that separated this case from the others.

There was one pattern that was difficult to ignore, and that was the April-November cycle. Carmen Colon was murdered in November, Wanda Walkowicz in April. Michelle Maenza in November, and now Michelle McMurray in April.

As for the age difference, the medical examiner pointed out that the killer might not have known just how young Shelley was. Dr. Edland said that Shelley was "unusually tall for her age, just under five feet tall."[188] She was taller than Wanda Walkowicz, for example, who was small for her age. Shelly weighed 58 pounds, the medical examiner noted.

During the autopsy it was discovered that Shelley had numerous scratches on her neck, and on both the front and back of her body. She had abrasions and bruises on her back and on her face. The scratches on the neck appeared to indicate that she was strangled with hands.

There was no evidence that she had been beaten, but there was evidence that she had been the victim of a "traumatic rape." Police admitted that they still didn't know how the killer got into the apartment, how he left, or how the body got to the place where it was left. Authorities did admit that they were withholding a few clues regarding the crime scene in order to use them while questioning suspects.

This time police were not asking people to call in with tips. Fantigrossi opined, "We don't need any more confusion in this investigation. It is confusing enough as it is." By April 13, analysis of the semen found at the crime scene indicated that Shelley's killer was not the Walkowicz and Maenza killer.

Since Fantigrossi believed that Carmen's killer was not responsible for the later murders, this meant the four double-initial victims may have been killed by as any as three different men.[189]

Police now believed that Michelle McMurray's killer, after raping the little girl twice, staged a burglary, removed the girl's body from the apartment via a bathroom window, walked across the roof onto the neighbor's roof where he tossed the girl down toward the driveway.

Fantigrossi showed frustration at a press conference when asked if the RPD was the only agency investigating the new murder. "If any agency thinks they can come in here and clear these cases, I welcome them to. I told the boys that I don't care if the Boy Scouts bring this guy in. I want the bastard."

April 13 was also the day that Shelley was buried at Riverside Cemetery on Lake Avenue, following a 30-minute private funeral service at the Gates Baptist Temple on Lyell Road, where the little girl attended Sunday school, which began at 10:00 a.m.

Approximately 50 relatives attended the service. A canvassing of the neighborhood revealed that Shelley's mother might have been out of the apartment leaving her daughter alone for longer than she had claimed, and plans to re-interview the mother were forthcoming.

The McMurray case didn't resemble the previous double-initial cases, yet there was no differentiation when it came to the community's moral outrage. Zephaniah Whitfield, president of the Afro-West Indian Social Club, was giving a speech at the Church of the Most Precious Blood to an audience of 100 people, including local government and religious leaders, when he listed off the names of the four murder victims and asked the unanswerable question: "What on God's Earth is there in a seven-year-old girl for a man to rape her?"[190]

Michael Macaluso Jr.'s CDC sponsored the meeting. Macaluso took the opportunity to reinforce its message that porn was the major cause of the degeneration of society's morals.

On April 16, police asked the public to help with the McMurray case, but with a caveat. The tip lines for the double-initial killings had previously become cumbersome because so many of the "tips" were actually theories, or reports of unrelated men who seemed suspicious. Police wanted the public to know that people should call the McMurray tip line only if they had *facts to report*.[191]

On April 17, police announced that they had found five witnesses who helped them meticulously account for Mrs. Ruggles time away from the apartment, but no witnesses that could help them with the crime itself.

Lieutenant Louis Campanozzi, head of the RPD's violent crimes detectives, said, "We're taking some affirmative actions to settle some questions regarding one potential suspect." He refused to elaborate.[192] Off the record, word was there were two guys: one of Mrs. Ruggles barroom pickups was hinky as hell, and the building's super had trouble making eye contact.

Two days later city detectives raided an apartment at Hillendale St., one that belonged to the pickup who turned out to be a 21-year-old-year-old man we'll call Scott Berry. While searching for evidence in the rape-murder, they discovered four pounds of marijuana and some marijuana plants. Also confiscated were some items of clothing, which were being examined by evidence technicians.[193]

Berry told police that he knew Mrs. Ruggles from school, and had run into her recently in a tavern and became re-acquainted. Since then he had been to her apartment once, staying about 20 minutes.

He was released the next day, the 20th, after pleading not guilty to the drug charge, which was eventually dropped because drugs weren't mentioned in the search warrant. And the sad McMurray case faded from the public consciousness.

In 2001, Detective Fantigrossi's nephew, Police Investigator Joseph Dominick, son of the Joe Dominick who originally worked the Shelly McMurray case, was handed cold-case duty and went to work on this one. As far as he was concerned there was only one suspect that looked good. He was the superintendent of the apartment building, a man named James Pressler, who had been interrogated at the time of the murder and, according to RPD Sergeant Mark Mariano, considered a "person of interest."

Dominick didn't give up on the case and put together a solid circumstantial case against Pressler—the theory being that the removal of the body through a bathroom window and across a rooftop required someone who knew the structure well. He then contacted authorities in Florida, where Pressler moved years before.

In 2007, two sheriff's deputies from Monroe County, Florida tailed Pressler. They watched as he smoked a cigarette. When he was finished he discarded the butt and they picked it up. The DNA from saliva on the butt matched that found at the McMurray crime scene. It was the oldest (31 years) cold case to be solved in Monroe County (N.Y.) history.

The current lab technicians sang the praises of the original crime-scene investigators who so carefully gathered evidence in 1976. The killer had been 33 at the time of the murder, and 64 at the time of his arrest.[194] Pressler had been living in Florida for 20 years, most recently on Big Pine Key.[195]

At the time of Pressler's arrest it was unclear if Deborah Ruggles was aware that her daughter's killer was under arrest. Ruggles had long-since left the Rochester area and authorities were attempting to "track her down."

Like many men who rape and kill little girls, Pressler didn't last long once inside the justice system. In fact he never made it back up to Rochester to face trial. While being held in a Florida jail, only days after his arrest, Pressler reportedly complained of chest pains and died in Lower Key Hospital.[196]

In 1995, the Associated Press reported that a prisoner in a maximum-security prison had claimed that he knew the DIK's identity.[197] The informant told Wayne County Sheriff Richard Pisciotti some "interesting things" that Pisciotti felt were "worthy of further investigation." Communication between the two began when the informant sent Pisciotti a map of the Eddy Road area where Michelle's body was found. This suspect wasn't cleared until twelve years later when DNA from the spittle on a discarded cigarette butt (same method used as with Pressler) was used for comparison purposes.

Pisciotti said that people didn't realize the toll cases like this took on police officers. He'd lived this case over and over in his mind: "In my mind, these little girls can never rest in peace until we find this guy."[198]

Detective Andy Sparacino expressed similar sentiments. It had bothered him for all these years: "What happened to these little girls just tore your guts out."

In the beginning of March 2009, D&C crime reporter Gary Craig wrote a two-part series on the double-initial cases.[199] State Police Investigator Thomas Crowley said that, among cold cases, this one was particularly active. That was because police still had hope of finding the killer. "We feel like we are making progress," he said, adding that the four agencies investigating the murders, RPD, MCSO, Wayne County Sheriff, and the State Police, were in regular communication to "discuss possible new leads."

Wayne County Sheriff Pisciotti, who photographed Michelle Maenza's autopsy, said he still reviewed her file regularly and looking at those images made it feel like "it happened yesterday."

MCSO Investigator Nicholas DeRosa, who had gone to Puerto Rico in search of Carmen Colon's uncle, told Craig that he'd never stopped suspecting Miguel Colon. Flight. His Caddy cleaned with heavy detergents. Carmen's doll in the car. DeRosa said he was sorry that the case was never presented to a grand jury. He thought there might've been enough there to indict Uncle Miguel in Carmen's murder.

MCSO Investigator Robert Russello had his own favorite suspect for Carmen, a fellow named James Barber, who worked in the Bull's Head area where he had no friends or family, left the area soon after the murder, leaving behind many of his belongings. On the day of the murder he penciled in info on his work time card (he was an assistant chef at a local country club) rather than use the clock punch. Most importantly, he was wanted in Ohio for assaulting and sodomizing a 15-year-old girl. Barber was now deceased, and his family DNA rang no bells.[200] According to Patrick Crough, Barber was not a suspect for Wanda and Michelle because he left the Rochester area soon after Carmen's murder.[201]

Craig interviewed Wanda's younger sister Ruth (pseudonym) who spoke of her own post-traumatic stress. Wanda was abducted on a rainy Monday, the day before Ruth's birthday, and to this day she had "dark moods" on gloomy Mondays.

Craig revealed that "recently" (sometime soon before March 2009) the newspaper had received a letter from a prison inmate claiming that a relative of his had committed at least one of the murders. A check with police revealed that this informant had frequently made these same claims. A swab of the informant failed to make a familial match with the case's extant DNA and the matter was dropped.

Crowley told Craig about another unnamed suspect who had passed away in 1974 and had been accused of acting suspiciously at the time of the 1973 murders, having expressed his sexual desire for female children and becoming overly emotional regarding the murders, despite not knowing the victims.

Yet another suspect was ratted out by his friend's sister. Police found no mention of the man in their files but did find his name on the log of attendees at one of the victims' funerals. This suspect also died in 1974. Both of these suspects, Crowley said, yielded no match through familial DNA samples obtained from relatives in Nevada and Alabama.

And there, with a limp and a lurch, the DIK investigation moved slothfully through the first decades of the 21st century—that is, until a new suspect exploded into the headlines: a Rochesterian, now in California, a man who had been arrested for killing street women with double-initialed names. The kicker was: One of the California killer's victims was also named Carmen Colon. Now *that* couldn't be a coincidence, could it?

Joseph Naso

In a story replete with odd ducks, Joseph Naso (pronounced NAY-zo) may be the oddest duck of all. He was a genuine weird-o, a man who could be stunningly peculiar in a variety of ways, some of them deadly.

He was born on January 7, 1934 in New York State. He may have been strange to begin with, but his behavioral idiosyncrasies were exacerbated by abandonment and death. His father left home when Joseph was young. His mother died soon thereafter. Joseph's moral compass was left to spin in the wind.

He made his first appearance in the Rochester *D&C* on August 23, 1948, as Joe Naso. He'd just competed in a Gannett Youth Club-sponsored Monroe County Junior rifle championship tournament designed to teach proper care and use of firearms.[202]

His first publicized trouble came on March 23, 1953,[203] when the tiniest of all items in the newspaper read, "Joseph Naso, 19, of Tillou Rd., Fairport, was fined $10 in City Court yesterday when he pleaded guilty before Judge Thomas P. Culhane to a charge of driving with improper lights." It is difficult to imagine why this was considered news worthy. City Court must have handled many traffic cases, moving and stationary on that day, yet it was Naso who received the one-inch item.

Four months later, Naso again made the papers, this time by being one of two local men who had enlisted the previous day in the Air Force. His address in this item was on W. Spruce St. in Fairport. He served in the Air Force from 1953 to 1957, discharged abruptly amid charges of sexual impropriety.

On April 26, 1958 we get a better idea of the dangerous man Naso had become.[204] He was charged with second-degree assault and attempted rape by the MCSO in connection with an alleged attack on a "21-year-old Central Park[205] woman." Central Park was a street in the city of Rochester.

He waived examination before Perinton Peace Justice Robert Gurney and was ordered held without bail for the Grand Jury. The victim told sheriff's deputies that Naso offered her a ride home from a Cortland Street bus stop on Thursday evening, April 24, but instead of taking her home he drove her to White Haven Memorial

Cemetery on Marsh Road in Pittsford, where the attack took place.

The deputies asked her why she accepted a ride from a stranger. She explained he wasn't a complete stranger; he was more of an acquaintance. They had previously met at a dance.

Bizarrely, Naso failed to realize that non-consensual sex might hinder his chances of future romance with his victim. After the attack, he dropped her off at her house and waited outside, just in case the girl wanted to invite him in to meet her parents.

What happened was, the victim's mother came running out and wrote down Naso's license plate number, which led to his prompt arrest.[206] But not so quick that he didn't have a chance to write about the sex attack in his journal, an entry that wouldn't be discovered by authorities until his 2011 arrest as a serial killer.

Cutting a deal in which the attempted rape charge was dropped, Naso pleaded guilty to *second-degree assault with intent to commit rape* on September 10, 1958[207] and two weeks later was placed by County Judge George D. Ogden on five years probation with a suspended sentence of two-and-a-half to five years.[208]

According to author C.L. Swinney, Naso was again arrested for rape early in 1960, and again avoided doing any time—this time because the victim refused to appear in court.

Naso was working as a printer, and living on East Ave. (a block east of Goodman) in September 1962, when he married the former Judith E. Weiermiller (born circa 1938) of Rundel Park, where she was a neighbor of my father Ben Benson. She was younger and would have been a ten-year-old girl when my dad across the street was coming home from the army.

The Nasos had a baby boy in 1963, a kid with health problems. Joe and Judith were divorced in 1980. During the mid-1970s, Naso lived in the East Bay, both in Oakland and in El Cerrito. During that time he took classes at Merritt College in Oakland. He attended the College of Alameda for one term during the fall of 1975. There were reports that he'd gone to Peralta Community College, but a rep from that school denied that he was ever a full-time student or received a degree from PCC.

On January 10, 1977, the Marin County Sheriff's Office operator received a phone call from an adult male calling from a pay phone. The operator later said the man sounded as if he were in his thirties. The caller reported the location of a body but hung up when he was asked his name.

A deputy went to the spot, a rural area near Fairfax, California. While walking along the shoulder of the road, the deputy spotted the body of a five-foot-two teenager, leading to the presumption that the call had come in from the killer himself.

The victim was found to have been strangled and bound with panty hose, dumped in tall brush along the eastern slope of White's Hill, alongside of Lagunitas Road, not far from Sir Francis Drake Boulevard, about four miles east of Lagunitas.

The victim, in essence nude, was curled into a ball and on her right side. She wore four pairs of pantyhose, one on her legs and pulled partially up, one stuffed into her mouth, a third tied around her neck, and a fourth around her face holding the gag in. The pantyhose on her legs were inside out. Perhaps her killer had redressed her. Her feet were bound together with a white cloth belt.

Marin County Medical Examiner Dr. Ken Holmes, assisted by his partner Dr. Erving Jindrich, performed the post-mortem procedure. The victim had red hair, freckles, and a tattoo, still unusual at that time. There was severe bruising on the left side of her face. They found strangulation marks around the neck, marks consistent with ligature strangulation, which was listed as the manner of death.

The pantyhose removed from the victim's mouth yielded semen samples from two different men. Human skin found beneath her fingernails was carefully scraped and bagged as evidence. Defensive wounds, bruising and cuts, to her hands and arms indicated that she'd fought her attacker. The body was found to have only one lung, which helped identity the victim as 18-year-old Roxene Roggasch, who'd had her other lung removed when she was only three days old. Fingerprints completed the ID.

A check of Roxene's background revealed that she'd had two abortions before she was 15, and had been a sex worker on the International Boulevard stroll in Oakland at the time she dated Joseph Naso.

A troubled woman, she'd tried multiple times to commit suicide despite trying to raise a son. She was last seen on her way to the MacArthur Bay Area Rapid Transit (BART) station in early January 1977, where she sometimes solicited johns.

Marin County lead investigator Detective Rich Keaton called on Roggasch's stepfather Vernon Ashby in San Jose to say they found Roxene.[209] He and Roxene's mother Beverly drove up to Marin County and officially identified the body.

Detective Keaton talked to Roxene's brother Larry and learned heartbreaking details of her childhood. Both parents were alcoholics, drug addicts, and abusive. When she was six her father was killed in a gruesome construction accident. Her mom remarried when Roxene was eight, bringing Ashby into the family. According to Larry, Ashby was worse than their natural father. Roxene ran away, lived for a time in San Jose, and even got a job with a traveling circus, before returning to the Oakland area where she met a guy named Benjamin Bennett.

Police did not immediately think serial killer, or one of Roxene's johns for that matter. They had two early suspects, each suspected of working alone. It was doubtful they'd ever functioned as a team because they were archenemies. A chatty and angry woman from Roggasch's stroll—referred to in police reports as a confidential informant—told cops the killer was her own nasty-ass abusive layabout pimp, the super alliterative Ronald Ray Rochelle.

The other suspect was Roxene's boyfriend Benjamin Bennett, who ended up in jail after Roxene's disappearance because he searched for her recklessly. Bennett looked at first like a better suspect than Rochelle. He was a powerful love broker with a large chunk of the International Boulevard street scene to himself. Bennett, in emotional stress over Roxene's murder, was *eager* to talk with investigators.

He'd seen a guy, didn't know his name, who toured the block as if he were in the produce section of a grocery store, squeezing breasts like he was choosing a melon. This john had a weirdly delusional sense of domain—a photographer with an expensive-looking camera, all the time smacking his lips like he was enjoying a tasty morsel.

The guy was cheap and cruel as well, tried to shortchange a girl once, made her pick the money up off the floor, with that camera around his neck, tried to trade a photo session for sex, and gave off unhinged vibes. He didn't spin like the rest of the world. There was something about his axis, something fundamentally *off*.[210]

Roxene had a stack of unpaid bills. She was desperate for

money and would have gone off with any guy, even one she didn't like, even Mr. Shutterbug. Which, according to Bennett, she did.

Roxene told Bennett they were going to Shutterbug's place, an apartment around the corner on Foothill Boulevard. When Roxene failed to return from the trick, Bennett went looking for her, but pounded on and eventually kicked in the wrong door and was arrested. He knew the freak with the camera lived near there. *He* was responsible for Roxene...

But cops didn't listen and the solid lead was lost. All police wanted to know from Bennett how often he hit Roxene. Bennett was in jail for a long five weeks before they turned him loose. By that time Roxene was long buried in Oak Hill Cemetery in San Jose. Rochelle was cleared soon thereafter and the investigation was left without a suspect.

On August 13, 1978, a California Highway Patrol officer, answering a report of a cow shooting, drove tentatively down Carquinez Scenic Drive between Port Costa and Crockett with his window open.

The officer stopped his car when he smelled decomposition, and then followed his nose to a swarm of flies at the edge of a large clearing. There were no people around, but there were cows. He got close enough to see the swarm wasn't about a cow, but rather a naked woman, severely decomposed, baked in the 100-degree heat, and partially missing due to animal and insect activity.

The officer radioed in his discovery and asked for backup from the county sheriff, whose jurisdiction this was, and reminded the dispatcher that a coroner would be needed as well. When several members of the sheriff's department arrived, the highway patrolman left the scene and never again heard anything about the case.

The deputy coroner performed the autopsy. Skin was found under the fingernails, at least those fingernails that had not been chewed off by coyotes. Partial prints were recovered from several fingers.

At first the case was listed as a Jane Doe, but those partial prints turned out to be enough to identify the body as that of 22-year-old Carmen Lorraine Colon, a street woman who'd been busted numerous times in Alameda and Contra Costa counties. Most recently, she worked on West MacArthur Boulevard and Broadway in Oakland.

She was Carmen Colon, found in Contra Costa County, California. Her body had cooked in a cow field for close to a week.

Police located Carmen's sister who was too upset by the news of Carmen's death to be coherent, but she did manage to tell police that her sister had met a man who was taking photos of her in his apartment. The guy was an oddball, but she didn't mention his name. The sister had warned Carmen not to stop going with the man.

There wasn't much of an investigation. Because of the decomposition, the Deputy Coroner couldn't even call it murder. The cause of death was listed as "inconclusive." The case was quickly put on a back burner and eventually became inactive all together.

On January 16, 1980, in Alameda County, Mrs. Judith Ellen Naso filed for divorce from her husband Joseph. Soon thereafter Joseph took a job as a superintendent at an apartment building on Leavenworth Street in San Francisco.

Now a frisky bachelor, Naso took photography classes and tested his skills on big-city women, models, students, and women on the street—whoever he could talk into it. He'd tried to talk them out of their clothes. If that failed he'd dive under the table and try to photograph up their skirts. Things often went poorly, but usually he didn't kill them.

In the meantime, Joe was a *bad* super. He ignored small problems and fixed the big ones only if he feared being fired. One day a woman came to his door and said she was answering an ad in the paper. Was the apartment still available? Joe said it was, saw to it that she got it, and, when the time came, helped her move in. She said her name was Sharieea Patton. One thing led to another and Joe started photographing the woman in all kinds of sexy attire, in all kinds of strange poses. They had several sessions together, but Joe overstepped boundaries and Sharieea ceased being cooperative.

On January 4, 1981, a woman jogged beside Paradise Drive in Tiburon, only feet from San Francisco Bay. During this morning's run she saw two black trash bags between the running path and the water. They stunk to high heaven. She took a few steps off the path to get a better look and saw the bags were alive with maggots, a sight disturbing enough for her to call 911 to the Marin County Sheriff's Office.

The dispatcher didn't prioritize a littering complaint and it wasn't until hours later that a deputy showed up at the scene looking for "suspicious trash." He found the trash all right, but didn't want to get too close. He called the California State Parks Department and told them to come pick it up, as it was their responsibility. Parks said they had nobody available to do that. Only then did the deputy take a closer look. He put on rubber gloves and used a knife to open up one of the bags, revealing human remains.

Now the scene, against a backdrop of the lapping bay, became crowded. Parks sent two rangers. Crime-scene officers pulled up and went to work. Drs. Ken Holmes and Ervin Jindrich, who had attended Roxene's autopsy, arrived and donned protective equipment to examine the contents of the bags.

"Adult female," Dr. Holmes called out.

Despite the decomposition he found ligature marks on the neck. The body had not been dismembered but rather bound with pantyhose into a tight fetal position. The pantyhose reminded the medical examiners of the Roxene Roggasch case.

The body was ID'd as that of Sharieea Patton, 56 years old. Her daughter came forward and identified her mother. A friend had seen a composite drawing in the paper and alerted the daughter that she'd better check it out.

Police learned that the victim most recently lived on Leavenworth Street and over the course of her life had used a series of surnames (Lafern, Anderson, Duvalle, Withrow, Heckert). She was born with the first name Lillian in L.A. in 1923. No dad was listed on her birth certificate, mom being a model who got in trouble. She grew up in a farmhouse near Fresno with her mom and stepdad, and after high school attended the University of Washington. Lillian changed her name in the 1940s for reasons unknown to the awkward Sharieea. She married, had a son, divorced and left the boy with his dad. She moved to San Francisco, married again, had a daughter, moved to New Mexico, where she was possibly widowed. She married at least two more times after that.[211]

Police went to Sharieea's apartment house and talked to her neighbors. They heard a sad tale of a woman new in the city from Lake Tahoe who couldn't find a job and was desperate to pay the rent. She'd lived for many years in L.A., and had even worked for a time as a clerk with the LAPD. Following that job she traced debtors on the run for a repo company. Cops wondered if she'd made an enemy during that time, but found no evidence of that. She'd applied for many jobs since arriving in San Francisco, but those leads also led to no suspects.[212]

Someone suggested cops talk to the super, who was peculiar, a guy named Naso. He'd been seen with the victim looking like he had a major crush on her, but in a creepy-crawly way.

Police talked to Naso and found him shifty, evasive, and careful in what he said. He gave them no probable cause to arrest him. What particularly irked cops was Naso's air of superiority, like he was getting off on handling his interrogation with such verbal finesse.

A couple of months later Naso quit his super job, left San Francisco, and moved to Yuba City, California.

On September 7, 1982, 37-year-old Cheryl Linn Carter, without taking her car or her purse, without contacting her family (which included two small children, ages seven and nine), left her home on Palmer Creek Road southwest of Healdsburg, California, and was never seen nor heard from again. Her children came home from school to an empty house. There were no signs of foul play. Just poof! Mommy's gone. She was described as five-six and "very thin." She had short brown hair, hazel eyes, a fair complexion, and suffered from severe allergies.[213]

Four and a half months later a decomposed body, caught up in the swollen waters of the Foss Creek, was found by a gardener snagged on debris just outside the tasting room of a Healdsburg winery. Police thought they'd found Cheryl, but a dental comparison proved to be no match. The mother of two would remain forever missing.

During the early morning of September 19, 1993, a man was walking his dog on the Simpson-Dantoni Road, a meandering country road along the Yuba River, near a rural community called Linda in Yuba County. It was a particularly beautiful stretch of road, lined with majestic and old weeping willow trees. The man had walked his dog there before, but not in a week or so. The terrier smelled something and led the man to the body of a naked woman on her back with her arms neatly folded across her chest as if she were in a coffin. The dog whimpered as the man held the leash firm to keep the animal from getting too close.

The man did not linger at the spot but instead walked briskly through the willows, and up the driveway to an adjacent dairy farm belonging to a man named Tony Luis.[214]

The body was assumed immediately to be that of Pamela Parson, for whom a missing persons report had been filed 48 hours earlier. The coroner found ligature marks on the neck and determined cause of death to be strangulation.

A background check revealed that Parson had grown up in the town of Linda. At the time of her disappearance she was waitressing at a small off-the-beaten-path sandwich shop. Word on the street was she was also a meth head and turned tricks.

On August 6, 1994, a 31-year-old Marysville, California, a down-and-out woman, drug-addicted and on the street, by the name of Tracy Lynn Tafoya went missing. Eight days later a morning paperboy was biking down a dirt road off of Highway 70, that ran next to the Marysville Cemetery, when he saw the face-down body of a naked woman at the bottom of a drain-off ditch. The odor was overwhelming. The boy biked hurriedly up to the main road, waved down a car, and the driver called the Yuba County Sheriff. First responder to the scene was Sgt. Joe Million.

When the coroner arrived he immediately thought of Sharieea Patton. There still was no thought of a serial killer, but it did occur to the coroner as he performed the autopsy that the same man killed Sharieea and this woman.

She'd been dead five or six days. There was bruising at the back of the neck and she was badly scratched up, leading investigators to believe she'd been pushed out of a moving vehicle and allowed to roll down an incline.

The ligature marks on her neck were faint but visible. Despite the decomposition, partial fingerprints were taken. These weren't necessary, however, as Tafoya's estranged-but-caring husband heard about the body, knew who it was, and ID'd the remains. The identification, as it turned out, was easy despite the extensive decomposition. Tracy Tafoya had been missing a finger, the result of a childhood lawn-mower mishap.

The husband told investigators that the last he heard from Tracy she said she had a modeling job, and was making legitimate money posing for a photographer.[215]

He provided a brief bio. She grew up in Yuba City, married and had five kids, one dying of Sudden Infant Death Syndrome. A divorce followed, depression, drugs—then a rebound and her second husband, the guy telling the story. They divorced as she deteriorated again, but he never stopped caring and had stayed in touch. Tafoya was buried on August 18 in a Sutter County cemetery.

In 1994, Joseph Naso moved from Northern California to Reno, Nevada, into a house on Medgar Avenue in what was known as Lemmon Valley. In November 1995, Naso was arrested for shoplifting panties from a ladies shop in South Lake Tahoe. He was given probation. By this time the creepy man with the camera was also rich, having made keen investments in real estate and coins. He could afford to misbehave.

In November 1997, he moved back to California, to Sacramento, where he lived until 2004 and as far as we know he didn't kill anybody during that time.

In 2004, the bleached skull of an adult white woman missing its lower jaw was found near Tahoe National Forest, east of Sacramento. Naso, according to his notebooks, remembered dumping a body there. It belonged to an obsessed Bob Dylan fan who he picked up hitchhiking. Forensic anthropologists estimated the skull had been in the sun for more than a decade.

Soon after the discovery of the skull, Naso thought it might be time for him to once again move on. He kissed Sacramento goodbye and moved back to Medgar Avenue in Reno. Bouncing back and forth between Nevada and California when the heat was turned up had proven to be an excellent strategy.

When he did get into trouble and spent time in jail it was because he was a bad theif. On July 5, 2009, Naso reported to the Nevada Department of Public Safety, Parole and Probation division. Naso was out on probation from an El Dorado County jail, and one of the caveats of his freedom was a search-and-seizure waiver out of El Dorado County with an interstate compact agreement with the Nevada Department of Public Safety (DPS).

Naso was on probation in California, but since he'd moved to Nevada that state was keeping an eye on him. His probation was scheduled to end on June 21, 2012. The parole officer always chose the time when Naso had to report to his office, and that visit was required to be at least once a month.

Sometimes Naso blew off his visit to the parole officer, so the parole officer had to come to him. Visits to Naso's home were always unannounced and made at the discretion of the officer. That officer was allowed to search Naso's home whenever he chose.

Visits to Naso's home were made on September 10, 2009, December 9, 2009, and April 13, 2010. Public Safety/Parole and Probation Officer Wes Jackson carried out that last visit, and chose to execute his right to search-without-limit Naso's residence.

Just an eyeball scan of the main room brought results. Jackson spied a single round of .380 caliber ammunition in an ashtray. This discovery prompted Jackson to pat Naso down. In a shirt pocket Naso had a second bullet and a neatly clipped-out advertisement for a gun. Boom, probation violation.

When backup officers arrived, Jackson called the phone number on the advertisement and learned that Naso had attempted to purchase the advertised gun. Naso was arrested, placed into custody, and locked up in the Washoe County Detention Facility.

The search of Naso's home that followed was meticulous but rewarding. In the words of Chris Perry, acting director of the Nevada Department of Public Safety, investigators confiscated "10,000 pieces of potential evidence."

Jackson found photographs depicting some images that he prayed were not as bad as they looked. Those photos showed scantily dressed or nude women, some in bondage, bound with pantyhose and wearing only lingerie. Some were apparently unconscious; some were blue and uncomfortably posed, possibly deceased.

Searchers found a hand-written list, the *List of 10*, referencing ten women (nine called "girls" and one called a "lady") and ten corresponding locations.

It read:

List of 10

1) **Girl near Healdsburg Mendocino Co.**
2) **Girl near Porta Costa**
3) **Girl near Loganitas**
4) **Girl on Mt. Tam**
5) **Girl from Miami near Down Peninsula**
6) **Girl from Berkeley**
7) **Lady from 839 Leavenworth**
8) **Girl in Woodland**
9) **Girl from Linda**
10) **Girl from MRSV**

When investigators compared the list with unsolved homicides, the item at #3 proved to be an instant match. It seemed to correspond with the unsolved murder of Roxene Roggasch, date January 11, 1977, dead by ligature strangulation. Authorities noted that Roxene worked very close to Naso's East Bay residence at the time. As a result of this evidence, Judge Ryan Petersen would determine that there was probable cause that Joseph Naso had been responsible for Roxene's death.

#1 interested police in Healdsberg. They had a disappearance; a young mom named Cheryl Carter had vanished.

#2 apparently referenced the murder of the adult Carmen Colon in 1978. To shore up this link, investigators noted that Carmen also worked on streets near Naso's home. Nail clippings taken during her post-natal examination yielded a partial foreign DNA file that included Joseph Naso as a possible contributor. Judge Petersen would deem this evidence sufficient probable cause to believe in Naso's guilt in the murder of Carmen Colon.

#9 corresponded with the murder of Pamela Perkins, a sex worker/waitress originally from the town of Linda, Yuba County, whose body was discovered on September 19, 1993 off Simpson-Dantoni Road in Linda. Found in Naso's residence were writings and logs about Pamela and a calendar that detailed her daily activities, indicating that Naso was obsessively stalking her.

During an interview with investigators, Naso admitted that he had taken photographs of Perkins. He also admitted that on

September 18 and 19, 1993 he had sold items at various flea markets, including at the Marysville Flea Market, one-and-a-half miles from where Perkins' body was found.

At the time of Perkins' murder, Naso lived in a two-story home on Cooper Avenue in Yuba City. During a search of Naso's safety deposit boxes in Reno, Nevada, in a zippered black bag inside an envelope, were 66 photos, some of Perkins, along with clipped newspaper articles regarding her death.

As a result of this evidence, it would be determined by Judge Petersen that there was probable cause that Joseph Naso had been responsible for Pamela's death.

#10 referred to a "Girl from MRSV", which was taken to mean Marysville. This jived with the murder of Tracy Tafoya, found next to the Marysville Cemetery. The location of the dumpsite was "near Naso's residence" at the time. In Naso's safety deposit box, police found newspaper clippings and photos related to the death of Tracy Tafoya. In Naso's home also were handwritten notes that referenced the disappearance and death of Tafoya. Judge Petersen would deem this evidence sufficient probable cause to believe in Naso's guilt in the murder of Tracy Tafoya.[216]

The other six names on the list of ten did not link up so quickly with actual cases, but were considered worthy of further study.

With the news of Naso's arrest, his neighbors on Cooper Avenue in Yuba City were among the first interviewed. Neighbor Darlene Cummings said, "One day I had a garage sale and he asked if I had any women's underwear to sell." She remembered the request as "very creepy," even creepier now that the man was an alleged serial killer.[217]

Back in Rochester, Guillermina Colon and her daughter Maria recalled first hearing the news.[218] In Spanish, Guillermina said, "I got up at 5:00 a.m. and turned on the TV. The case came up and it surprised me. I thought to myself, what's going on? Because the only thing it showed was the photo of the girls. Sometimes when I'm sitting here alone, I look at Carmen's picture; I think it was my daughter. The only thing I ask God is the person responsible is found. So many years have passed, every suspect ends up not being the one."

Maria added that she had a photo of Naso saved on her phone

and added in accent-free English, "It eats me up inside, wondering if it's him. I look at him as a sick person. Strange how they're both Carmen Colon. The only difference was one from Rochester, one from somewhere else, and eight years apart. If it was him it would be such a relief for my mother. She'd be able to live in peace knowing he was caught."

Because the Naso cases took place across a swath of jurisdictions, Marin County District Attorney Ed Berberian was chosen to supervise Naso's prosecution for all three Northern California counties involved.

Putting together the case for the people, Berberian knew, was going to be a complicated process. Just the list of law enforcement agencies with a hand in the investigation was impressive. There were: both the Investigations and the Parole & Probation divisions of the Department of Public Safety, the Washoe County Sherriff's Office, the Washoe County District Attorney's Office, the FBI, plus the Marin, Contra Costa and Yuba county sheriff's offices.

Scientific analysis of the evidence continued, tightening Berberian's case, replacing conjecture with inalterable fact. Sad sack Naso lived in the El Dorado County Jail, and his chances of seeing freedom again were dismal.

At first Naso was in for probation violations. After doing that time, in April of 2011, he was released and promptly re-arrested by the Marin County Sheriff's Office, this time charged with four counts of murder.

When Rochesterians learned the names of Naso's alleged victims—PP, CC, RR, and TT—they were startled, and then relieved. The DIK had been captured! Two Carmen Colons. Finally…finally…

New York State Police Senior Investigator Allan Dombroski reported, "The investigation revealed that Naso most likely left Rochester in 1969 but he had family here and would travel back and forth."

On April 12, 2011, Marin County authorities released a detailed timeline for Joseph Naso. There was nothing obviously in the timeline to discount Naso as the killer of any of the three Rochester victims. The following day Naso was arraigned on four counts of murder with special circumstances and ordered held without bail.

On April 14, 2011, reporter Shannon Moore from the Fox affiliate in Reno went to visit Naso's residence, and found a "boarded up home with a trashed yard dried up and picked apart."[219]

Neighbors described Naso as "creepy," and one woman complained that he would scratch at her windows and hang out in her yard. Another neighbor stated that he always suspected Naso was up to *something* because, as soon as he bought the house he built a tall wall around his property—and people with tall walls were hiding something.

The reporter went to a nearby bar and met a woman named Kerri Clay, who said that she'd had an encounter with Naso, one that she'd never forget: "A gentleman came into the bar with a big portfolio and camera. He had more than a thousand photos of young girls. He said, 'I take pictures.'"

Clay said that she had a granddaughter in need of a senior portrait, and Naso agreed to be her photographer. He gave Clay a business card and offered her what Clay considered to be "a good deal" on the photos.

Clay said, "I later threw the card out because I got to thinking, I had second thoughts. The guy seemed suspicious. It was the photos in his portfolio, all female. No boys. No couples. Just women, from two-year-olds up to age 40. It looked like all of the photos were taken out in the woods someplace, not in a park or anything, but away in a remote area."

Now that she knew the guy might be a serial killer, thoughts of the encounter became terrifying: "I came this close to risking my granddaughter's life. I could be looking at him like I'm looking at you and not know the difference. And then put my granddaughter in harm's way—all because someone gave me a deal."

Neighbors with Naso stories turned out to be easy to find. He'd resided in many places and had always acted memorably peculiar.

In the days that followed, Naso's DNA was compared to that suspected of being from Rochester's DIK. No match. Despite fresh investigation in Rochester, and mind-blowing coincidences, *no evidence* connected Naso with the Rochester murders.

Dombroski noted that like Kenneth Bianchi, Naso could not be ruled out as the Rochester killer on DNA results alone.[220] There was the possibility that the Rochester DNA was of an origin other than the DIK. Nobody knew if the DIK was a lone nut, or if he had accomplices. Nobody knew what happened to Carmen, Wanda, and Michelle during their last hours.

Former FBI profiler Gregg McCrary, who had worked with the local police on the Shawcross case, said that the police were wise not to rule Naso out based solely on the DNA. "In a case like this," McCrary said, "you have to keep your options and hypothesis open because we don't know the answers."[221]

There were strong factors that led investigators to believe that Naso was, at least in part, a copycat, that there were *two* Double-Initial Killers, *at least*, not one, acting separately, and that the Rochester guy preferred children while the Northern California guy preferred adults.

On April 13 reporters Karl Fischer and Robert Salonga, working for the Bay Area News Group, located Joseph's ex-wife Judith coming out of her Oakland apartment.[222] She explained that the FBI had asked her not to talk to the media.

"I'm in shock over my ex-husband's arrest and knew nothing about any murders," she said, and hurriedly retreated back into her apartment and for the rest of the day refused to either answer the door or the phone.

The reporters had better luck next door. A woman identifying herself as Gwendolyn Friend said she'd been Judith's next door neighbor since 1997 and thought of Joseph as a conscientious ex-husband, who visited twice a year to check up on the welfare of his ex.

"When was the last time?" one of the reporters asked.

"Early 2010, I guess."

Gwendolyn remembered thinking Joseph was a little odd. He had difficulty making eye contact with her during their infrequent conversations. "He didn't seem like that kind of person but I guess you never know. Never in my wildest dreams did I think he would pop up on TV as a serial killer."

Naso's writings brought some mild good news. The notebooks contained a fact-and-fantasy combo. Not all of the women on the list had been murdered, and apparently at least some of them had merely been stalked without their knowledge. Some didn't know they had been targets until police investigators came around checking on their welfare.

A man named Thaddeus Iorizzo told reporter Matthias Gafni of the *Contra Costa Times* that his wife Margaret Prisco was #7 on Naso's list. In 1981 when the stalking occurred, Prisco was 23 years old and lived in San Francisco's Mission District.[223] Naso was their downstairs neighbor.

Prisco must have been a Naso favorite. He filled three notebooks with fantasies regarding the way he would have liked to torture her. The notebooks referred to her as Peggy Prisco (double initials), something she was never called. It was an indication that Naso didn't know her well, and perhaps that he enjoyed alliteration.

Thaddeus and Margaret lived in Upstate New York in 2011 and admitted that they hadn't thought about the acquaintance they referred to as "Crazy Joe" in the 30 years since they stopped living near him. That is until Iorizzo received a phone call from Detective William Thurston of the Nevada DPS.

"I just want to know if your wife is still breathing," Thurston said.

"Yeah, she got up and went to work today. So, yeah, she's all right," Iorizzo replied.[224]

Prisco was understandably troubled by the news that she'd been in Naso's dirty notebook, even after all these years. "It's disconcerting," she said. She couldn't stop thinking about how young and vulnerable she was at that time, living in San Francisco and walking around without her guard up. She and her husband had since moved back east but back then they were filled with the adventurousness of youth, moving to San Francisco almost as a whim.

Iorizzo told the Associated Press that he and his wife just threw their bags in their yellow Volkswagen bus and drove Route 66. They ended up in San Francisco with flowers in their hair, Golden Gate Bridge or bust. Iorizzo was a musician, played the bass, and already had a gig lined up in the Bay Area.

They moved into a studio apartment, Prisco got a job working for a used-car dealership and Iorizzo moved furniture, and they got by, all but oblivious to the building's superintendent, then 47-year-old Joseph Naso, who had the bounce of new bachelorhood in his step. After 18 years of marriage he was officially divorced from Judith.

Interaction with Naso was not frequent but occasionally memorable. Naso, the couple later realized, knew that they were from the same area of Upstate New York as he was because they had used Upstate New York references on their rental application. One morning, Iorizzo was heading for the garbage chute to empty his trash and encountered Naso already there, pushing two stacks of pornographic magazines, tied together with twine, down the chute. Iorizzo could see that some of the magazine covers featured photographs of women in bondage. Naso denied ownership of the magazines.

"This isn't mine, this isn't mine," Naso said and left without finishing his task, so Iorizzo had an opportunity to untie one of the bundles and look at the magazines.

"This is disgusting! Who would look at stuff like that?" Iorizzo recalled saying.

That occurred in the morning. That very afternoon Iorizzo was practicing his bass, the thumping going right through the walls of the apartment complex. Naso came to complain about the noise in a pair of boxers, a tank top, and slippers, and holding a bottle of tequila. He screamed, "I'll kill you! I'll kill you!"

Iorizzo recalled replying, "Yeah, bring it on, Joe. You'll be seeing stars!" Iorizzo said that he had a baseball bat, a Louisville Slugger with Harmon Killebrew's autograph on it, waiting for Naso in case he attacked.

"How can you forget someone who threatened your life? It was the only time anyone had ever threatened my life." Iorizzo recalled. "That is something that stays with you. Crazy Joe."

After that Iorizzo noticed strange things happening in their apartment. His metronome was moved. His clothes were out of place. He announced that the place had gotten a "freaky vibe," so he and Prisco moved out in the spring, and never thought about Naso again until they saw his mug shot on TV.

Prisco, who became a computer programmer, said that her husband remembered Naso better than she did.

Iorizzo agreed that this was true: "Each time I crossed paths with him the hair on the back of my neck would stand up. You'd get a real creepy feeling. He was pure evil. I'd say to myself, 'Stay away from this guy. He's nuts.'"

Prisco had not been provided with details of what Naso wrote about her, but she was curious. Though fearful that the notebooks' graphic detail would keep her awake at night, "It would set my mind at ease to see if there was a threat," Prisco said.[225]

On April 14, 2011, Naso made an appearance in a Marin County courtroom. Reporter Justin Burton from the *San Francisco Gate* wasn't much impressed with the accused man. He was old, bald, stoop-shouldered, and pathetically burdened by the shackles on his wrists and ankles.[226]

Naso wore his prison striped red-and-white shirt and red sweat pants, didn't speak during the hearing but swiveled in his chair and nodded several times when his lawyer was making arguments in his favor. Naso's four-count indictment ran five pages, and he donned glasses to read it.

At the hearing D.A. Ed Berberian told the judge that the defendant had assets "approaching one million dollars" and could afford to hire a private defense attorney rather than be appointed a public defender.

After the hearing, reporters peppered Berberian with questions regarding the double-initial angle in the case, but Berberian refused to address the issue, saying only that "everything will come out in court."

In June 2012, Naso wrote a letter to KRNV-TV, News 4 in Reno in which he claimed to have been wrongfully arrested, that he had completed a one-year term in the South Lake Tahoe jail and was exiting that facility when we was "arrested without a warrant".[227]

Naso loved lashing out at society in his writing, and was most prolific regarding the medical mistreatment of his son Charles, who was schizophrenic and could be violent when off his meds. Naso had two children but only mentioned Charles. David was his other unmentioned son. Some thought it unusual for a guy like Naso to care so much for a mentally ill offspring. Others have suggested his interest was monetary as he could pick up extra social security money for tending to a sick kid. While living in Yuba City, Naso said that he could take care of his son better than the health-care professionals who'd tried. He called those workers incompetent and bragged that he no longer allowed them inside his home. He always believed in the sanctity of the home. What a man did inside his own four walls was nobody's business.

Roberta Fletcher, president of the local chapter of the National Alliance for the Mentally Ill, remembered clearly her sometimes terrifying encounters with Naso regarding his son. She said, "I made sure I was never alone with him."[228]

She remembered one particularly scary encounter. She was walking down the street and saw him approaching. "I ducked into a store and went to the very back. The next thing I knew, I heard, 'Hello, Roberta.'"

Now, the kind of creepy Roberta felt, it wasn't serial-killer creepy. It never occurred to her that he wanted to kill her. He just seemed like a strange and very lonely man, and instead of running for her life, she merely impressed upon him that she was "not available" for dates.

Now that she knew, it felt very strange. She knew him during the time when he was committing some of his murders. She knew him when he was an *active* killer.

He'd told her he had moved to Yuba City from San Francisco because he hoped his son would receive better care. She remembered him being well-dressed, intelligent, and polite.

At the time she found it unusual that he was evasive whenever she asked him about his work history. She was surprised to learn that he'd been a professional photographer. She never got the sense that he was a photographer, or an anything for that matter. She thought that he was independently wealthy and didn't have to work.

Now that she knew about the double-initials thing, she figured she was safe all along. But she would never forget the way he focused on her when they had conversations, his eyes demanding more information, like maybe he was a police detective or a private investigator or something.

In addition to his list of ten, Naso implicated himself in the murders on his desk calendars. The entry for September 15, 1993, read, "Stayed in Yuba City all day long. Took care of some old business." That was the last date that Pamela Perkins was known to be alive.

On another calendar, in an entry for August 6, 1994, Naso wrote, "Picked up a nice broad in Marysville. 4 p.m. She came over for four hours. Took photographs. Nice legs. She ripped me off." That was the last day Tracy Tafoya was known to be alive. Hers was the body found alongside Highway 70 near Marysville Cemetery.

Authorities back in Monroe County were still interested in Naso as the Rochester DIK, despite an attempt to match DNA that "didn't work." The fact that one of Naso's California victims was named Carmen Colon was simply too much to ignore. If it was a coincidence, it was one of the wildest ever. Some argued that Carmen Colon, the adult, rarely told johns her real name, so there was little chance Naso ever knew. There's nothing in his writings about her name, or double initials, or the alphabet. He called Margaret Prisco by the name Peggy, that was it.

At the very least, Naso was a copycat killer, right?—perhaps creating an homage to the Original DIK.

In January 2012 there was a preliminary hearing to determine if there was enough evidence to hold Naso over for trial. First Naso refused to pay for a lawyer, and then he refused to be repped by a public defender. He insisted on acting as his own lawyer.

One of the first witnesses, Nevada DPS probation officer David LeBaker testified that he had searched Naso's home in 2010, found his journal, which in part read:

"Girl in north Buffalo woods. She was real pretty. Had to knock her out first. 1958."

"Salina, Kansas girl I followed and met at Fred Astaire dance studio. She was gorgeous. Great legs in nylons, heels. Had to rape her in my car on a cold wintery night. Snow storm."

"Outside the front door I overpowered her and ravaged her. I couldn't help myself."

LeBaker testified that the diary appeared to document rapes and sexual assaults of underage girls. One item described a young girl on a bus in Arkansas.

LeBaker testified that his next step was to search Naso's dresser drawers and in them found women's lingerie. In the other bedroom, LeBaker discovered the list that referenced the four victims in this case, plus six others.

Near the list, he discovered a cache of photographs, some depicting unconscious and nude woman. "Some were in awkward, unnatural positions yet appeared unconscious," LeBaker said. His gut feeling was that they were not just asleep, but had been rendered unconscious—or were dead.

Some photos were pinned up on a poster board. Some, he noted, were difficult to identify because they showed the woman from the waist down only. The photographs of clearly alive models were just as disturbing, as they showed the contorted visages of women in terror.

There was other stuff about the place that painted a picture: at one end of the house was a room with a bolt on the door so it could only be opened from the outside. In the middle of the door was a flap, like the food slots found in the doors of prison cells. That room's window was the only one in the house fitted with metal bars. It wasn't just a room, it was a cell. He was equipped to keep prisoners.

During cross-examination, Naso asked, "Are you familiar with the details of the sexual assault laws in other states? You know the age of consent and other laws can differ from state to state."

The witness replied, "If I heard that someone digitally penetrated a young woman, I would say that's sexual assault."

Next on the stand was Nevada probation officer Wesley Jackson, who testified that in April 2010 he went to Naso's home in search of probation violations. "In Mr. Naso's bedroom I found mannequin parts, and one full female mannequin in a red dress."

Jackson thought it odd that there should be so much female garb when there was no female living on the premises. Later during the search of Naso's garage, more mannequin legs were discovered. One mannequin had her legs up in the air and was wearing panty hose. Officer Jackson checked Naso to see if he too was wearing pantyhose, but the old man had socks on.

Naso himself handled cross-examination. Awkward wasn't the word for it. Take this example from the cross-examination of Nevada Department of Public Safety Detective Richard Brown:

"Detective Brown, you have an obsession with my photographs and my lifestyle, don't you?"

"Only as they pertain to this murder investigation, but yes."

"You are obsessed with my journal."

"I have read it repeatedly, yes."

"You called it a rape journal, why did you call it that?"

"I call it a rape journal because in it you write things such as, 'I had to rape her. I raped her in an alley. I raped her in the front seat of my car.' You used the word rape."

"That, in my culture, and where I come from, that refers to making out, scoring, getting to first base." Naso said.

There were audible gasps in the courtroom.

Naso continued, "I use that term loosely. It's just a fantasy."

Other evidence presented against Naso at the hearing was circumstantial in nature. Naso was in possession of newspaper clippings regarding the Perkins and Tafoya murders and, on a calendar, had written that he was in the same town as Perkins on the day she disappeared. Naso, court documents stated, had been living in the Yuba City area with his mentally ill son at the time of Parson's murder, and hard evidence indicated that Naso had photographed Perkins.

On January 12, 2012, Richard Tafoya took the stand to testify regarding his memories of the day his wife disappeared 17 years earlier. He lost his composure, broke down in tears, and had what the prosecution later termed an "anxiety attack."[229]

Court took a short recess and when the hearing resumed, Tafoya was far more composed. He apologized, saying, "I never had to deal with this before." He testified that his wife had been a drug addict and a prostitute, identified her in photos found in Naso's safe deposit box, and identified items of clothing she was wearing in the photos as lingerie they had purchased together.

The following day, an 80-year-old woman testified via video feed from her home in Florida. Her name was Betty Clarke (pseudonym), and she told the court that she met Naso during the 1990s when they both lived in Sutter County. She answered an advertisement that Naso had placed seeking a caretaker for his disabled son. She did not get the job but she and Naso hit it off and commenced a sexual relationship. There came a time when Clarke moved to Florida, and she only saw Naso twice after that.

"You had to break off the relationship, isn't that correct, Ms. Clarke?" asked prosecutor Rosemary Slote.

"Yes, I did."

"And what was your reason for breaking it off?"

"I don't remember."

"I show you now photographs of a woman wearing lingerie,

her hands bound together up near the ceiling with cord, in another [photo] bound on a bed, apparently unconscious, and I ask you if you recognize that woman."

"I do."

"And who is she?"

"That's me."

"Can you explain how you came to be in those positions?"

"No, I don't remember."

This answer did not disappoint Slote. It supported the prosecution's theories that Naso routinely drugged his victims, sometimes into unconsciousness, so that he could pose them without resistance.

Once Clarke's memory started to fail on the stand, it continued to do so. She struggled and eventually failed to verify written police statements she had made alleging violence and threats by Naso. Nonetheless, despite her faulty memory, the statements and photographs did exist, and that was what mattered. Slote ended her direct examination, and it was Naso's turn to cross.

"You still look good, Betty. After all these years you still look good to me," Naso began. "When we were together, Betty, we had a good time, didn't we?"

"Yes."

"Do you remember the day trips we took, the dinners out we had?"

"Yes."

"Do you remember holding hands and taking long walks."

"I do," Betty Clarke said, and she giggled.

At the prosecution table the ladies were pinching themselves to make sure they hadn't slipped into the twilight zone.

Naso seemed pleased with the witness's giggle, but that was the high point of his cross-examination.

"Do you ever remember me mistreating you?"

"Yes."

"And how was that?"

Silence.

"And how was it that I mistreated you?"

Betty couldn't answer.

"Do you remember me driving you so that you could give piano lessons?"

"What I remember is you threatening me that you would blackmail me about the piano lessons I taught."

"How did I threaten you?"

"I wish I could remember better," she said.

"I wish I could, too," Naso replied, concluding his questioning.[230]

There was action outside the courtroom as well. Police in Healdsburg, California, announced that they had a case that might explain the "Girl near Healdsburg" notation in Naso's list.[231] The Healdsburg victim was recovered from Foss Creek in 1983, and thought at first to be the body of the missing Cheryl Carter. Dental records indicated that it wasn't Carter, but that didn't mean it couldn't have been Naso's girl in Healdsburg. On April 28, 2011 the body was exhumed, a second autopsy was performed on the 29th. DNA was collected. The body was very badly decomposed but Healdsburg Police Chief Kevin Burke said he believed that there were sufficient DNA samples taken from the body nonetheless. Unfortunately, results were "inconclusive."

Marin County Sheriff's Detective Ryan Peterson testified that he had been among the first to question Naso regarding the incriminating items found in his home and bank deposit box. "Naso called the items part of his secret hobby," Peterson testified. "He said, 'It's kind of like my dark side.' Naso asked me if I was married. I said I was not and he told me, 'It's like a boss cheating on his wife with his secretary. There are things you don't want other people to know about.'"

On cross-examination Naso made a point that he remembered the ride differently, that he had not answered any questions but rather said he wanted to "take the Fifth Amendment against self-incrimination. Isn't it true that I said I wanted to take the Fifth and you said 'We can talk about that later'?"

"No," Petersen said solidly.

The prosecution rested. Naso called no witnesses.[232]

Prosecutor Dori Ahana delivered the closing argument that the People had presented enough evidence to have Naso held for jury trial, that Naso was a sexually deviant serial killer who "actualized his sexual obsessions," who drugged and photographed his victims before strangling them, stripping them nude, and discarding them in rural areas.

Naso bound and gagged his victims. "He sought dominance and control. There was dehumanization by the defendant of women," Ahana said. "We have presented dozens of photos, some of the victims in this case, some unidentified, some appearing unconscious or dead, some splayed in unnatural positions." Items found in Naso's safety deposit box revealed him to be a caustic collector who "kept mementos of his conquests."[233]

She reminded the judge that the unusual poses that Naso placed his models into, poses he felt were "erotic," mirrored the poses in which his victims were found. The victims were strangled, and this was in synch with testimony from Naso's exes and sons of exes, that Naso choked women, and liked having sex with women when they were unconscious.

Naso delivered his closing argument while sitting alone at the defense table, an array of paper before him, each sheet crowded with his manic handwritten notes. "The Prosecution gives a nice speech, but it is completely false. All of their so-called evidence is circumstantial. There is nothing wrong with my interest in glamor photography. My interest in pin-ups and cheesecake is natural. If I seem passionate, it is because it is my art."

The prosecution, he said, had made him seem like a hypnotist or some kind of mind-control expert or something. Not true. "Your honor, I do not have power over women. It is true I have had many dates with women but it has nothing to do with power. It has got to do with rapport. I have rapport with women. I can make them comfortable, willing to pose nude or in lingerie. That doesn't mean I committed any of the crimes for which I'm charged. I did not."

Naso turned and stared at the prosecutors. "I could probably get half the women in this room to disrobe voluntarily. I do not need to coerce women. They will do my bidding for my photographs."

The statement and manner drew Judge Sweet's ire: "Stop looking at the prosecutors, Mr. Naso. Look at me when you deliver your remarks."

The defendant looked at the bench and continued: "I never used drugs to knock a woman out. I don't know a drug from a potato. I have the technique. The talent. I don't have to look for models, they look for me. These are people I have worked with in my photography. They were *customers*."[234]

Naso complained that the prosecution tried to make so much hay out of his photos and his journals and his lists. He snorted a little laugh. "Sex, prostitution, and erotic images are Americana!" He referred to his exhibits. "Your honor, I am demonstrating that I am not unique, that this goes on all over the country. They are merely photo shoots and notes about models. Most of the models in those pictures are alive and well."

Not all. There was Pamela Perkins. He explained to the judge that he'd come upon Pam by chance. He lived in Yuba City at the time, was driving down the road, and there she was. Hitchhiking. "She wanted to come to my home for sex, but I wasn't interested in sex. But I said she has nice legs, she can model for me."

And he *didn't* abuse her. He abused none of them. He wished the four dead women named in his indictment were still around, because they could testify that he never "laid a hand on them." He certainly didn't abuse Tracy Tafoya, one of the women he was accused of killing, although they might have "dated or whatever."

The prosecution couldn't believe their good luck. Naso, who was so *not* a lawyer, had just admitted to having a relationship with Tafoya. Until that moment there was no evidence physically linking Tafoya and Naso. The line that Ahana had used in her opening statement was that one of the photos discovered "might have been" Tafoya, but that statement was based on evidence that probably wouldn't hold up under scrutiny. Tafoya's husband was unable to I.D. the Naso photos as of his wife, but he did say that he thought he recognized a pair of panties the model was wearing as those of his wife. Naso had also apparently written about Tafoya on a number of occasions. She seemed to be the final item on his list. Plus, in one journal, in an item dated August 5, 1994, the date of Tafoya's disappearance, Naso wrote, "Met Tracy. Put it to her." [235]

"There is no evidence that I committed these murders. Did I leave my signature or anything that belongs to me?" he asked. "You heard my ex-wife say that she doesn't remember losing her pantyhose or leaving them in a restaurant. I said, 'Be sure to tell the truth.' Her pantyhose did a lot of traveling. They left the house and never came back."[236]

The week finished before Naso did, so he had to conclude his close on Monday morning. Over the weekend it was reported that the

Naso hearing had jump-started a few cold-case homicides with double-initialed victims.[237] The most notable of these came out of South Lake Tahoe, California, where authorities were taking a fresh look at the murder of 17-year-old Kathleen Keohane in 1976. She died of blunt force trauma to the back of her head that fractured her skull, and was found beneath the Truckee River Bridge. No suspects. No motive. The other South Lake Tahoe case was the 1976 demise of Marina Mitchell who in 1976 disappeared in the American River Canyon. After weeks of searching, her remains were found in a shallow river in a state of extreme decomposition, so much so that it was impossible to determine the cause of death. There were no gunshot or knife wounds on the body, and authorities didn't think she drowned. Back in 1976, Investigator Mike Mergen said, "We may never know what she drowned from." Keohane was murdered four months before Roxene Roggasch.

And Naso knew South Lake Tahoe. He'd been arrested there on burglary charges in 2008. Asked in court why he was in the county at all, he replied that he was "visiting an old friend." Perhaps the best link between the South Lake Tahoe cases and Naso was the eyewitness report of Mitchell's boyfriend, Steve Haslett, who said that not long before she disappeared a "strange-acting man" was lurking in the vicinity of the Strawberry cabin where they were staying, and he was trying to take photographs of Mitchell. Haslett said he caught the man and the man ran to a car with Connecticut license plates and sped off.

On Monday morning, Naso's closing argument petered out to a finish and Judge Sweet ruled for the prosecution.[238] The prosecution announced it would be seeking the death penalty. Judge Sweet tried in earnest to get Naso to accept a defense attorney, but Naso wouldn't listen.

His self-representation made everyone nervous. He was a mistrial waiting to happen. The trial was expected to last months, and no one wanted to have to start over because Naso spontaneously did something stupid.

The *Chicago Tribune* reported that the prosecution had a new witness, a 74-year-old woman prepared to testify that Naso raped her in 1961 when she was a student at the University of California at Berkeley. Story was he picked her up at a bus stop. Reporting the incident to authorities was an ordeal in itself, as investigating officers seemed to think this was a stunt she was pulling to make a boyfriend jealous.[239]

Awaiting trial, Naso wrote a letter to the newspaper: "As a result of the Marin County D.A. targeting me as a serial killer expert, and with fabricated charges against me, the media has been misguided. It's high time for me to set the story straight. I'm not the guilty one. I plan on another true story in the near future before trial. The fact of the matter is, never in the thousands of photo sessions I've had, I never forced anyone to pose for anything. My resumé of glamor, pinup, and sensual—or even *erotic*—photography was always performed with knowledge and consent."[240]

He wrote a second letter to KRNV, My News 4. He called the letter "The True Story, Part 2" and in it he claimed that it was ridiculous for people to call him a serial killer. Even if he had committed the murders he was accused of, the tag would still be false. "Serial means succession," he wrote. The four murders he was to be tried for occurred in 1977 and 1978, then 1993 and 1994. There was nothing serial about it.[241]

Naso had plenty of time to craft his letters. A full two years passed between his arrest and the start of his trial in the spring of 2013. During the wait, Naso's grip on reality further slipped. He was even a problem during jury selection. Naso noticed that Rosemary Slote was demonstrative with her hands when questioning jurors, so when it was Naso's turn he flailed his hands wildly in an effort to mock her. The act was so crude that one prospective juror told the court that she found the mocking objectionable.[242]

A psychologist would have had a field day analyzing Naso's courtroom behavior. It seemed that the more he thought about his own behavior, the creepier it got.

In sharp contrast, Slote brought her A game. During her opening statement, she accused Naso of four murders, and promised evidence that would link Naso to a fifth, that of Sara Dylan.[243]

Slote went through each victim one by one, describing each dumpsite and the condition of the body when discovered. Some jurors wiped tears from their eyes as she humanized the victims.[244]

Then she turned on Naso: "He is a sexual deviate, a serial rapist and murderer who drugged and photographed his unconscious victims before strangling them and dumping their bodies in rural areas," Slote said, pointing at the defendant. She read from his diary, beginning all the way back in 1958 when Naso raped an acquaintance, a "gorgeous chick" in a cemetery. A 1961 entry written at Berkeley included the charming, "I pulled up her skirt and put it to her."

As Rosemary Slote promised, the prosecution's case was overwhelming, with Naso's own writings serving as a chillingly remorseless confession. As witness after witness took the stand, Naso was reduced to shrugging his shoulders and interjecting that he was an artist, a horribly misunderstood artist. He once again cross-examined his ex-wife, producing this memorable exchange:

"Did I ever so much as slap you? Kick you? Push you?"

"Not if I was conscious," she replied.[245]

On August 20, 2013, Naso was convicted of four counts of murder. A penalty phase followed, during which the same jury would decide if Naso were headed toward life in prison or death row. During that phase, the prosecution introduced evidence connecting Naso with two other deaths, not just that of Sara Dylan, but also a previously undisclosed *sixth* victim,[246] 56-year-old Sharieea Patton, murdered in Marin County, 1981.

In her penalty-phase closing, Dori Ahana told the jury that the death penalty was warranted because of Naso's "lifetime of devastation, lifetime of violence."

She had a two-minute timer, which she started, and everyone in the courtroom waited silently as it ticked down from 120 seconds to zero. It seemed like a very long time.

"That is how long the victims in this case suffered, two minutes spent struggling for air, in mortal terror. He enjoyed their suffering. He enjoyed their pain: tying them up and dumping their bodies like garbage."

As she spoke, she showed the jury grisly crime scene photos. The jury deliberated for four hours before returning to the courtroom with a recommendation for execution. In November, Naso was officially sentenced and took up residency on death row in San Quentin.[247]

From the moment he was arrested for murder until he moved in to his new home on Death Row, he never mentioned anything about a victim's initials being important to him. Sure he had referred to

Margaret Prisco as Peggy Prisco, even though no one else called her that, but in his writings, in his photos, which covered decades of sex crimes, there was no mention of a victim's initials mattering.

That said, according to Naso biographer C.L. Swinney, Naso was in Rochester at the time of all three of Rochester's double-initial murders.[248]

Deviance Germinated

In June 2016, private investigator Donald A. Tubman dug out some facts about Theodore Frederick Given, Jr., the Gates child rapist who had lived so close to Michelle Maenza. Given, Tubman determined, was institutionalized in a maximum-security psychiatric hospital for the criminally insane, kept from society due to a civil commitment. He'd been in prison for the great bulk of his life, but was out at the time of the Walkowicz and Maenza murders. He was now 69 years old, five-feet seven-inches tall and 157 pounds. Hair brown, eyes blue. He had a tattoo on his right arm.

He was listed as Risk Level 3, a "Sexually Violent Offender." There was a new mug shot, too, taken in April 2016 that showed Given with gray/white hair, slicked back on top, with glasses and a Fu Manchu moustache and beard.

Given had served his time for the 1974 "attempted rape" and had been set free to rape a child again. During his time in the system he "had not really" been treated for his child-rape problem, although in his last couple of years he was subjected to some experimental behavior modification sessions which, in retrospect, didn't help much.

He was released from a state maximum-security prison on parole in March 1984, but returned to prison on December 31, 1985 when he was found prowling in a vacant mobile home. He was paroled again on February 7, 1986.

I did some googling on Given, and quickly pulled up his dad's obit, 1986. Ted Given Sr., died in Florida at age 66. He had eight kids, six sons, all surviving. Fought in WWII, crossed Europe in a tank.

I found a July 1986 article from a small daily newspaper serving New York State's Finger Lakes region. Ted Given Jr., 39 years old, was on an auto-theft spree, so everyone was advised to be on the lookout. He'd stolen six autos in the New York State's Twin Tiers region. Given was also wanted in connection with a car theft in Wyoming, and a suspect in two New York State auto thefts, one from a grocery store and one from a restaurant parking lot. Both vehicles were eventually found unharmed. A man matching Given's description was seen in the restaurant parking lot, and he'd been seen the previous Monday night, July 28, about a mile south of Dundee on Route 14A in a Camaro reported stolen from Savona, Steuben County. State police chased him but lost him along the east side of Keuka Lake. The car was found abandoned, stuck in a hedgerow in a farmer's field, leading police to believe that Given escaped on foot. State Police said that a car was subsequently stolen in Waterloo, but police couldn't be certain that this was related to Given's flight.[249]

It was only weeks later, in September 1986, that Given threatened and overpowered an eleven-year-old girl before raping her. He broke into her house, where she was home alone, and, wearing a bandana over his face, raped the girl in her bed. Days later, the *D&C* published details regarding the attack on the little girl under the headline, "Man is sought as the rapist of girl, 11."

In a juxtaposition that must have driven Mike Macaluso berserk, the article ran alongside a heavily illustrated ad for the Lyell Theater's presentation of *Wild Things II*, starring the limber Amber Lynn.

According to the article, the man they were seeking broke into the girl's split-level, suburban home, where the girl was staying home from school that week because she was ill. The man apparently first knocked on the door on Monday afternoon, the day before the attack, and when the girl answered he asked her about buying a van that was parked on the lawn. The girl said her mother would be home later and that he should return and talk to her then.

The attacker returned on Tuesday morning, between 8:00 and 8:30 a.m. and cut a hole in a screen to open a first-floor window. Both of the girl's parents were at work. He entered the house, walked up to the second floor where the girl was sleeping. His face covered with a bandana, he covered her face with a pillow and raped and sodomized her. The girl described the man as wearing a large cowboy hat, with "maybe a feather" in it, a green coat, blue jeans, and a brown belt with a knife casing.[250]

Two days later, Barker put out an APB for Given. He described the search as "statewide" and "up and down the seaboard." An arrest warrant for a separate parole violation had been issued, but authorities were eager to discuss with him the much larger issue of the Parma child rape. The APB said that Given "could be armed with a semi-automatic handgun."[251]

On a morning in November, the MCSO received an anonymous phone tip that Given was holed up in a cheap motel on Mt. Read Boulevard. Two investigators staked out the hotel at 11:30 a.m. Given was seen leaving the motel around noon. He got into a car, and pulled away. Investigators followed him, eventually blocking his path at the corner of Mt. Read and Lyell. According to MCSO Captain of Detectives Anthony M. Ciaccia Jr., Given offered "some resistance but quickly surrendered." Weapons were found in his motel room and his car was reported stolen in Cleveland, Tennessee, which is a place.

Given was charged with first-degree rape, first-degree attempted sodomy, and first-degree burglary for the Parma attack.[252]

It had been quite a manhunt, with authorities always "one step behind" as Given traveled from Rochester to Florida, Alabama, and Tennessee, before returning to Upstate New York. He came back because, police theorized, he had relatives in Newark, N.Y.

In March 1987, Given admitted in court to the Parma rape before Monroe County Court Judge Patricia Marks, who would later be the judge in my book *Betrayal in Blood*. Given was successfully prosecuted by A.D.A. Terry M. Servis and sentenced by Judge Marks to 12 ½-to-25 years in prison.

Twenty-three years later, in 2010, there was concern in the Rochester area because Given, now 63 years old, was scheduled for release on May 27 from the Mid-State Correctional Facility in Marcy, Oneida County, after serving the maximum time allowed under his sentence.

Two weeks before his release date, a court hearing was held. Monroe County Court Judge Frank P. Geraci Jr. ruled Given to be a Level 3 offender, considered to be the highest risk of committing new crime.

"The court finds that he is an extreme risk to this community," Geraci said.[253]

At that time the plan was for the free-again Given to live in Wayne County and report with high frequency to a parole officer who specialized in high-risk sex offenders. He would, of course, be returned to prison in the wink of an eye if he stepped out of line.

At the same hearing a Public Defender named Jon Griffin argued in vain that Given had been miscategorized as a predator by sloppily prepared background reports. Griffin's heart could not have been in it.

Because Given had been convicted of first-degree rape he was required to participate in the sex offender counseling program while incarcerated. In 2003, he was removed from the program due to poor performance, participation, and progress.

In September 2005, Given re-enrolled in the program but was soon placed on probation status based on his lack of honesty, insight, and empathy. Because of this, his "good time" credit was withheld by the Time Allowance Committee, assuring that Given would serve his entire sentence.

Given sued to have his time for good behavior returned but Judge Lynch of the New York State Supreme Court dismissed the suit, stating that Given's failure to successfully participate in the sex offender counseling program was adequate reason to withhold his good behavior time as it demonstrated that Given had refused to address the very conduct that resulted in his incarceration.[254]

Even after his complete sentence had been served, no one wanted to release Given. He was eventually civilly committed to an institution for the criminally insane, under lock and key, and there he remained.

During the summer of 2016 I wrote a letter to Ted Given at his insane asylum home. I told him I was a true-crime writer researching the double-initial cases. I briefed him on my book *The Devil at Genesee Junction*, that I had a strong interest in Rochester-area cold cases.

"I don't know if you are familiar with the double-intiials case," I wrote, "but your own criminal history makes you a unique expert witness. I was hoping you might be able to advise me as to what possibly made the killer tick. Do you believe the double-initials were just a coincidence, or would it have been possible for the killer to determine his victims' names and kill only girls whose names started with the same letter?"

My letter had the look of something that would be intercepted by authorities long before it reached Given, but was an interesting experiment anyway. Unless I was ignored completely, always a possibility, I might learn something.

On August 1, 2016, Given wrote back—and his letter was a lot longer than mine. He said there were a few different reasons why he was responding to my letter and all of them did not "employ coincidence" dealing with the Double-Initial Killer. I should learn right off the bat, he wrote, that the guy was called the Alphabet Killer, not the DIK. I should get it right.

At his age, with mortality "staring back at him in hi-def" every time he stood before a mirror to shave, his guard was lower than it had once been. So there he was, at his typewriter, replying to questions he knew were curve balls, disguised behind some interest of what made killers tick! He made it clear: he had me figured out, and he was answering anyway.

I was delighted.

He didn't know how familiar with prison psyche I was, but he'd been in the inside for 50 years. Must be some sort of record. Rule number one was to be very suspicious of everything. Rule number two was that the prettier you were when you came in, the harder rule number one was going to be literally pounded into you.

Given explained that he'd been a pretty one, and got it from the first day he walked down the chow-line while 800 to 1,000 convicts "squatted on his ass" as he passed, chirping, making kissing noises, screaming over the mess hall din: 'That one's mine!'"

He wanted me to know that he had to fight past a whole army of suspicions about why I contacted him specifically about the double-initial murders in Rochester, especially since he had a history with Rochester's BCI concerning those cases back in 1996 or 1997, whenever his name came up during one of their cold-case investigations.

There was a voice inside him saying, "Whoa, back off this guy." He remembered other members of the media who had been interested in talking to him. Former talk-show host Sally Jesse Raphael. Oprah! They wanted to pick his bones the same way I did now. Back then it was because of a TV guy who'd been a victim-offender reconciliation advocate. He wanted nothing more then sensationalism. Ratings. Ted had seen media hype, ducked it, and my letter was causing some of those alarms to go off. He thought it was strange that I had referred to him as a unique expert witness. It was if I were calling him a criminologist—and he wasn't sure what he thought of that yet. He'd have to "chew on it" a little bit. Truth was he *had* used the word criminologist to refer to himself. He'd even called himself a *penologist*—mostly when meeting with the pretty college girls that ran his violent offender civilian volunteer workshops.

There was a time when a guy with his troubles could lie about his record in prison. It was nobody's business what he was in for. You could hide behind any damned story. Then the Department of Corrections website made it impossible.

He said it was important for me to remember, that we were not pen pals. His facility had a rule against it. We had two choices. We could be friends or I could become his "proxy guardian."

Theodore Given believed that he and I would have difficulty getting our letters to one another because the powers that be would be reading them and judging them counter productive to his rehabilitation or whatever.

The main benefit of becoming a proxy guardian, he explained, was it limited how The Man could restrict our communications. In the long run, he said, it might not make any difference because, if they wanted to, they could declare any communication inappropriate and order it discontinued. He reminded me that if I were on the New York State or Federal Sex Offender Registry I would not be permitted to correspond with him. I also would not be allowed to pitch a business relationship. Total control, he concluded, was *their* motto.

The letter was fascinating, and I read it repeatedly. Sure, it was paranoid. The man had spent his life in institutions. He was used to being part of a machine, with no volition. But it wasn't psychotic. There was even unexpected humor. He'd used the word penologist to describe himself when meeting with a pretty social worker.

My favorite part was Given's issue with the moniker for the Rochester killer and his reference to "looking in the mirror" less than a sentence later.

I hadn't known about the BCI investigation, or the interest from Oprah and Sally Jesse, but that was interesting too.

I wrote back: "Thanks so much for getting back to me. Let's make it 'friend,' it sounds so much less complicated than 'proxy guardian.' Bottom line: I find you an interesting guy, Mr. Given. I want to learn your story, and I don't even care which part of your story you tell or in what order. If you don't want to answer the questions in my previous letter, what about telling me about what your life was like as a kid, and why you first started getting into trouble? Tell me what you think about when you look in the mirror. Please, tell your story under *your own* terms, and there may come a time when I am in a position to enhance your legacy. My offer to send stationery and stamps stands. Let me know."

On August 20, I received a thick packet from Given. There was a long letter and a stapled-together package that purported to be a detailed timeline of Given's life. The letter began: "Dear Good Ol' Buddy Michael Benson" followed by my typed address, and the date. As in his first letter, he opened with paranoia, wondering how I got his name and address. What made me think he would know how a killer thought? He'd never killed anyone, but he "sure as hell" tried once to kill one of the nine guys that had raped his "sweet, little-boy ass" when he was 16. That was why he was deadened. Calloused. And he had therapists by the dozen telling him it was a contributing factor that twisted his thinking when it came to ten and eleven-year-old girls, and the "creeped out" things he had done in 1974 and 1986. He'd been investigated by both Rochester police and Wayne County sheriff's detectives. If I didn't know about that, why was I contacting him? He wanted to know the path that led me to him. And I'd better tell the truth. One iota of distrust and he was done with me.

He admitted that his knowledge of modern-day investigative techniques was limited. Where he was he wasn't even allowed internet. But he wondered if maybe I'd found him on a website, where he'd heard there was some basic info re his criminal history.

Because of his Mental Hygiene Law, Article 10 civil confinement, he said he obtained N.Y. State Attorney General records of his criminal history: court records, rap sheets, pre-sentence investigation reports, prison history records, and psych records dating to the 1960s. Nearly 4,500 pages of records. He had typed up a Table of Contents for the bundle, which in itself functioned as a poor man's biography. That was what he'd enclosed with his letter. As Given put it, his entire life was on record.

Given looked back at the Big Picture. He'd seen a lot of prisons. More than 50 of them—in six different states. He'd broken bread with Mafia dudes. That was when he was in a fed pen in Georgia, 1968 or 1969.

He'd known members of the psycho-killer hall of fame as well: Son of Sam David Berkowicz. Also Herman Bell, who wasn't a household name but was seriously badass. He was a former killer for the Black Liberation Army. They made a TV movie about him: *Badge of the Assassin*. He was also the quarterback when the prison team played the kids from Plattsburgh Community College.

Ted had even had a bunky in Danbury Federal Correctional Facility named Philip Berrigan, one of the two (brother) Jesuit priests who dumped pig's blood on draft records in protest of the Vietnam War. Given and Berrigan worked together in the Education Department. Given thought he might have been mentioned in one of Berrigan's poetry books.

Given befriended William Addison (pseudonym), who owned his own law firm in Manhattan. He was 73 at the time and in for tax evasion. Given cut Addison's hair. A few years later Aberson sent one of his law partners to Attica to make sure Given was okay after the riots there.

Given claimed he was in a famous photograph from the Attica riot. It was in the McKay Commission Report. In the middle of the book were about a dozen photos offering a panorama of the prison during the riots, and Given was right in the middle of one of them, a kid 20-years old or so, fist raised in a power gesture.

His one major regret was that, when he got out of Attica about a year after the riots, he didn't immediately go to Addison and ask for a job—in the mail room, whatever. He could have turned his whole life around, no more crimes, but he didn't do it.

Instead, he remained addicted to what he called his "glitz and glitter fast life," living not in the actual world but in the world he fantasized about as an inmate. Living not by society's rules, but with a "prison mentality." In his mind, the world owed him for the time he'd spent inside. He needed to do some double living to make up for lost time, two blondes on each arm. He wasn't back in free society for long before he realized that his fantasies tended to spend rather than make money. When the reality of the streets didn't meet up to the rich standards of his prison fantasies—broke, no job—he went to what he knew, burglary.

My "expert witness" comment was still stuck in his craw.

Prison was full of murderers. Why not ask one of them? He'd never killed anyone, what did he know about the mind of a murderer? That said, he was perfectly willing to fill me in on his biography. Though he didn't want to make any comments involving the murders I was interested in, he was more than willing to talk about himself, and he again wanted me to know that he had 4,500 pages of documents that comprehensively covered his many treks through the justice system.

I noted that Given's enclosed list of documents did nothing to alibi him for the murders of Wanda Walkowicz and Michelle Maenza.

Up until the statewide prison guards' strike of the late 1970s, about two or three years into his first sex offense bid, he maintained an airtight prison persona as an organized crime tough guy. He lived in constant fear, however—fear that any day a guy from Rochester would show up and "blow me up, run a wire on me in the yard." One day one of those Old School guys he'd attached himself to would tug his coat and he'd be shamed or worse on the prison basketball courts, hangout spots, etc. His secret needed to be kept. He was a child rapist, lowest of the low in the prison caste system.

When the prison guards went on strike, National Guardsman guarded the prisoner population. Everyone was locked in. After the strike's second day, antsy inmates banged, screamed, and harassed the baby-faced Guardsmen, threatening the State Police who were manning the gun towers and walls. Someone got smart and let out the prisoners with clout and influence in the population. Given happened to be the elected chairman to the Inmate Liaison Committee. So he was among those let out to browse through the cellblocks, taking down grievances, gripes, and echoing hollow promises from the cops—just to stretch out the time for the strike to run its course. After each excursion, Given gave the captain reports on how dudes were handling the lockdown.

The local TV and news reporters were camped outside the prison gates, waiting, rooting for carnage. The captain arranged for them to come into the administration building. The other inmate reps and Given were brought in. They sat around a table—prison brass, reporters and prisoners. Given sat next to a guy with a shoulder-held camera and immediately told him, "Do *not* film me!"

The dude nodded, but as the interview went on Given could see cameraman angling the camera toward him. This time Given raised his voice: "Dude, do not film me!"

That cameraman shit, but he said, "I'm not. The camera is off."

Given grabbed the lens of the camera and slammed it down toward the table and said, "Then don't point it at me!'"

That night, on the cellblock's radio system, the six o'clock news reported some of the meeting. Given heard himself say, "You can't lie to these guys! They know the deal. For six days they've not caused you guys hassle other than a few screams and bitches. You've got to give something back, gallery rec, something!"

Being on the radio fighting for prisoner rights did not bring the reaction that Given had perhaps hoped for. Mostly he heard grumblings from those in his block that he'd sold out and was working for The Man. Some came to his defense but not many.

In 1978 or 1979, Given was transported to Rochester briefly so he could testify for the Federal District Court prosecutor who was trying to build a case against William Mahoney, Chief of Detectives. Given was asked about his allegations that Mahoney had abused him before Given confessed to his 1974 sex crimes.

"He tore my balls off! Well! It seemed like it…" Given told me. And with that, he announced, he was going to close the letter, but not before telling me he was as suspicious as ever.

He was still adjusting to his new shrink keepers. He could be less guarded and it would be OK, but it was hard to let go of a lifetime of suspicion. "I can read their demeanor, I can't read yours," he said, and signed it Ted Given. Beneath that he noted that he was keeping a copy of the letter, "no shit" he wrote after, and made reference to the enclosed index of all documents about him, which he referred to as his timetable.

In his following letter dated August 29, 2016, Given wrote saying, should I stop getting letters from him it was because they had discovered something about our, that is his and mine, "unspoken relationship." They would confiscate my letters. They wouldn't allow him to respond. They would force him (or me) into the Court to resolve the matter. They're not afraid of the Court, Given opined, so they will easily stop our correspondence. All they had to do was say my letters were counter to his treatment, and I was through. He told me that the Courts almost always sided with them, not surprising; the other side was criminally insane. If I didn't hear from him in 30 days, I was to contact his primary therapist, whose name and number he gave me. He said he was currently in the middle of a longer letter, which he would send me when it was finished.

That longer letter did come, dated September 3, 2016. Ted said he remained concerned that I thought him guilty of things for which he hadn't paid his debt to society, and no such guilt existed. That said, he was willing, perhaps eager, to discuss the crimes for which he'd been punished. His psyche program urged him to be completely open and honest about his crimes in the hopes that it would make him more empathetic toward his victims. He was learning what his crimes did to his victims and what they had experienced. He didn't have to look any further than his own life to see how sexual assault, abuse, horror, could potentially lead to a life of hell, crime and transformation from "a victim into a predator in the ultimate."

Given compared prison versus the mental wing. There was a world of difference. He was still locked up but the head game was completely different. He wondered why, if I was so curious about what made him tick, why was I unwilling to be his proxy-guardian. He said that if I'd read up on my Mental Health Law, I would see the advantages of taking that role. It would give me access to his treatment plan. I could be in on teleconference video meetings with his treatment team. I could access his mental health assessments. "That *is* having a look into how I think," he wrote. "Read up on it," he suggested.

Of course, I still had no intention of being his proxy-guardian. I didn't like the way it sounded, like maybe I was on his side. I was trying not to let my loathing get in the way of my research. I tried to forget that Ted spent the great bulk of his life caged at the taxpayers' expense because he was too much of an animal to walk among us.

He told me that he'd had one of his sisters, one of the few members of his family with whom he maintained contact, and had her google me. (I guess I passed muster.) He said, if it was OK with his family, he would introduce them to me.

There wasn't too much they could offer me, he supposed. He was separated from his siblings when they were just little kids, and through the years they'd had little to no personal contact. He recalled that I'd asked him how a criminal lured his victims into his car. Before he could answer that question, he said he needed to explain his mindset back in 1974. Before the sex offense that year, he claimed, all of his crimes were property crimes. It was burglary that got his juices flowing. He'd "gotten a taste for it" and it gave him an adrenaline kick, a rush.

When he got out of Attica in 1972, part of him wanted to commit burglaries and feel that rush again, but he tried to stay straight. In the legit world where he'd convinced himself he would thrive, that he'd be making big bucks like a rock star. They were daydreams allowed to become excruciatingly vivid during years of incarceration. Truth was, he'd been lonely. He missed his family. His brothers and sisters were in Florida, in a foster home somewhere.

Many of his prison fantasies involved financial success, but the great bulk of them were masturbatory. In prison, he looked at magazines—*Playboy*, *Gent*, *High Society*—and paperback books.

All of those dirty photos blended into one another, except one. The one of *her*. That image, the *one*, seared its way into his memory, got into the fabric of his sexual arousal and wouldn't let go. The photo was of a ten-year-old female lying naked beside a swimming pool, and it was in one of those nudist-colony magazines popular back then. Completely naked men and women, and sometimes families, were shown engaging in wholesome activities. There was a lot of volleyball and badminton. This photo showed the healthy Caucasian family at poolside, the little girl lying on the deck, on her side, face to the camera. According to Given, the photo was "the spark that initiated" the crime. He first saw the image as a 16-year-old kid in Woodbourne Penal Institution (1963-4), and used it for "arousal and ejaculation," and it became the "mental foundation upon which the sexual deviance germinated." Not only did the photo make his sexual buzzer go off, and how, but he told me it was directly related to his 1974 sex offenses.

He began to sound defensive. He was so young, naïve, immature, a mere farm boy, still trying to develop his own sense of masculinity even as he was bombarded by the "perverse nature of the prison environment." Nine different dudes had raped him more than 100 times in two years. How could you blame him for having his sexual appetite bent by the experience?

He noted that back in those days, in the tiny ads in the back pages of men's magazines, he'd find photos of children in provocative poses from films and magazines produced in foreign countries. It was child pornography, available by mail order in the back of a newsstand magazine. He was desensitized to the demon in pedophilia. He didn't even feel guilty about it. He had himself convinced it wasn't that bad.

So, in essence, his reasoning went, he taught himself that sex with a pre-pubescent was okay. In his fantasies, which he carefully groomed over the years, he "lovingly and tenderly made love" to his imaginary child sex partner.

When Given was released from prison in 1972, a federally funded ex-con program called Occupational/Vocational Rehabilitation enabled him to enroll for free in the Lincoln Continental School of Beauty to study to be a cosmetologist.

The school was located on Front Street in Rochester, a location notorious as a homosexual pick-up spot, and there was a bathhouse right next door. He'd heard that male beauticians were mostly homosexuals. Because he was such a homophobe from his prison experiences, he talked himself into a negative attitude regarding the school. Even though there were beautiful women attending the school, he let the negativity get to him, he kept looking at his fellow male students wondering if they were gay, and eventually he quit.

In hindsight, it was a huge mistake. He had been given a chance and he blew it. He was fucking up left and right, in fact. For a while he lived in a YMCA, where parole paid his rent! During the first days of his freedom, he found the nearest porn bookstore—they weren't that hard to find back in those days, before internet porn, especially in run-down areas. He went from store to store, a search for the golden ticket.

He'd ask the guy working there, "Got any nudist colony magazines?" He was looking for that photo—the photo of *her*. He paged eagerly through many nudist mags in hopes that he'd find her. While he was there, he'd check the pedo racks and pick up some pigtail porn as well. Then came a routine search of his room at the Y, the discovery of his deviant smut, and next thing you know he was outdoors and his rent-free digs were gone.

As a further affront to his fantasy of highfalutin living, he'd been forced to move in with mom and dad in their two-room apartment on Parcells Avenue just off Webster Avenue, sleeping on the couch. So, as the steam built in Given's pressure cooker he was sleeping on a couch about 200 yards from Michelle Maenza's house.

Theodore wrote, "I was told by those BCI investigators to the Alphabet Murders that one of the little girls who had been abducted from a house just around the corner from where I lived in that time period." He explained that it was that proximity that caused him to become a suspect. Well, that and the fact that there was something about the car he had at that time that fit a witness's description.

Given skipped past 1973 to his 1974 crime in Gates. He said that the sex crime snuck up on him. All he was thinking about was burglary—honest.

This doesn't sound like the same guy who spent the first weeks after his release scouring adult bookstores. But he says he was back into B&E, and experience tells us that many rapists are breakers and enterers first, that they get off on violating others, in private space, property, and then in body.

Given was once again a B&E man. A good one. He would go into the suburbs and countryside to break and enter. He swears, scout's honor, that he never set out to commit a sex crime, and he especially never set out to commit a sex crime against a child.

Sure, he still fantasized about having sex with *her*, with—as he put it—"the perfect ten year old girl as she stretched out at poolside, her little hairless vaginal cleavage peaking seductively from the narrow delta of her slender hindquarters." But he never thought of that as part of his *criminal* career. When he thought about crime, he thought about breaking and entering.

Folks thought he prowled around in his car like some sort of predator seeking his prey, seeking to abduct a child to rape, but nothing could have been further from the truth.

His recall was different. He'd been on the road for hours, starting in the early morning until mid-day, and he was scanning the houses on the streets he cruised, looking for his favorite type, for a house that talked to him, said, "Break me, enter me." But he wasn't having any luck.

He was on an unfamiliar road, one he didn't think he'd ever driven down before, and he came upon a small village. He didn't like villages because they had local law, small-town cops that cramped his style. Even when the little villages were too small to have local police, they had "neighborhood watches." For one thing, he'd driven his whole life but never had a driver's license, so he tended to drive where he wouldn't get pulled over.

Nightmare in Rochester

When it came to hamlets there were too many eyeballs, and he was skittish about houses with a lot of windows right up next to each other. As he was driving along this unfamiliar stretch of road through the hamlet, he saw a turn-off near the last house in a row of houses. He turned into the lane with the intent of turning around, but saw that he was on a dead end, and at the end of the street was a dirt parking lot next to a soccer field.

He was tired of driving, so he pulled into the lot and parked, to rest. He positioned the car so he could see the backs of a row of houses about 50 yards away. Always scouting for the ol' B&E.

His windows were down. He lit a cigarette and turned the engine off. There were a couple of precious moments of complete relaxation, and then...he heard voices. Kids. Laughter. Coming from the soccer field behind him.

Given reparked his car so he was facing the road he'd just come off of. The soccer field was behind him now. He cocked himself sideways so he could see out both the front and back windows of his car.

There was a narrow opening and pathway onto the soccer field with high brush and some trees on either side, so he could not see where those delightful childish noises were coming from.

There was a time when thoughts of burglary and the happy sounds of children playing competed for control of Given's brain. He got out of his car and pretended to stretch. He smoked another cigarette. He gradually strolled more and more toward the pathway onto the soccer field.

His head was on a swivel. He had to be completely aware of his surroundings now. The further he got onto the soccer field, the more exposed he felt. About 20 feet to his right, there was a block-and-wood structure about the size of a two-car garage. He thought it might be an outhouse and a concession stand. In front of the building was a kiddie's play area. Two female children were sitting on the swing sets.

A jogger ran along the back part of the field. Given began walking along the field's edge, knee-high grass to his right, mowed grass to his left. He turned and continued walking, passing within ten feet of the children. He kept an eye on the jogger, thinking the jogger might be the adult there with the kids.

In the high-grass field was a heap of junk stuff: boards, tin roofing, large stones. Given stopped to sort through the junk, waiting for the jogger to pass. The little girls were now walking toward him and the jogger was nowhere to be seen. The jogger had either left the field, or stopped behind the concession stand.

As they approached, one of the little girls asked, "What are you looking for?"

She looked so familiar. He was certain he'd seen her before. The other little girl was tiny and also looked a little bit familiar but not as much. Then it hit him. The girl who spoke was the spitting image of *her*—the little naked girl in the magazine.

As Given put it, he felt "the spark." Suddenly he was that 16-year-old kid in prison masturbating, getting the "sexual buildup and the orgasmic rush." The real-life moment, he wrote, "flipped his script." Now, instead of surveying the area for B&E opportunities, he surveyed her, eyeballing the little girl up and down. The more he looked at her, interacted with her in conversation, the more aroused he became.

Given blamed fate. If it had been any other little girl, he was convinced, he would have been fine. But this was too much for him to resist. Fate had put before him the ultimate temptation—in a secluded area!—and he was nowhere near strong enough to resist.

He recalled now that in that original nudist magazine, there were three naked girls by the pool, but he only focused on one of them. In his mind-movies he always directed the other two girls out of the picture so he could focus on the object of his desire. That was sort of how he felt now. There were two little girls but only one mattered to him. The other was simply going to have to be managed so she wouldn't interrupt the romance.

"What are you looking for?" she said again.

Given replied, "I'm helping my nephew, he's about your age. I'm trying to find baby rabbits for him. They usually can be found under stuff like this." He pointed at the junk pile.

He walked slowly along the edge of the soccer field toward the back edge where there was a more heavily wooded area. He could still partially see the houses, which meant folks in that house could see him. There was a narrow pathway into the secluded area with heavier underbrush. The girls followed him. Inside the secluded area, Given stopped, and sat on a fallen tree.

"What are you girls doing here? Where are your parents? Do

you guys have pets?"

At this point, Given reminded me that he had no specific memories of what was said, but it was along those lines. He did remember luring them to that secluded site, that he did not act sexually toward them—touch or otherwise. He and the girls left the secluded area because he still felt nervous. The jogger was on his mind. He told himself he had to "keep it moving."

He wrote that rape was not a part of his thinking at that moment. To him it was what they call "grooming"—foreplay, if you will. He wanted the girls to feel comfortable with him.

He reached out and touched her on the shoulder. "Innocently! Nonchalantly. Not threatening," he wrote. He didn't sense any uncomfortable response from her, which fueled his confidence. She was trusting. "Of course!" he wrote. "She was a little kid."

Conversation began to wane. He coaxed the girls back out onto the soccer field. They strolled along the other side of the field's edge, heading back toward the front, stopping now and again to look under debris in the ditch. They saw a small snake under some debris but left it alone.

He continued to become more and more sexually aroused by her. He saw her movements as seductive. When she leaned down he could look down her shirt and see her chest. He felt as if she were teasing him...But he couldn't decide what to do with the other one.

To the girl he desired, he said, "I've got to go over there and see if my nephew found any baby rabbits. You guys can wait by the swing set. When you see my car over there, come over and I'll show you the baby rabbits."

At this point in the letter there was a pencil sketch of the soccer field and locations as he recalled them. The girls walked back toward the swing set. Given headed toward the pathway he had pointed to. He wanted to see if the pathway could accept his car so he could move his car to a spot that could be seen from the swing sets but not from any of the houses. Such a spot did exist and he moved his car to it. Given opened up the trunk of his car and stood at the back, sneaking glances toward the swing set so as not to appear overly anxious. He noticed the girls starting toward him across the field. He turned to see them and waved. He bent down and pretended to look for something in his trunk.

As the children approached, he calculated distance and space.

Then, getting between the girls he said, "They're in the trunk." As the girls looked down into the empty trunk, Given wrapped his arms around both of their waists (a girl on each arm), lifted them off their feet and tipped them head first into the trunk. They stretched their hands out to break their fall. He brought down the trunk lid slowly so as not to crush or catch their little fingers and said in a raised voice, "Be quiet! Keep your mouth shut!"

He hurriedly got behind the wheel, started the engine, and rolled up his car window so he couldn't be heard outside. "Relax and be quiet," he yelled toward the back.

Given now wrote that he knew this area slightly and had broken into houses out there before. He knew of one house that was hidden off a long driveway. The house was empty and the lot overgrown. He knew he could get in there through the cellar door. He chose someplace close for the girls' sake—you know, gas fumes and exhaust. He worried carbon monoxide was getting into his trunk.

At the empty house he pulled both girls out of the trunk, and was somewhat surprised that they weren't in hysterics. Terrified, yes, but both were "very docile." He led them both into the basement. He felt totally committed, focused, zoned, as if he were in a trance. He was living his fantasy out—but there was a key difference. In his fantasies his diminutive lovers weren't afraid. They were into him, aroused.

But not in real life, he realized, that wasn't the way it worked.

He found a cord on the dirt floor and used it to tie the one he wasn't interested in to a support beam. He led the other girl to the second floor, into a bedroom that had a mattress on the floor under one of the broken windows.

He told her to strip. She seemed not to understand, so he pulled her shirt up over her head. He turned her so that her back was to him and pulled down her shorts and underwear. He told her to "bend and spread'em." Again, she did not understand. He touched her just as if he were a guard and she was being strip-searched.

At this point, as an aside, Given noted that he understood how sick all of this sounded.

He tried to rape her on the dirty mattress but could not get an erection, so the mission was scrubbed. He put the girls in his car—in the back seat this time, not in the trunk—and drove back to within 50 feet of where he'd abducted them. The entire event probably took no more than 45 minutes, from first parking to rest, to dropping off his victims. *(Author's note: Police records say the girls were gone for three hours.)*

The girl who had remained in the basement was the only one who spoke. "You lied," she said.

Given didn't know exactly what she meant. He eventually came to the conclusion that she was still angry that he had no baby bunnies. He tried to portray the incident as a lesson he'd been teaching them: "Don't ever let someone catch you like that again!" he said.

As they exited the car on the passenger side, the basement girl reached back into the back seat to retrieve a broken piece of a coloring book crayon. He hadn't noticed it earlier. He figured she must have clutched it in her hands the whole time.

That was all he had to say about the 1974 "incident." He said a lawyer from the Mental Hygiene Law Legal Services called him to tell him they received a copy of the State Mental Health Examiners report opposing his release onto Strict and Intensive Supervision and Treatment (SIST). The key word there was release. There wasn't going to be one.

The lawyer told him he would send him a copy of the report so he could critique it for him and that he'd be up in about a week to discuss Given's obtaining an independent psychologist to do a report as to his fitness for release.

He told me he would be going to court for his annual discharge review in February or March 2017. If I wanted to attend that court appearance, Given said he could ask the lawyer to submit the appropriate court papers, a petition, to permit my attendance.

Otherwise, since this was to be a mental-health hearing in a civil court, it would be closed to the general public. Attendance would only be permitted by Court order. It was up to me. He signed off, "Chow! Namaste! Ted Given."

I wrote back thanking him for his honesty. Scheduling prevented me from being at his hearing. I sent my regrets. I had more questions than I ever. I asked:

You mentioned something about having siblings in foster care. Why was that necessary? Where were your parents?

Have you ever had a speech impediment, stuttering or

stammering or anything like that? You made a comment in court once about stuttering and I was wondering if it was just something you said or an actual problem.

Regarding the 1974 incident, how did you get caught? Were you perhaps less careful about witnesses on the drop off than you were on the pick up?

Do you remember the makes and models of the cars you drove between your release from Attica and your arrest in 1974?

You lived on Child Street in 1974? I spent the first five years of my life living on Campbell Street, right around the corner from there. You were arrested there. Tell me how that went down.

There was a witness after the murder of Michelle Maenza who saw the killer and his victim in a car with a flat tire at the side of the road. He reported the incident, and later, weeks later, claimed he saw the man again and wrote down the guy's license plate number. Because of that, police interrogated a man from Lyons, N.Y. who looked a lot like the composite drawing in the newspaper, but who had an alibi and passed a polygraph. I know you were living in Rochester at that time, but I was hoping you had heard through the grapevine who that suspect might have been, he being from one of your hometowns. If not, never mind.

You have spent a major portion of your life in institutional care. During times of freedom, you've (as society would put it) messed up. Do you feel that, in some ways, you function better in an institution? Is freedom in some ways harder to handle?

And, getting back to the 1974 incident and your timely erectile dysfunction, do you have a theory as to why that happened?

On September 22, Given responded with a short letter, warning me of a delay in our communications because he was processing into a new Treatment Mall Programming Schedule and had just had his one-half year Individual Service Plan (ISP) review with his Treatment Team. He was also engaged with his attorney preparing for his Annual Court Review for possible discharge. "So, there's a lot on my plate at the moment," he added. He said he was making a list of priorities and I was at the bottom of it.

In other news, he'd just gotten an okay from his long, lost estranged sister that he could start writing to her, first contact in 30-plus years. They had a lot to catch up on. He was going to ask her if she had any objections to him writing stories for me that featured her. Once she gave the okay, Given would introduce me to various members of his family. They could confirm some of the stuff he told me about. He promised to get back to our correspondence in a week or two. He signed off, "Thank you for keeping an interest in me. Theodore F. Given."

On October 3 I returned to my favorite subject: *Judging from your letter before last, I have to believe that you think the double-initial aspect of the crimes I'm investigating now is a load of bullshit, just a coincidence. If that guy was anything like you (and I know that's generalizing, but it all happened a long time ago and assumptions need to be made) then the crimes began (him picking up the girls in his car) spontaneously because he happened upon the opportunity. People say, "What are the odds that all three girls would have the same first and last initial?" But that coincidence scenario is more likely than one in which he researched these girls so that he knew their names, assumingly discarding potential victims because their names weren't correct for his needs, and then managed to find them all in vulnerable spots, walking a city street, each on a late afternoon, two of them returning from running an errand. Another question occurs to me: Why would a guy only want to attack girls with the same initials in the first place? How would that help to get him off? Why would he care? If it were a symbol of something, wouldn't he have felt compelled to explain? The only answer I can think of is that he read a book called* The ABC Murders *by Agatha Christie, in which a guy killed victims with the same first and last initial, in a town that also began with that initial, because one of the victims was an enemy he needed to kill and the others were window-dressing, crimes committed to make police believe they were after a serial killer. I'm just thinking out loud, but I would be interested in your opinion on these matters. The FBI calls it profiling. You use all of the available evidence and try to paint a picture about what the killer is like. You and he are going to have some things in common; other things will be different. Where do you stand on all of this?*

A letter from Given dated October 2 arrived on the 5th, crossing paths with my last letter. Given said he was going to talk about his childhood and events that led to his delinquency—both events he remembered and family lore. For instance, according to a story his mother used to tell, he was about nine when a family pet jumped up on him and knocked him down into a deep mud puddle, where he almost drowned.

His dad told him that he started up his father's car when he was about five and drove it into their "shitter," that is, the outhouse. The collision disturbed a bees' nest under one of the wooden cutout seats, and a bee stung little Ted on the "pecker." True or not, he had no idea, but it was funny as hell to hear his dad tell it.

When he was a kid, his parents went out at night to country and western bars, square dances, stuff like that. Sometimes the Given kids were dragged along. He remembered his mom showing him a two-step waltz dance. He had to be pretty little because he remembered his head tucked into her belly.

Soon thereafter, his mom began showing signs of alcoholism. She became mean-spirited when she drank, and violent—mostly toward his dad. He didn't remember mom ever beating any of the kids, but he did remember a lot of arguing between mom and dad.

He gave me a list of his siblings, with their ages—two older brothers, now 74 and 72, still living "somewhere in Florida." He had a younger brother who was about 67 and his kid sister was 63. He had two younger brothers, and then the baby, a girl, who had recently passed away, the first of the siblings to go. Dad and then mom had also passed away.

There was intrigue built into the family tree. Given's oldest brother, from what Ted had been told, was conceived while dad was overseas during World War II. Mom had a fling with an old high-school boyfriend, a grocery store produce supplier. Years later, the paternity issue caused dad and his brother to become estranged.

That brother moved out at age 16 to live with his grandparents. The whole thing was kept very hush-hush, and Ted admitted that his knowledge was "fragmented."

Given recalled one of his brothers, wasn't sure which, chasing him through an apple orchard "hell-bent on killing" him. At least, that was how the memory felt. He was nine, ten, eleven, somewhere in there, and they lived in rural Wayne County up near Lake Ontario.

His dad worked as a migrant worker, so they moved every two, three, four months. Crops were seasonal. He worked for farmers. And all of the migrant workers and their families lived in shacks.

Nightmare in Rochester

The Givens were one of the few white families. There were many Native Americans, he remembered, and the rest were black. Given's dad was usually hired as the foreman to these crews. Dad used to have kids walk behind a wooden flatbed wagon through a plowed dirt field. They had to throw big rocks on the wagon, rocks that would later be piled into hedgerow field dividers.

They went from farmstead to farmstead. Naturally, the kids were never in the same school for longer than a few months. At one time or another they lived in each of Wayne County's townships. Bottom line: no friends.

His dad was wounded in the war, blast to the foot and leg in Germany. Returning stateside, he was a frequenter of the Geneva V.A. hospital. Eventually, 1959-1960, he had to get his big toe amputated.

Dad couldn't work and they went on welfare. This brought shame and self-loathing into dad's psyche. He took part-time jobs, janitor, cleaning jobs. Mom never worked. The family just got bigger and bigger, poorer and poorer.

One summer, while living out in the country, with dad in the hospital, their landlord told his mom to get out because the rent wasn't paid. Without a car or a phone, mom marched her brood alongside the country road toward their grandparents' house about seven miles away. The youngest sometimes rode in a child's wagon, and they took turns riding the family's lone bike.

One time they went with their mother to the town square with other village poor people waiting for an Army Surplus food truck, from which they'd receive rationed cans of apple butter, peanut butter, blocks of American cheese, and powdered milk and eggs. Sometimes they'd use a wagon to haul the stuff. Each of the kids would carry two or three items back to the shack.

And, ah yes, violence. He recalled one incident in which mom threatened dad with a shotgun. He must've been young, because again, the memory was fragmented. He was in the back seat of a car with two of his brothers. His mother was in the passenger seat, Dad driving. Both were drunk and arguing. His mother started pounding on his dad, forcing him to pull to the side of the road. Mom jumped out of the car, went to the trunk and got a shotgun. She pointed it at dad with the barrel of the gun over the head of Ted's sister. Ted jumped forward and grabbed Ann and pulled her over the seat and into the back. That was where his memory ended. Mom didn't pull the trigger.

Memories now came vividly, as sharp as a fresh pain. Another incident occurred when they lived in a Wayne County hamlet called Marengo, a small cluster of homes between Clyde and Lyons. He was 13 or 14; the Given kids were at a table eating toasted cheese sandwiches. Mom and Dad, sober, got to arguing. Dad slapped mom and she ran around the table to get away. He grabbed her blouse and tore it off her. Mom continued her escape in her bra.

About the same time they moved again to a house on Route 104 on the fringe of Alton, N.Y. One night Ted's parents came home blasted from a beer binge (probably after receiving a welfare check). Dad roused the kids from their beds and made then come down to the kitchen where mom was sitting at a breakfast nook with a strange man, both drunk.

"See what your mother has bought in our house!" dad said. "She's a *whore!*"

Ted claimed he yelled back at his father so dad told him to go back to bed. Instead, Ted grabbed a knife out of the sink, and went over to the nook where mom and the strange man sat, oddly mute. Ted waved the knife in the man's face.

"Get out!" Ted screamed again and again—and the man did leave.

Mom went into her bedroom.

Ted got up in dad's face and said, "Don't you ever do that again!" He was terrified dad would kick his ass, but he didn't.

One morning, dad woke up and his whole face was puffed up. It grew increasingly worse for two days until it was blown up like a balloon. Mom, at some point when the kids weren't around, had hit him between the eyes with a high-heeled shoe. That was a time when all the money went to booze with the barest of foodstuff in the house.

There was a kid that lived next door, down a hill a ways. He'd come up to play with Ted and his siblings, and they'd go to his house, too. One day, Ted went onto the kid's closed-in back porch to knock on his door, and saw a lay-down freezer. There was no answer at the door, so he peeked into the freezer and saw stuff wrapped up: various packages of meat, and even a tub of ice cream. Ted cleaned out the freezer and brought everything home to feed his siblings.

Parents were boozing. This might have been one of his first delinquent acts, other than sneaking change out of mom's purse and dad's pants pockets while they slept to buy candy.

The increasing boozing and welfare check misuse caused the Welfare Department to eyeball Ted's parents. He and one of his brothers were placed in separate foster homes. Soon enough, he was being handled by the system as a troubled kid. His delinquent behavior escalated to running away, stealing stuff out of parked cars, parking meters, and burglarizing cottages along the Erie Canal.

He remembered good times. His dad would take the kids fishing. They used either bamboo fishing poles or a tree branch off of Sodus Bay Bridge. He remembered catching some sort of eel-looking creature.

"To this day, I hate having one of those things on my fishing hook. Whew!" Given wrote, although it's hard to figure what he meant by this. He hadn't been fishing for some time.

He remembered his father holding him on his knee and letting little Ted steer the car. He remembered the family being taken to Lake Ontario to swim. He remembered one Christmas when he and his brothers and sisters spent a long night looking down from their bedroom through a grate. They could see the "X-mass" tree[255] at an angle and waited for Santa Claus to bring the (church donated) toys. He remembered going out trick-or-treating and using his mom's upper false teeth as a part of his Halloween costume—Buckteeth Face.

Sex criminals in his position, he wrote, went through a program that required them to establish a "timeline and pathway" for their sexual history, beginning in childhood. The idea was to help them explore possible origins for their sexual deviancy—not an "explain-all", but merely a baseline. Given told me that he had been introduced to sexual behavior at an early age, Today he would be considered a victim of sexual child abuse. The sexual behaviors he began exhibiting at age seven, he now realized, went beyond mere childhood curiosity/exploration.

In Given's first sexual memory he is in a kindergarten classroom on a bench with a little girl with long yellow hair. She looked like Shirley Temple. One of them, and it might have been her, initiated a visual exploration of their privates. "Show me yours,

I'll show you mine." There was no touching. She lifted her dress and pulled down her panties and he unbuttoned his fly and pulled out his pecker. That was all he remembered of that incident. He didn't remember what led up to it, or what followed.

Another memory, around the same time: he was sitting in the bench-style front seat of a car between a female on his right (perhaps his grandmother) and a male on his left (grandfather) with his brothers in the back seat. In the memory, he is looking down at his own skinny legs. He is in shorts, and his legs are wet because he is crying very hard. The male on his left had just pinched him very hard between his legs, on the upper inner thigh. Something he couldn't explain made him feel it had something to do with sexual behavior. It also fed into his adult suspicions that there was incestuous stuff going on involving his grandfather and his grandfather's daughters when they were little girls.

In Given's next memory he was about ten or eleven and up the road from his grandparents' home in the countryside visiting a friend's house. He and the friend, who was the same age, were out in the barn playing around bales of hay. His friend's twin sister, who was slightly developmentally disabled, was with them. Show me yours, I'll show you mine occurred. However, this time his friend showed him how to insert his penis into his sister's *virgina* (Author's note: *spelling his*).

His next sexual event occurred soon after that one. Using the lesson he'd learned at his friend's house, he attempted to insert his penis into someone else's virgina. She screamed and kicked and he ran away. To this day he hoped she didn't remember that. Even before he attempted to engage in a sexual act, he'd been excited by women in the Montgomery Ward catalog, women's section, girdles and bras. "*Adult women,*" he emphasized.

He then moved the subject briefly to Nancy Jennings (pseudonym), his only-ever adult girlfriend. She was around just about the same time as his 1974 sex offense. He was just getting involved romantically with Nancy, a beautiful blond 20-year old. "I fell in love with her. Really! I think!" he wrote.

Another thing he learned in his psyche classes was that he suffers from intimacy deficiency, and had difficulty forming "loving relationships." If that was true, then what he felt for Nancy through all those years and now in his old age was a rare and precious thing, and messing up instead of being with Nancy remained a significant regret, one that haunted him. He had really screwed up.

That was where the letter ended. It was unsigned, and had been typed, single spaced on the backs of order forms for a men's clothing outlet.

We continued exchanging letters for many months after that, but he never really opened up to me again. I'd never learn if he thought all of those double initials were a coincidence. His letters became shorter and mostly schemed to improve his life, something I had no intention of doing. He apologized for his lack of verbiage, "But the fact of the matter is I'd slipped into the 'doing time' mental state. After all, there are so many physical reminders of this 'treatment facility' that there's no real difference than a prison." He sounded sad, "I have cognitive distortions within the thought processes. My letters will reflect a lot of psychobabble. I'll have to pluck out my past letters box, all those letters you've written and make myself a schedule (of one hour) to devote to answering questions you've posed in previous letters. But not right now! I have to psyche up to this discipline."

But he never did.

Wendy Jerome

An examination of Ted Given's "timeline" revealed that he served a decade for his "attempted rape" and had been set free to rape again. During his time in the system he "had not really" been treated for his rape problem, although in his last couple of years he was subjected to some experimental behavior modification sessions which, in retrospect, didn't help much. He was released from Attica on parole in March 1984, but returned to prison on December 31, 1985 when he was found prowling in a vacant mobile home. He was paroled again on February 7, 1986 and stayed free until his arrest for the breaking and entering child rape in Parma in the autumn of 1986.

Did anything horrible happen to young girls in Rochester during Given's 1984-6 glimpse at freedom? That question leads us to the tragic tale of 14-year-old Wendy Jerome, a freshman at Edison Tech high school, a brunette with red highlights in her hair, whose favorite color was purple, who wanted to grow up to be a cosmetologist with her own business, who spent her last days in the Tech print shop printing business cards.[256] She loved the band Journey, took a babysitting course, and was a member of a group called Teens on Patrol.

At about 10:45 p.m. on Thanksgiving night, November 22, 1984, the beaten and raped body of Wendy Lynn Jerome, was found lying in an alcove of School 33 at 500 Webster Avenue in Rochester by a man who said he found her body as he was walking by, taking a shortcut that evening.

School 33 was the school Michelle Maenza was attending, and walking home from, when she was taken. Wendy's body was found at the kindergarten entrance to School 33. The location was less than three blocks from Wendy's home on Denver Street.

Because her mother was at work—as a nurse at the Beechwood Nursing Home—Wendy and her dad prepared the Thanksgiving meal, ate at 4:30, and did the dishes afterward.

While Marlene napped, Wendy asked her father if she could go visit her friend Susie. She had a birthday card for Susie that she wanted to deliver in person. She left home just before 7:00 p.m. Susie lived on Alexis Street a few blocks away. Wendy arrived safely at Susie's house, left there at about 7:30 to return home, and was never seen alive again.

Wendy's curfew was 8:00 p.m., which was about the time Marlene awoke from her nap, realizing immediately with a mother's instinct that something was wrong. She came downstairs saying, "Where's Wendy?" Wayne said she went to Susie's house. Marlene called there and there was no answer. In fact, there was no answer for hours. When Marlene finally reached Susie's mom, the woman said, "Marlene, hang up the phone and call the police immediately." By that time the body had been found and police knocked on the Jerome's door only minutes later with the bad news.

The location of her body was not on the route between the two homes. There was a four-inch cut in her throat. Her pink hoodie had been removed and placed over her beaten face. Between the rape and the murder, she'd been allowed to get dressed.[257] The school grounds where the body was found were adjacent to Webster Avenue Park, which was small but contained a popular playground. Police said that bloodstains were found on the school wall about 30 yards from the body. The body had been left near the east side (kindergarten) entrance to School 33. Police did not wait till morning to investigate the area, but set up lights so the search for clues could begin right away. Also searched was a "burned out garage" nearby that contained trash and rags.

Relatives identified her body, and the story appeared in the Friday morning paper. Eleven years had passed since Michelle Maenza's murder, and there was no recognition in the press coverage that Wendy's body was found only about 300 yards from where Michelle was seen in a stranger's car by young Cynthia Nicoletti.

Lt. William Mayer of the RPD Physical Crimes Unit told the *D&C* that, although the area where the body was found was well traveled, this was not necessarily true on Thanksgiving, when there was no school, and folks tended to stay home.[258] He said the killing was "brutal" but refused to be more specific.

"Those details are known only to us and the killer," Mayer

175

said.

The body was autopsied on November 23. That same day, a fire truck was brought to School 33 to wash away the "large quantity of blood."

Detectives put together a timeline of Wendy's last hours. Only four hours passed between Wendy leaving for Susie's house and police knocking on the Jeromes' door.

The medical examiner said that the cause of death was "massive head injuries." District Attorney Howard Relin said that he didn't want to go into details, but that there were "multiple stab wounds."

Wendy had been beaten in the head with a blunt instrument, possibly a hammer. Police, Relin said, were questioning a man found near the crime scene covered in blood. He claimed that he, too, had been assaulted. Susie was too upset to say much about Wendy, just that she "was a nice, sweet, caring girl. I knew her about three or four years. We sat on the bus together. We saw each other at school. In the evening we did a lot together."

Susie's mom added, "We've been asked by the police not to talk about her death. All I can say is that Wendy was a nice, pleasant, lovable, and well-mannered little girl. She was a doll. You must understand this is a very trying time for us. We loved her."

Wendy had a ten-year-old brother, William, surviving paternal grandparents, William and Rita Jerome of Macedon, and a maternal grandmother, Goldie Sawdey, who lived in Texas.

There were no updates published in 1984 on any progress regarding the murder investigation. The man found covered in blood was not mentioned again, leading one to conclude that the blood was his own and he had been, as he'd claimed, an assault victim.

In the *D&C* "Letters to the Editor" section on December 15, School 33 vice principal G.E. Mancuso, complained that a *D&C* reporter had decided that School 33 was in a panic and was looking for quotes to support that assumption. The problem was, there was no panic, just a quiet sense of shock, which, Mancuso claimed, probably did not make for as good of a story. Two more readers, R.L. Hane and D. Mallette, wrote to compliment the police who went about their job of investigating the murder in a most professional manner, while remaining kind and respectful to the victim's friends and family. One letter gave special thanks to Sgt.

Ray Miraglia. Then there was a letter from the Jeromes, thanking everyone, friends and strangers alike, who had sent condolences.

After the New Year, concerned neighbors and other citizens, desperate to do something but not knowing what to do, threw money at the mystery. Neighbors went door-to-door collecting money for a reward fund, hoping that greed would unearth information that conscience could not.[259] Two "sister" groups were collecting money: the Northeast Area Development, represented by their Safety Organizer Nancy Beagle and president Carol Johnstone, and the Beechwood Neighborhood Coalition. A man named Ted Extale was also involved in setting up the fund. Canisters were placed in stores. Businesses were solicited for donations. The Kiwanis Club gave $200. More so than during the double-initial terror, there was frequent use of the plural, mentions of "Wendy's killer or killers." This was perhaps because both a knife and a hammer had been used in the attack, possibly indicating two perps. There was no mention of the double-initial cases, or the proximity between the Jerome and Maenza cases. Not only did Wendy have differing initials, the M.O. was different. True, the murder occurred in November, same as Carmen and Michelle, but Wendy was a little older, and beaten and stabbed rather than choked. Her body was left urban rather than rural.

The fund drive, all in all, included 25 people and they worked North Goodman Street, Bay Street, Culver Road, and East Main Street. Johnstone said that there had been talk of raising a reward fund immediately following Wendy's murder, but they decided to wait until the police were out of leads, which by all indications was pretty soon.

On the evening of February 1, in cooperation with the fund drive, Channel 10, WHEC-TV re-enacted the murder on its six o'clock news as part of its *Crimestoppers* segment. The TV station was offering its own $1,000 reward. The morning newspaper also printed an address where money could be sent. As usual, all tipsters were assured anonymity. The door-to-door effort eventually raised $1,700.[260] In April, 30 volunteers posted 500 posters across the city—in libraries, banks, stores, the Hall of Justice, and the Public Safety Building.[261]

The posters read: "*A KILLER is walking free on our streets wanted for the murder of 14-year-old Wendy Jerome...This could have been your friend or daughter."*

Police noted that, despite the wishful thinking of the community groups, there were no known witnesses to the murder. The reward was supposed to be available for one year only, at which time the money would go to *Crimestoppers*, but when the year was up, the time period was extended.

In May 1985, to improve neighborhood safety, there was a call for School 33 to keep its outside lights on all night.[262] Up until that point school policy was to only put the lights on if there was a school activity after dark. Han DeBruyn, president of the Webster Park Neighborhood Association, made the request. It wasn't just fear of another murder, DeBruyn said, but the darkness around the school made it a welcoming nocturnal teenage hangout. After some discussion of the electricity bill and miniscule school budgets, Superintendent Laval S. Wilson tepidly agreed to keep the lights on for a year and "see what happens."

In the meantime, there was turbulence at the Jerome home. Wendy's dad thought mother Marlene was spending too much time clinging and suffering over Wendy's belongings, and so threw out the little girl's Smurfs, miniature Care Bears, and diary. Marlene responded by throwing Wayne out.

It was revealed to the public for the first time in 2012 that an empty pack of cigarettes and a lighter were found near the body. There were also hairs, belonging to an African-American male, were found at the crime scene, as was usable DNA— but there was never a hit on CODIS. That was odd, and in some ways limited the list of suspects. Investigators took a fresh look at the unnamed 22-year-old African-American man who discovered Wendy's body. He was not considered a serious suspect at the time but committed suicide about six years after the murder without ever being DNA tested. On the night of the murder, the man had behaved oddly, visiting the home of a friend and then returning to the school alcove before calling 911 to report the body. According to the D.A.'s office, "He indicated that he was on his way to a bar, and cutting through the school and saw someone lying there and thought the person was intoxicated. He got closer and saw blood, went to a friend's house to confirm what they were seeing. They went back to the house and, it's odd, a lot of back and forth from the crime scene, before calling police."

*   *   *

On September 12, 2018, I spoke on the phone with New York State Police Investigator Thomas Crowley, who told me that, as I'd expected, our investigation was not the first to take a serious look at Theodore Given as the DIK. Ted had said so himself, saying "BCI" had suspected him. He said that DNA comparisons had been made between Given's DNA and that found at Wanda's crime scene without a match.

The Girl Who Saw the Killer's Face— And Other Eyewitnesses

Following the publication of my book *The Devil at Genesee Junction* about the 1966 Chili murders, my first public appearance was at the Scottsville Free Library in Scottsville, New York, November 2015. It was Local Author Night. I drew a nice crowd, and was asked, now that I'd finished writing about the murders of George-Ann Formicola and Kathy Bernhard, what did I plan for an encore. I said I'd like to sink my teeth into that double-initial thing, and this made everyone happy. So, between paying gigs, I scoured archives and data banks and put together a fairly detailed assemblage of facts about the three murders. I checked into a few of the most popular suspects, and began my correspondence with Ted Given.

Don Tubman and I, still a well-oiled machine from the *Devil* days, went back to work. The person I wanted to speak to most was Cynthia Nicoletti, the girl who'd stood at the corner of Webster Avenue and Ackerman Street as Michelle Maenza, a girl she knew well, and her abductor zoomed by recklessly in a piece-of-crap dented up American car, almost creating a crack-up as it turned toward the northeast.

Don found her and I interviewed her by phone, first on a Saturday evening, and then again on Monday morning. More than four decades had passed since Cynthia saw what she saw.

At that time, she said, her family lived on Lamont Place, which was the dead-end street just north of Webster Crescent, where Michelle lived. Cynthia remembered Michelle as mentally disabled and as a girl who was picked on a lot at school. Cynthia's recollection was that Michelle's family was very poor.

Cynthia still felt guilty because she was, on occasion, one of the kids who picked on Michelle, although she did not pick on Michelle on the day she was abducted.

Cynthia said she was on her bicycle, and was headed northeast on Webster Avenue, headed for her girlfriend's house on Copeland Street. Cynthia saw Michelle walking ahead of her. Both she and Michelle were just about to Ackerman Street heading in the direction of the public library on Webster Avenue. Cynthia passed Michelle on the bike. She remembered that she found it strange that Michelle was not with her mother, and that she and Michelle spoke briefly, although she doesn't remember what was said. Maybe it was mostly things she wanted to say, things she wished she'd said. She does know that she did not tease Michelle at that time. She remembered that she had been *nice* to Michelle. Cynthia continued on Webster Avenue and Michelle turned and headed up Ackerman in the direction of the shopping center.

Cynthia picked up her girlfriend Mary Kay at her house on Copeland and Mary Kay rode on the back of Cynthia's bicycle. She dropped Mary Kay back off at her house, returned to Webster Avenue, took a right, and headed toward home. She got to the northwest corner of Ackerman and Webster Avenue, just a few feet from where she'd encountered Michelle a few minutes earlier, when a car approached rapidly from their right, from the direction of Goodman Plaza. The guy cut the corner so severely from Ackerman onto Webster that Cynthia had to back up to avoid being hit. He turned left on Webster Avenue. She later came to believe that the guy was trying to run her over. For a moment she was looking right at him, and, as he passed her and turned left on Webster Avenue, she saw Michelle in the backseat of the car, her face in the rear driver's side window, screaming.

She got a good look at the car and the man driving it. The car was a tan-colored two-door, beat up with rust on it. She could not tell the make of the car but mentioned that it "might have been a Ford."

Later she got into a car with a detective and drove around looking for the car, but she didn't see it.

The man, she said, was "scruffy." I said that in 1973 that described a lot of men, and she added that she didn't mean "hippie scruffy." She meant "dirtbag scruffy."

Cynthia said that she went home and hid in a bag that contained her mother's wedding dress. Her mother found her and it was then that Cynthia spoke up. However, based on official reports, Cynthia's mother did not call police until it was known that Michelle was missing. Cynthia told her parents and the police that there was something familiar about the man, that she thought she had seen him before, and she associated him with a pizza parlor at the corner of

Bay and Goodman, with the generic name Bay Goodman Pizza. She said she thought the joint was still there. She didn't know if he worked there or if he had been a customer there when she went in with her father, but she always believed that he was a guy from the neighborhood. (She later said she thought he might have been a customer who sat in the corner at the bar, which was why she always told her father that she knew the guy.)

Cynthia said the detectives took her very seriously and talked to her every day for a while, and a couple of policemen stayed at her school (Corpus Christi) with her. Her teacher was Sister Rita.

The first time she rode around looking for the car with the detectives her mother came along, but after that her mother gave them permission and she rode with just the cops in the car.

She remembered that a reporter (she thinks it might have been Warren Doremus of WHEC-TV, then Channel 10) came to her house and they showed where they lived on TV, which made her mother very angry. Within a year or so Cynthia's dad moved the family to Henrietta.

Cynthia said that the neighborhood at that time was considered safe, that kids were allowed to go places by themselves, and everyone looked out for each other. Of course, all of that changed after Michelle.[263]

Two days later, Cynthia called me back to tell me that she had been trying to get the memories to flow, which was hard because she had been blocking them for so long, but she now thought the tan car was parked up Ackerman street waiting when she encountered Michelle the first time that afternoon. Cynthia was very eager to be helpful.

Cynthia believes that "the composite drawing" of the guy might be based on her statements to the police, but that she hadn't seen it in years. She wanted me to send her a copy of the drawing (as she was "off the grid" and hadn't a computer). I said I didn't think that was a good idea. I would rather send her an array of photographs and have her rate them in terms of how much they looked like the guy she saw.

She told me she was willing to do a drive-around with Don Tubman, which she thought might help her memory. She said she was willing to put herself "through hypno-therapy" if I thought that would help.[264]

I sent Cynthia a package of nine photographs of men, some considered double-initials suspects, some random. One of the photos was of me when I was 20. Cynthia picked number eight. Number eight was a photo of Theodore F. Given, Jr.

On the following Sunday afternoon, Don Tubman picked Cynthia up at her home in a Monroe County suburb and drove her to her old neighborhood, hopeful that, seeing the streets once again might help her recall the details of what she saw on the day of Michelle's disappearance.

Don parked his car on Webster Avenue and they toured the neighborhood on foot. Cynthia struggled at times because so much had changed. There were abandoned properties. The corner of Ackerman and Webster Avenue looked very different because houses that were once there were now gone and there was nothing but vacant lot between that spot and the Goodman Plaza.

They went to look at the Bay Goodman Pizzeria but discovered that the building now housed a social-work group. At the corner of Ackerman and Webster Avenue Don urged Cynthia to relax and try to "go back to being a little girl again."

Cynthia took it very seriously and closed her eyes. She said that she still remembered Michelle being in the back seat of the car, but now recalled that she was waving her arms over her head and was making a fuss.

In a conversation with me on October 24, Cynthia said that she was a tad disappointed with her experience walking around with Don. She had expected an "Oh shit!" moment, when her memory would burn through with great clarity, but that hadn't happened. Regarding the array of photos I had sent her, she said that she couldn't be positive, but there was something about #8 (Given) that made her stop and stare. It was his chin, the longness of his face. His eyes burned into her brain, she said.

Next on my list to speak to was Linda, the girl who'd been with Wanda Walkowicz when the pair was stalked on the Saturday night before Wanda's disappearance. Don found her, and on a Friday afternoon I spoke with her.

"I grew up in the same house as Wanda Walkowicz," she told me. The house had been divided into four apartments, and the Walkowicz's lived upstairs from Linda's family on Avenue D. Linda and Wanda were the same age.

"We went to school together, and became real good friends. She had red hair, I had red hair. We used to play tricks on her mother, on my mother. We used to spend the night at each other's houses," Linda said.

Wanda was her best friend, and to this day she keeps a photo of Wanda, hair the color of an Orange Crush, on the wall of her home. They'd known each other since they were five. I asked Linda about Wanda's chipped tooth, and she remembered that Wanda had been running down the sidewalk, fell, and hit her face. The tooth was never repaired. She said that Wanda's mother was "a good person but she was drunk most of the time," and the same was true of her boyfriend Junior (Paton Raney Jr.). She remembered Junior as being a nice guy.

Looking back on it as an adult, Linda wondered if Wanda ever received any adequate parenting.

I asked her if any police or reporters had ever spoken to her about Wanda and she said I was the first. She said that she lived in the same house as Wanda for years, but not long before Wanda disappeared, her family moved five blocks away to an apartment on Harris Street, a north/south street that ran parallel to Conkey one block to the west.

"We were still really close to one another, just a few minutes walk," Linda said.

Sometimes there were four of them hanging out because Wanda's sister Ruth and Linda's sister were the same age as each other and they were there, too. Because Joyce was a drinker, Linda remembered hanging out more at her own house than at Wanda's.

She said that maybe two weeks before Wanda disappeared, she and Wanda were walking from her house to Wanda's house along Harris Street when they were followed by a man in a dark woolen hat and a coat, medium-build, maybe five-foot ten inches tall. It was too dark to see his face at all. Her memories were foggy in spots. She remembered her first inkling that there was danger: "In the bushes, the hedges that we had to pass, you could hear something scraping on the ground. I said, 'Let's run.' And we grabbed each other's hand and ran." They ran into Wanda's house and up the stairs and into the Walkowicz apartment. They heard the man opening the downstairs door and coming up one flight of stairs to the landing before he stopped and said, "I'm going to get you next time."

I asked if her mother had called the police and she said she didn't know, and there was no way of asking her mother as she'd passed away.

"It could have been," she added. "It's a big possibility."

I suggested that it was possible that Linda had seen "the guy." She acknowledged that was true and said, "All I know is that I was scared after that and wouldn't go outside alone anymore."

Linda remembered playing with Wanda earlier on the day she disappeared. Because of the incident where they were followed, Linda told Wanda that if her mother ever asked her to do something by herself she could come get Linda so they could be together.

Linda remembered her own mother being angry with Joyce for sending Wanda out by herself to buy milk and cigarettes when she knew there was a man out there grabbing kids. Linda wasn't sure if her mother was referring to the Harris Street incident or to the murder of Carmen Colon.

"Back in those days we were allowed to buy cigarettes for our parents," Linda noted. No reporters ever spoke to Linda but she did remember the day that she and her mother went to Wanda's wake: "I was in a flowered jacket and I remember seeing Wanda in that casket and that just blew me away." The TV cameras tried to film Linda's face. Her mother was very cautious about stuff like that and covered up her face. "She didn't want the guy to see it on TV and think I was the girl who'd seen him." Linda figured the killer must've been watching Wanda for a while. She was never alone, hardly ever certainly, and yet the one time she was out by herself he was there to grab her.

In a lot of ways Rochester was a small town, she said. When she grew up she worked with a person who was a cousin of Carmen Colon.

Gidget

I sat pondering the great confusing maelstrom of swirling facts that kept us from clearly seeing the double-initial murders. Some of the fog was permanent, but I tried to isolate spots where there was work to be done.

My first thought was that the Carmen Colon murder had been under-investigated. Police felt Carmen's murder was not only separate from Wanda and Michelle's murders, but that it was all tied up in the dysfunctional Colon family, a world of half-siblings and attempts at murder/suicide, a place they didn't want to go.

After Miguel Colon shot his wife (Carmen's mother) and her brother before turning the gun on himself, they figured he was the guy. It was his Cadillac that had been washed out with detergent, his Cadillac in which was found one of Carmen's dolls. He was the one who split for Puerto Rico saying he'd done something wrong. As far as many investigators were concerned, Miguel Colon did it, case closed. One down, two to go.

But how much did we really know about the Colons and Carmen's sad life? Had Carmen's mom ever been interviewed in Spanish by a woman with no men present?

I wanted to create a man-free Spanish-speaking atmosphere for Guillermina Colon, to see if she would open up about the days and years leading up to Carmen's murder.

For help, I went to Christine Green, a journalist originally from San Jose, California, now living in the Rochester area, literary arts columnist for the *Democrat and Chronicle* and *(585) Magazine.* She had been a friend of the investigation from back in the Genesee Junction days and was eager to help.

Christine recruited into the fold her friend Deb Sperling, a former newsstand magazine reporter who was writing obits for the *D&C* and transcribing college lectures. Deb's husband was from Argentina and she spoke Spanish, although she was not confident about understanding Puerto Rican dialect.

On December 19, 2017, I wrote a letter to Christine Green and Deb Sperling saying that the investigation needed to speak to Carmen's mom because she might know who killed her daughter. I urged them not to be overly optimistic because we had only a small

Nightmare in Rochester

hope of getting her to say anything revealing, or anything at all for that matter.

In the past the family had circled the wagons during interviews, offered press releases that oft seemed defensive and spin doctored. Initial reports agreed that Carmen had been a troubled child, but the family said again and again that she was happy, happy, happy.

There was an early report that her aunts and uncles didn't like Carmen, that they left her behind and made her cry. The family couldn't wait to correct this notion: her aunts and uncles loved her, loved her, loved her.

There was no reason to think the family has suddenly become chatty, but we couldn't know for sure until we attempted an investigation in Spanish and without men to disrupt the rapport. Along with location suggestions, since we still didn't know where Guillermina lived, I offered a list of questions the ladies should ask should they get the interview.

Christine, Deb, and I planned a meeting for January 12, 2018 in Henrietta. Christine sent me the report of a study on human trafficking in Puerto Rico sponsored by actor and singer Ricky Martin, himself the victim of childhood sexual abuse. The report said that poverty was such a severe problem on the island that young girls were often expected to be earners, and were frequently shipped to the U.S. mainland to make money.

The meeting with Christine and Deb went great. Who wouldn't want these lovely ladies in their home? I suggested they bring food. By the evening of the January 12, Deb sent me her first report. She'd found that Guillermina had five Facebook profiles, was religious, had a house in Puerto Rico that survived the hurricane but with roof damage in need of repair, once drove a school bus, and had a large scar down her right arm from her gunshot wound.

On February 25, 2018, we mailed a letter to Guillermina to the two addresses we had for her, written by Christine Green and translated by Deb. It read: "Dear Ms. Colon, My name is Deb Sperling. I am a friend of renowned author Michael Benson. Michael is researching the case of Carmen's untimely death and the impact it had on her family and friends. I am hoping that I can set up a time to talk with you about the case at your convenience. Michael and I know the basic facts of the case and what happened to poor Carmen, but we want to learn more about you, your life, and how your loss has impacted your life. We are victim advocates and we want to hear your story. I know this must very painful to think about. I realize that our inquiry may feel intrusive, but I promise we offer nothing but sympathy and our deepest respect. We in no way mean to exploit you, Carmen, or anyone else. Michael is Rochester born and bred and has been personally touched by the violence of murder. He is a justice-seeker and one of the kindest people I know. If you'd like to talk further I can be contacted at [deleted]. I look forward to hearing from you. With respect, Deb Sperling."

As this was going on, the state police used the TV news and social media to fish for new clues regarding the Wanda Walkowicz murder. A TV channel opened up its Facebook page for Wanda comments. One woman replied that her ex-husband had been the man to identify Carmen Colon's body. I messaged her, asked who her ex was, and in 24 hours had arranged to speak with Angel Colon, who had indeed been one of two relatives that volunteered to go to the morgue to ID little Guisa.

On the afternoon of March 20, Angel Colon called me and said he'd like to speak with me that evening, when work was over and he was home. At that time I asked him what he remembered about the day Carmen disappeared. He said he was 18 and in school and they called him out of class and told him to go home. He remembered family and friends going out in cars to search for Carmen. He remembered that during the search there was great concern because Carmen was in "special school" and "very friendly."

"She would go with anybody," Angel said.

He remembered detectives coming to the house and asking for a volunteer to ID the body. He went to the morgue and yes he was the one who said he saw a dried tear on Carmen's face—although he had since been told that it might have been something the medical examiner used to clean off her face. Her eyes, he said now, were filled with blood.

He said the Bull's Head neighborhood was still nice in 1971, and there was no real concern about Carmen being out by herself. The thing that worried the family once Carmen disappeared was that there was a bar at the time at the corner of Main and Brown and with bars you never know who was coming and going.

I asked him if police had questioned him and he said no. At this point he got off track and began to defend his Uncle Miguel.

Turned out Angel was not Miguel's brother, but his nephew. Angel's mother was Miguel's sister. He has the last name Colon because his dad remained in Puerto Rico and he didn't even meet him until he was 35 years old. He had mom's maiden name as his own. As for Uncle Miguel, he says that everyone was lying when they said Miguel fled after Carmen died and was found by police in Puerto Rico. Angel said Uncle Miguel was in Rochester all the time, and according to his memory it was Miguel who accompanied him to the morgue to ID Carmen. (1971 reports said it was Julio Colon that went with Angel.) If Miguel acted funny at all at the time it was because he was living with Guillermina and she was in social services, so he wasn't supposed to be in the house.

Angel said he had read that Miguel killed himself because of Carmen, but this wasn't so. He killed himself much later (20 years later) and did it because of personal and financial problems. The personal problems he could only guess at. Angel knew the financial problems were real as Uncle Miguel came to him not long before his death and tried to sell Angel a gun. He said Uncle Miguel suffered plenty when Carmen was killed, but admitted that he did have a temper.

It is Angel's belief that one person killed all three girls. He said that, according to Guillermina, Carmen's grandma died because of what happened to Carmen, that she "got crazy."

Asked if he had contact info for Guillermina because a lovely Spanish-speaking woman wanted to interview her. He said he would call her and give her my phone number and that she would be happy to speak with me. I again said I'd prefer she be interviewed in Spanish and he agreed that that would be nice.

He used the word "suffer" a great deal. He would say, "We suffered. The family suffered." Perhaps in response to public feelings (now mostly forgotten) that they didn't like Carmen and one of them might have killed her. He said a couple of things emphasizing that he was the same generation as Carmen. "We grow up together," he said, although he was at least eight years older. He used the term "special school" only once and afterwards referred to Carmen's mental handicap as "being the way she was."

On March 22, 2018, Angel again called me, and gave me Guillermina's phone number, adding that she would appreciate being interviewed in Spanish. I forwarded the number to Deb and

Christine.

The ladies followed up on the lead and on the afternoon of April 7, Christine and Deb sat and chatted with Guillermina and her daughter Maria in Guillermina's city apartment. The building was run down, but her apartment was spectacularly clean. A large pot of heavenly-smelling soup was on the stove.

Christine noted that it was a small sparsely furnished one-bedroom apartment. Christine saw no family photos. There was a stereo system in the living room. Deb spied a flat-screen TV in the bedroom. There were a couple of plants, a plain couch, and a small table with four chairs.

Guillermina was tiny, less than five feet, wore glasses, and had short hair dyed red with grey roots peeking out. She wore jeans, a blue sweatshirt, a blue and white polyester blouse, and black sandals. She was well put together but understandably nervous. The ladies were there to talk about the worst days of her life.

Maria, Carmen's half-sister and daughter of Miguel, was a tall woman who looked particularly statuesque next to her tiny mom. She wore fashionable light jeans with holes, a pink shirt, pink sneakers, and large gold hoops. There was an Apple watch on her right wrist and a gold religious medal around her neck. Christine couldn't see who was on the medal, a saint or perhaps the Virgin Mary. Maria had tattoos on her arms. She had long, long dyed red hair. Her makeup was artistically done and she looked considerably younger than she was, thrice a grandmother.

Christine's first impression was that the women were determined to block the investigation. Maria was on the phone and Guillermina seemed hesitant and quiet. The women settled in the living room and Christine began to ask questions in English which Deb translated into Spanish. After a bit, Christine felt the room get comfortable and relax.

Christine asked, "Just talk about your life here. You grew up in Puerto Rico, right? When did you come to live in Rochester?"

Guillermina said she first came to America when she was nine, 1954, 1955, something like that. She came directly from Puerto Rico to Rochester. She came to live with her father while her mother remained behind in Puerto Rico. She was sent back to Puerto Rico for a year because she was afraid of the snow and didn't want to go to school. She was in Puerto Rico until she turned 14, at which time she returned to Rochester.

Deb asked, "What was your adolescence like in Rochester?"

Guillermina replied, "I don't think I had an adolescence." She explained that her life had been hard. Her parents separated. There was no happiness, much violence. "My mom had married another man," Guillermina said. "My stepdad—it wasn't easy."

Deb asked, "How old were you when you had Carmen?"

"Fourteen."

"Her father was Justiano?"

"Yes."

"How old was he?"

"In his early thirties."

Christine and Deb tried to learn about the relationship between Justiano and Guillermina, but didn't have instant results.

"Were you married?"

"No."

Maria tried to help: "You and Justiano weren't boyfriend and girlfriend?"

Guillermina replied, "No, nothing. He was with my sister."

Maria read her mom and added, "There's a story behind that, but that's personal, so she can't really explain that relationship with that man, which is my uncle, but there was nothing as boyfriend or girlfriend. She just ended up pregnant."

Deb persisted, "There was nothing romantic?"

"No," Guillermina said, "I don't know how to even tell it. No choice. I was 14 years old. I was still a girl."

Deb thought that painted a clear-enough picture and moved on: "Did your family help you with Carmen when she was a baby?"

"No. I always struggled alone. I still struggle alone."

Guillermina's father took her and baby Carmen to Puerto Rico to live in a new house he'd built there. Her mother wanted her to give Carmen to her grandfather.

"She didn't want her to suffer with me," she explained. "Because I was working in houses with families."

She said Dad helped, Mom didn't. Christine got the distinct impression that no one helped much.

They stayed in Puerto Rico until Carmen was seven or eight years old. For much of that time Carmen stayed with Miguel's grandparents, Candida and Felix, who Guillermina referred to as Mama Canda and Papa Fele. When Miguel's grandparents came to Rochester, Guillermina and Carmen came with them.

Christine and Deb were confused about how, exactly, everyone was related to everyone else. Guillermina intimated that it was a web weaved at least partially in deception ("so many secrets") and hard to untangle.

Maria said, "There's all these half brothers and sisters. Everybody wants to be a part of the newspaper. They want to be known as Carmen's sister and brother, but nobody was there for my mom, you know? Like all these people in our family, nobody comes and visits her, ever. But when the topic pops up about Carmen, everyone wants to be a part of it, and act like they care. I'm sorry, I'm like very blunt when it comes to things like that."

Christine said, "I think you should be. And I think it's common. People who want to be a part of tragedy somehow to make themselves either famous or to be needed in some way."

Deb asked Guillermina, "Getting back to when Carmen was seven or eight, how was life in Rochester?"

Guillermina replied, "We came back in '68. After that," she turned to her daughter, "I had met your father [Miguel] in Puerto Rico, but I didn't like him. When I came to Rochester, he came too. And then we got together. We had Luz, and Maria, and then got married."

Christine turned to Maria, "And what year were you born?"

"1975," Maria replied. "Luz was born 1970."

"Any other children, brothers, sisters?" Deb asked.

"No," Maria said.

"Could you tell us a little bit more about Carmen's personality, her favorite things when you came here?"

"She liked to do exercises," Guillermina said, and then launched into a description of Carmen's final hours. "The day that she disappeared, she had on some little pants. I had just gone to the hospital with my other little girl, Luz, who had an ear infection. Luz was eleven months old—between ten and eleven months. Carmencita was playing and was saying I should do exercises like her so I would be skinny like her. When I went back inside my in-laws' house, she came in, too. She was always with her little sister. My in-laws were there. Mama Canda and Papa Fele. I always called them Mama and Papa as if they had been my parents."

When Carmen heard that Luz's medicine needed to be picked up and said, "Mommy, I'll go! I'll go!"

Guillermina continued, "She wanted to go. So I told Papa Fele to watch her, because the drugstore was on the same block. She didn't even have to cross a dangerous street or anything. He was always watching her. I put the Medicare form and the prescription in a little bag, and I put a coin in so she could buy something sweet. She arrived at the drugstore, but it seems that when my father-in-law went in, she had left the drugstore and she disappeared."

Maria added, "The grandfather was watching her from the house, right up the street. I guess in the little quick moment that he turned and went inside the house real quick, she must've came out of the store and that's when she disappeared."

This story was in contrast to the one reportedly told by the family immediately following Carmen's disappearance, that Felix had followed Carmen to the pharmacy on other occasions but this time did not because Carmen took off without notifying him that she was going.

Maria added, "It was on the same side of the street. She didn't have to cross or nothing. Just walk up the street to the pharmacy."

Guillermina said, "The pharmacy was here, and the house was here. He would go out to the sidewalk and watch her from the sidewalk. He could see to the door of the drugstore."

As I had walked it, I knew this was not true. Carmen had gone out of sight the instant she turned the corner onto Main Street. Their memories had blended Morrell's Cigar Store where Carmen bought penny candy on Brown Street and the drug store on Main into a single location.

"Who was the first that went to look for her?" Deb asked.

Guillermina answered, "Papa Fele went to look for her. He went with Compai Tonio, an uncle." [*Note: Antonio Colon. "Compai" is slang for "friend" or in some cases "godfather."*] He went to speak with the man from the pharmacy but the man knew nothing. Nobody knew anything. Compai Tonio decided that he had to call the police. Then the police didn't show up right away. Justiano and Miguel were working. They worked at Gerber. Maria's father and Carmen's father worked together at Gerber."

Gerber made baby food, and was known at the time for its big water tower, dominating the skyline along Rochester's western edge, with the Gerber baby painted on it.

Guillermina continued, "So they would get out of work around 4 or 4:30 and....at 5. But when my daughter disappeared, they were always saying that it was my husband. But it wasn't my husband, because he loved Carmencita a lot. He loved her like a daughter. He was her uncle. She grew up with him. Two years… with my mother-in-law, he was living with them. He always took care of her. Miguel didn't appear right away to talk to the police because my brother-in-law told him, 'Don't show up yet because you will get in trouble for living with a woman on welfare. It is fraud.'"

Guillermina said the policeman she dealt with was a "big guy, an older man. He was a really good person." He was the one who told her that they'd found Carmen's lifeless body. But other police came also, and they came for Miguel.

"They took my husband several times. They mistreated him. The same police told me I wasn't telling the truth. I told them 'I am telling the truth. I am not lying. It wasn't my husband. My husband was working at that time.' So they kept searching, until they found my baby's body, up in Chili. I was asking them to look for her. I was frustrated. I was saying to the police that they go into a building on Brown Street. I asked them to look there because I heard her crying in my mind."

Deb interjected, "I'm so sorry."

Christine asked, "What year did you marry Miguel?"

"It was 1979." She added that, the way she remembered it, Angel and Antonio were the pair who identified Carmen's body. Angel, they noted, was not a Colon brother. He was the son of Miguel's sister, Justina. He was a nephew.

Guillermina said that it was she and not Angel who saw the tear on Carmen's face. At Carmen's wake, in Felix and Candida's home, she saw a tear come out of Carmen's eye and became so distraught she needed to be hospitalized.

"I stayed in psychiatry for a long time," Guillermina added.

"She had to get mental help. She was depressed. She lost so much weight—80 or 90 pounds," Maria said.

Deb sympathized, "Nobody should have to go through that."

"It's the worst thing that could happen," Christine agreed.

Deb got back to business: "Let us know if we have our facts

wrong, but we understand that Miguel went to Puerto Rico a few days or a few weeks after—"

"No. He never went back to Puerto Rico," Guillermina said.

Deb didn't know how to handle the contradiction for a moment. Miguel's flight was documented. "Like, never, or not that year, or later...?" Deb sputtered.

Guillermina was adamant: "No. He went to Puerto Rico with me when my stepfather had a heart attack. And that was like 1977, I think, or around 1980-something. It was like '84, '85 that my stepfather had the heart attack and he went with me, yes."

Maria emphasized: "That was like years after..."

Deb hung tough: "He never went back before?"

"No. He went with me. And we went when my stepdad was in the hospital, very serious." There were other times, too, illnesses in the family, a death, but they were later and they had nothing to do with Carmencita.

There was no point in arguing. As with the changing geography of Rochester's Bull's Head section, Miguel not leaving was part of how Guillermina remembered things. Interestingly, Guillermina acknowledged that Miguel avoided police after Carmen's murder, because his brother told him he was a criminal, committing fraud.

Deb shifted gears, "Do you still have family in Puerto Rico?"

"I have a sister and two nieces," Guillermina said. She visited them a lot, spent many weeks there the previous year. She was on the island for Hurricane Irma in September 2017, but not for Hurricane Maria just a few weeks later.

"Lucky," Deb said. "Your sister and nieces are OK? Do they have light and everything?"

"Yeah."

Christine brought up Dominick Colon who said he was afraid after Carmen was killed. Did he fear a vendetta or something?

Maria noted that Dominick was known in the family as Cheo. She didn't really know why. Someone said it one day and it stuck.

"And Carmen, they used to call her Carmencita or Guisa," Maria offered.

"Why Guisa?" Deb asked.

Guillermina answered: "A nickname that they gave her."

Deb asked, "It doesn't have a meaning?"

The women laughed. They couldn't think of a nickname that meant anything.

Christine pointed out, "On her gravestone, it says Carmen G. Colon. So is that for Guisa? Or did she have a middle name?"

"I don't know," Guillermina said.

Christine turned soothing, "That's OK."

Maria said, "I don't know why they put the G."

"She didn't have a second name?" Deb asked.

"No," Guillermina said, ending the subject.

Deb put the conversation back on track: "The question was, why was Cheo afraid after Carmen was killed? We would like to know why he would've said this."

Maria took a shot at it: "Cheo was my father's brother. He doesn't do good with funerals and stuff like that. He went in, but he wouldn't go to the casket. He said it was like too much for him. He was a little weird." Maria stood. "Do you guys want some juice?"

Beverages were served. Deb used the bathroom. Christine kept an eye on a mouse that kept running back and forth in the kitchen, visible to her each time he went under the refrigerator. Christine and Maria chatted. Maria had always lived in Rochester. Deb came out of the bathroom and Christine went in. Maria and Deb chatted.

Maria said, "I wish that the whole true story can come out."

"That's what we'd really like to hear. Your story," Deb replied.

"I know. But she's not going to, that personal part..."

"It sounds to me like a lot of those two men, your father and the other father, were kind of difficult on her, I want to say. "

"My dad was pretty good. As for Justiano, I don't know. Our family is like so distant. That's just how our family is. There's a lot of secrets, a lot of fake family."

"Fake family in what sense?"

"They are quick to say they are a closer relation than they are, just to be a part of the story..."

"But there's no blood relation?"

"They don't ever check up on her, they don't care."

Christine returned and Maria began to talk about her father. She had been very close to Miguel, daddy's little girl. They clarified the timeline: Guillermina was in a relationship with Miguel, giving birth to Maria and Luz, years before she married Miguel.

"They got married when I was about four years old," Maria

said. "1979."

Christine said, "Miguel must've been a huge support to you during this whole ordeal. You guys must've really leaned on each other, right? While Carmen was missing, and the death?"

Maria answered: "But he was being...he was in a stressful situation because they were accusing him, and so, yeah, that was another stress for him, so..."

Christine asked Guillermina if she was worried about Miguel when the police questioned him.

"No," Guillermina said, "because I knew that he hadn't done it. And we felt really bad. He suffered a lot. When they killed another girl, they took him out of work. When they killed the other, it was the same problem. He was also really unhappy. He lost his job, because of them taking him out over and over."

Maria was her dad's number-one fan and in charge of the rehabilitation of his reputation. "My mother and father were married for 24 years."

Of course, that marriage ended in hideous violence. Christine pushed the subject in that direction. "Did that stress just accumulate over the years with him?" she asked.

Guillermina didn't get Deb's translation so Maria rephrased the question as: "How did you get along with Papi?"

Guillermina looked to Christina as she answered, "No, not always good. But he was very good. He was a good father."

Maria said her parents couldn't do bad things. They were always such *protective* parents. They kept their eye on the kids, never neglectful. Daddy absolutely. She always had to wear a tee-shirt over her bathing suit. "Because he would say there were so many perverts out here. He was very overprotective. And I just don't see him having anything to do with my sister's murder," she said.

Deb asked, "When the police questioned Miguel, would they question you as well in relation to all the other murders?"

They would not, Guillermina said.

Christine asked, "Did you ever meet or have any sort of contact with the families of the other two little girls at all?"

Maria said, "We met one of the sisters. Do you remember who it was? I can't remember which sister it was."

Guillermina said, "They told us that the parents of the other girl had already passed away. When they killed the second girl, I asked them to take me to the funeral home to see the girl and meet the mother. It hurt me a lot, because it was like re-living Guisa's murder. And then a year or so when the other girl was murdered, I couldn't go, because when…"

Maria took up the point, "Like she relived it every time this happened to each girl. For the one that was killed after Carmen, she actually went to her funeral. She wanted to meet the mom. She got really agitated. I had to take her out of there. For the third one, she couldn't."

Christine asked if they ever felt blindsided by Carmen stories popping up expectedly in the newspaper or on TV. Maria said if she saw something she'd call her mother to warn her and tell her about it.

Guillermina said that for years she would put flowers on Guisa's grave on her birthday, but this year, no.

"What was the story in the paper that struck you as a complete lie?" Christine asked.

Maria had one. "That Papi cleaned the trunk. And that they found the doll in the car."

Guillermina said, "Yeah. In the car, there was a brush, but it was for my hair. Because I was always brushing my hair in the car. And because of that they blamed him, saying that it was Carmen's. But it was mine."

"And the doll," Maria said. "The doll was one of the homemade ones with the threading that you put the toilet paper in and stuff it. My mom gave him that. And it was broken and sitting in the car. But I mean, like I always say, too, even if they did find anything of my sister's in the car…"

"You're family!" Christine said.

"They just wanted to find somebody to pin it on," Maria said.

Guillermina had some wind behind her sails now. Old anger was surfacing: "That time, for me, they didn't want to do the work of looking and looking and looking and researching to figure it out…Search the school, or search in a place where," she was speaking very quickly now, "all three of them…learning disabilities. Or some social workers, those kind that know where they were living, what their names were, the *situation* of the girls, that they had problems."

"And to know their double initials and all that stuff," Maria said. "It's somebody that had to know about these girls...They wanted to pin it on my dad because, like she says, at the time, when all the family came to be questioned, my dad was the only one that didn't come. But it was because my uncle had put fear into him that they were going to get in trouble because they lived together, and he worked and she was on welfare. Fraud stuff."

This statement rather neatly fit into the official story. Word was, when Miguel fled, it was because he'd "done something wrong". He said nothing about murder and he could have been referring to his belief that he would be arrested for welfare fraud if he spoke to the Rochester police.

Deb gave the facts one last push, "And this idea, and I'm sorry to press on this because I know it's a rumor, but the idea that Miguel did go back to Puerto Rico right after, where did that come from? Why did that get circulated so much, do you think?"

Maria suggested a cousin made the story up and it stuck.

Deb offered a face-saving option for the ladies, to see if they would come off of their revisionist version: "And I think also, even if he had gone back to Puerto Rico, it would've been a totally normal thing to do, to go back and visit relatives. So they take this and kind of spin it."

Guillermina and Maria didn't bite.

Christine got down to brass tacks: "So this is going to be the hardest question. Your father's passing, and that day. Do you guys feel comfortable telling us a little bit from your perspective what happened? All we have seen is the police report—well, I mean, what Michael read the police report and just wrote a few sentences about what that said. So that's all we know, and you know, what do you guys feel comfortable telling us about that?"

Maria began to cry.

Guillermina said nothing for a moment and then came in hot: "Things that happened between him and me, that no one needs to know, and no one needs to—only, there are things that have to happen in life that one can't solve. He was a good man. Nothing more. That's all I can say."

Through her tears, Maria said, "They were just going through their own personal problems, you know like every marriage has. I guess it was hard for my dad, so, that was his way out. Maybe the problems from Carmen drove him to that point, but I don't think so.

My dad had his gun permit, and he would shoot his gun in the basement.

"They said because he wasn't wearing earplugs that that started to do damage to his brain. I was 15 when that happened, and I remember I was going with some friends to New York City to go shopping. And my dad was OK with me going, and so I called him when I got down there to let him know I got there safe. I got down there two days before he killed himself. I called him on the 16th. I told him that I made it down there and I was fine. And it was a weird call because he wasn't himself. He yelled at me when I told him. He had given me permission, like he totally forgot. I think the 18th is when that happened. I got sick, for some reason, down there. So we ended up having to come back to Rochester, and um, I think we came back the 19th. It was the day after. I was in a car with a bunch of people and we're coming down Avenue A, and my kid's father, at the time which we weren't even a couple, didn't even know each other, stopped the car that I was in and he's telling the driver, he's like, 'Oh, you heard what happened? Some guy, he killed his wife and he killed himself.' We keep driving, we're coming up Treyer St., another person stops him, and he's like, *"Hey, you heard what happened? Some guy he killed his wife and he killed himself on Radio Street.'* And we go on Radio Street, and I go to my parents' house, and they don't answer, and I'm like next door to my uncle's house, and—I still don't know what was going on. My sister, at the time she used to live at a building on Clinton. And I went to my sister's building. She wasn't there, but her friend came home. And she gave me the news. It was *hard.* Because I had to see my mom in the hospital. And then, my dad was dead. I had a thought like I should've called and checked up that day, and what if I was there? I just don't want my dad to be remembered like that. I don't want people to think wrong of him because my dad was a good person. He was very lovable. And he loved his guitar. He loved playing music all the time. I was real close with my dad. He was a tall, big guy. And I remember he used to put on his big blue robe with a hoodie. He would come out of the shower with it on, and he'd be like, *In this corner...* Those are things I want people to remember about him. He was just a fun person. Lovable."

Deb asked Guillermina, "What can you tell us about that day?"

Maria answered anyway. "I know she made oatmeal that day

because I remember seeing like, you know, after my dad's death, my family went into that house. I remember seeing three fresh bowls. Nobody had touched that yet."

Christine asked, "So that happened in the morning?"

"Around one o'clock," Maria answered.

"I don't know exactly what time," Guillermina said. "I made the oatmeal. I ironed. I made the bed. My brother came in to help me. I went out of the bedroom and instead of going to the street I went to the sofa to call the police. And then he shot my brother in the back. I didn't know that he had the revolver right there. And then he shot me. And then he killed himself."

"That's what it was," Maria said, "The shooting in the basement made him lose his mind."

Deb established that the other shooting victim that day was Juan Melendez, Guillermina's brother. Maria said he was shot in the shoulder from behind.

Maria said, "When Juan fell he hit his head on the corner of the TV. You know, remember the old wooden—so it knocked him out, so he couldn't do nothing to help her. And then she was on the couch calling 9-1-1 and my dad came and shot her four times. The cops came and told him to put his weapon down and I guess that he shot himself in the head. He died before he hit the ground. Because of everything we've been through, I'm the same way with my kids. My kids are grown, my daughter she's visiting her family, and she went out last night with her cousins and I'm like *don't leave your children unattended*, and I'm always like, well, I want to know where they're at, where they go, who they're with. And they're like, *mom, we're grown*, and I'm like, *I don't care, you know, if God forbid something was to happen to you, I would like to know who you were with last or where*. And that's just, you know, from the way we grew up and everything we've been through."

Christine pointed out that, in the modern world, it always pays to be overly careful.

"You never know somebody's background," Maria said. "Somebody could seem so lovable or so sweet, but you just don't know their background, you know?" She once dated a guy who she later learned was on the sex offender registry.

Christine brought Maria's mind back to poor little Carmen. Who would want to hurt a little girl like that? It made you wonder.

Maria admitted that she did wonder. "Like, I've always wondered, on the ride, because you know we took the ride one day from here to where her body was found, and that's pretty far. So it always stayed in my head like, I wonder if she was dead before they took her on that ride, and if she was alive during that ride, her last moments, how she felt. That fear she went through. You know? So many things. Running on the street naked. Mom, do you know about the part where they saw her from the highway?"

Guillermina again spit venom, "If I see a girl I'm going to stop. To help her. To help her. And they didn't stop. I don't believe that."

The ladies ran through the most recent times they'd been talked to by the press. It seemed like the last time was nine years before, something like that.

"What about the police?" Deb asked.

Maria said to her mother, "When was the last time someone from the police talked to you?

"Years and years ago. I think more than 20 years," Guillermina said.

Deb asked, "Do you have any more photos of Carmen?"

"No," Guillermina said. "In Puerto Rico I have them." In the damaged house. "Roof gone. Everything wet."

Maria had photos on her phone. She said, "They're old, that's why they don't show good, but that's Carmen right there. And Mama Canda and Papa Fele."

Deb said, "Michael, I'm sure, would like to see those."

"Let me see if I have others. This is my daddy. You see how big he was?" Maria asked.

"Would you be willing to share any of these pictures with us?" Christine asked.

Maria nodded, "Yeah, sure. I'm trying to see if I can get..." She turned to her mother: "I was going to ask you a question, Mom, what color suit did she have on at the wake?"

"It was like a pink. Pink."

"It wasn't yellow?"

"No."

"All right," Maria said.

Christine said, "Now Carmen's biological dad, is he alive?"

"Yes. Justiano was married to Aunt Carmen, your sister, right? He was married to my mom's sister. "

Deb asked, "Before or after—"

"Justiano and Carmen had already been married for a year. They already had four kids," Guillermina said. "Nelson and Guisa are the same age."

Maria said, "But…oh my God."

Guillermina and her sister Carmen had been pregnant simultaneously, each with Justiano's baby, and it would be Guillermina's child who would be named after his wife.

"People think my uncle and my mom had a romantic thing. How do I explain it? Nobody knows about that. I can't say nothing, it's her business. But it sounds so confusing, right? She was 14 and he was already married to her sister."

Guillermina added that Justiano and his wife Carmen left Rochester and moved to Chicago when Carmen was born, afraid for good reason that Guillermina's parents would press charges.

"My family has a lot of secrets," Maria said.

Guillermina had had enough for the time being. "You want soup?" she said. "I made it because the weather is so cold. And this is good. Makes your body warm."

And so they had soup.

Christine asked if Justiano and Carmencita had a relationship.

"She was affectionate with him," Guillermina said, "but he treated her like a niece."

Maria said her mom used to drive a school bus. "They called her Gidget. My mom was a strong woman."

Twice widowed, she was. After Miguel's death, she married a man named Julio. They were married for 16 years and one morning Guillermina woke up and found him dead of an overdose.

Deb asked, "Does your mom have an active life?"

Maria answered, "No. She's never been able to work ever since my dad shot her. He left her hands—because he shot in her hand. So if you look at her hand, it's like kind of like disfigured the way it's shaped. And her middle finger is shorter. So she's got problems with that. And she's got an ugly scar like from here to here from when he shot her. What saved her here was her nameplate. She had a nameplate with her name. So when he shot her, it lodged the bullet halfway. So it didn't let it go all the way in. And the same thing with her fingers. What saved her fingers was her wedding band, when he shot her. If not, she would've probably lost her fingers.

Maria was in tune with the questioning now, we were interested in Justiano. She began asking her own questions, asking her mother: "How were my dad and my uncle? Did they get along?"

Guillermina said, "Yeah. They always played dominoes. There were times when the two of them would come out fighting over dominoes. Even though they would argue, they always got along well."

Afterword

On October 13, 2018, I lectured on the subject of the double-initial murders at the Gates Public Library, an event put together by librarian and friend of this investigation Hannah Baumgartner. Because of the popularity of the subject in the Rochester area and Hannah's considerable social-media skills, a second presentation had to be added, and the event(s) were moved to a much larger space. An overflow room was set up to watch me on a screen, and my lecture and slide show were live streamed on Facebook.

We had wonderful guests:

Maria Vasquez, who took the podium briefly to defend her father Miguel Colon.

Felix Colon, Carmen's half-brother was there. He told me his father Justiano was 89-years old and not feeling well.

Wanda's first cousin, John Spock, and Michelle's first cousin Geanine Maenza sat in the VIP section.

Law enforcement was there. Investigator Gary Galetta, and retired RPD Detective Mark Mariano.

Robbie Head from the RIT Barnes and Noble set up a table full of my books to sell.

Each presentation began with a screening of a spooky movie about the murders called "Fear in the Flower" made by Private Investigator Nicholas Fici many years ago when he was a student.

After the second presentation, a reporter/camera person interviewed me for Rochester Spectrum News and the one-minute piece ran every half hour all day Sunday. Again and again I called the case "an underground wound" that caused "community post-traumatic stress."

My team was there—co-author Don Tubman, my cousin Trina Treu, journalist Christine Green, my friend since fifth grade Paul Johnson—making things as easy as possible for me. Hannah instructed those who needed to speak to me about anything, to put their name and contact info on a piece of paper and I would get back to them.

One woman with double initials said she had met the killer.

She lived in a house on Clifford Avenue, not far from Conkey Avenue, same house where in 1967 two gypsy con artists were arrested for pulling a religious scam.

There was a woman who said her deceased mother complained that Wanda Walkowicz had been her bully.

A lady wanted to tell me her story. She said that as a young woman, Bianchi and Joe Naso had scammed her as a team. They were "photographers" looking for models.

And a defense attorney said he'd once represented a guy who claimed he'd given a false confession. During voir dire, the attorney interviewed Joyce Walkowicz, who was in the jury pool. Joyce said that she knew about false confessions. She came home one day and found her boyfriend Junior confessing to police that he killed Wanda. She said, "Officers, you are going to have to excuse Junior because he is out of his mind. I know he didn't do it because he was with me when it happened." There was no corroboration for the story, and for all the lawyer knew she might have been lying to get out of jury duty.

Gene VanDeWalle, the man who discovered Michelle Maenza's body, attended the Gates event and afterward gave me his contact info.

One piece of paper had the name Rodney J. Sullivan (pseudonym) on it, a suspect, a social worker who (so it was said) had all three cases and acted shifty and suspicious, strange behavior for a guy with that job. Sullivan worked for Child Protection Services and was interviewed re all three cases, although this may have been because the police didn't want to speak with female CPS employees re sensitive sex subjects.

A woman who worked with Sullivan was at the October 13 event and said Rodney was a weird-o who had trouble making eye contact and once lurked but wouldn't talk while she was bowling with her league. She said Sullivan was unkempt, greasy and smelly. We learned that Sullivan was now in his seventies, lived in the American southwest, worked in a rehab facility, and had a Facebook page in which *all* of his friends were very young looking females.

At the Gates Library event, Tubman spoke to a woman named Laura who had once been married to a Lyle Shane (pseudonym), whose father claimed to have heard a deathbed confession to the murder of Wanda Walkowicz from an employee of Shane's tree surgery company in the town of Greece. The employee was named James Grayson (pseudonym). He died sometime in the early 1990s, at which time he reportedly confessed to Shane that he'd killed Wanda. Tubman learned that Shane and Grayson had been arrested once together sometime around the time of the murders. They were kicked out of a bar, and came back, attacking the building with chainsaws, which they had handy being tree surgeons.

I found out that on March 28, 1980, James Grayson was sentenced in Monroe County Court to 20 years to life in prison for the February 1978 murder of his 66-year-old hunting companion. Phillips was found dead on his kitchen floor, shot in the back, off of Scottsville Road in Chili. Grayson, they said, tried to make it look like suicide. In April 1984 his conviction was overturned, and he pleaded guilty to first-degree manslaughter in the case, his sentence adjusted to five-to-15 years, which amounted to time served.

And so the leads continue to come in, of varying quality and clarity. There remains work to be done. And, as I told everyone back in 2015 when *The Devil at Genesee Junction* was published, this book may be finished, but the investigation goes on.

*   *   *

Come away O human child to the waters and the wild…

We sign off with this thought:
Let us never forget our stolen angels, dragged from their world of weeping into eternal rest.
And let us never forget the human hands that steal our children—steal them to sate a twisted instinct—for they are Evil, bubbled up from Hell, and should be vanquished.

PHOTOS

The victims were, from left to right, Carmen Colon, Wanda Walkowicz, and Michelle Maenza.

The building in which Carmen Colon was attempting to have a prescription filled. The bull's head sculpted at the top gave the whole neighborhood its name. (Photo by R. Jerome Warren)

Nightmare in Rochester

The stretch of Route 490W near which Carmen Colon ran into rush-hour traffic, naked, for her life as dozens of motorists passed without stopping. (Photo by R. Jerome Warren)

Stearns Road, about 700 feet south of Griffin Road. The spot where Carmen Colon's remains were found. (Photo by R. Jerome Warren)

Joyce Walkowicz and little Wanda. (Photo courtesy Joann Spock)

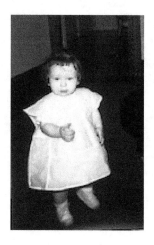

Baby Wanda. (Photo courtesy Joann Spock)

Joyce Walkowicz

Wanda Walkowicz's body was left off of a rest area in the town of Webster. (Photo by R. Jerome Warren)

The Goodman Plaza, where Michelle Maenza was last seen by her Uncle Phil. (Photo by R. Jerome Warren)

Witness Cynthia Nicoletti saw Michelle in a car squealing around this corner, and almost causing an accident. (Photo by R. Jerome Warren)

Michelle's house. (Photo by R. Jerome Warren)

Michelle Maenza's body was found near Mill and Eddy in the town of Macedon. (Photo by R. Jerome Warren)

The body of rapist Dennis Termini is disinterred in 2007 from Holy Sepulchre Cemetery for reasons of DNA comparison. (Photo by Mark Mariano)

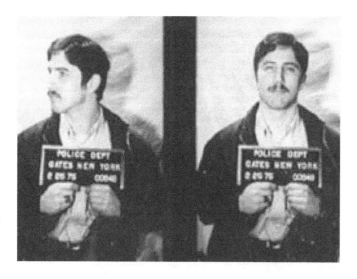

Kenneth Bianchi lived in Gates at the time of the murders and went on to become one of the Hillside Stranglers in Los Angeles.

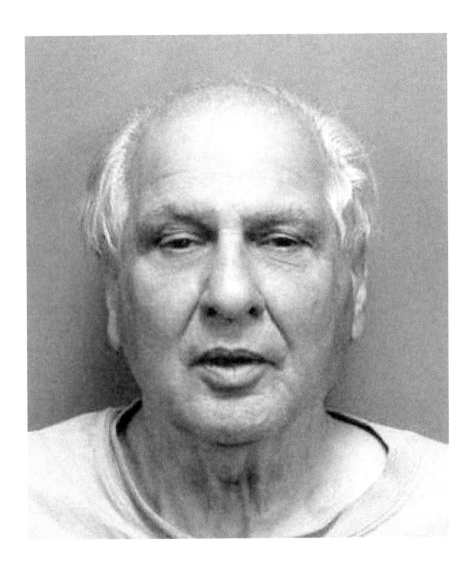

Joseph Naso is California's convicted double-initial killer. The kicker is he grew up in the Rochester area, and one of his West Coast victims was also named Carmen Colon.

Ted Given

Composite drawing of Michelle Maenza's killer.

At 1:30 p.m., Saturday, August 3, 1974—a little bit more than eight months after Michelle Maenza's murder—Ted Given abducted two nine-year-old girls in Lions Park in the Rochester suburb of Gates. (Photo by Matthew T. Benson)

Given lured the little girls to his car by promising to show them baby bunnies. (Photo by Matthew T. Benson)

Carmen Colon's mother Guillermina and Carmen's half-sister Maria still yearn for answers. (Photo by Christine Green)

The 1974 Gates rape suspect. (Courtesy Hannah Baumgartner, Gates Public Library)

Photos by Tom Baumgartner

About the Authors

Michael Benson is originally from the town of Chili, New York and is a Graduate of Excellence from Wheatland-Chili High School. He has a journalism degree from Hofstra University, and is the author of many true-crime books, including *The Devil at Genesee Junction*, *Murder in Connecticut*, *The Burn Farm*, and *Killer Twins*. He has appeared on the television programs *CBS Morning News, Snapped: Killer Couples, Evil Twins, Evil Kin, On the Case with Paula Zahn, Deadly Sins, Someone You Thought You Knew, Inside Evil with Chris Cuomo, Murder in the Family, Evil Stepmothers*, and *Southern-Fried Homicide*.

Donald A. Tubman is from the village of Scottsville, New York, where he still lives. He is a former Town of Wheatland police officer, investigator for New York State, and currently works as a licensed private investigator.

ENDNOTES

[1] Agatha Christie, *The ABC Murders*, New York: William Morrow, 2011 (originally published 1936).

[2] Some believed the victims were also found dumped in a town that started with the same initial as their names—although that theory required some creative geography. If that sounds a little bit literary for a serial killer, be aware that the book was made into a movie in 1965, a comedy entitled *The Alphabet Murders*, with Tony Randall playing the Belgian detective Hercule Poirot.

[3] In 1969, a disc jockey claimed that The Beatles had been hiding clues in their music and album artwork indicating that bass-player Paul McCartney was actually dead. Paul was fine, but the clues, some supposedly on the record backwards, kept Paul's theoretic death in the news for weeks.

[4] The Top 10 songs on AM radio at the time of Carmen Colon's disappearance were: 1) "Shaft" by Isaac Hayes, 2) "Gypsies, Tramps and Thieves" by Cher, 3) "Imagine" by John Lennon, 4) "Baby, I'm-a Want You," by Bread, 5) "Have You Seen Her?" by the Chi-Lites, 6) "Maggie May," by Rod Stewart, 7) "Peace Train," by Cat Stevens, 8) "Family Affair" by Sly and the Family Stone," 9) "Got to Be There," by Michael Jackson, and 10) "Yo-Yo" by The Osmonds.

[5] "Girl Is Slain After Motorists Ignore Her Pleading for Help." *Watertown Daily Times*, November 22, 1971, p. 1A.

[6] Interview with Guillermina Colon by Deb Sperling and Christine Green, April 7, 2018.

[7] Carmen's biological father Justiano Colon lived at 22 Alberta Street.

[8] The neighborhood got its name from a "bust" of a bull that poked out of the front of the building that housed the drug store. A 2016 visit to the area revealed the bull's head to be difficult to see because of the installation of fire escapes at the front of the building, fire escapes that did not exist in 1971. The building currently holds an Islamic mosque and library known as Masjid Al Haqq.

[9] Patrick Crough, *The Serpents Among Us: How to Protect Your Children From Sexual Predators*, Webster, N.Y.: Millstone Justice Children's Advocacy Organization, 2009, p. 236.

[10] Mark Starr. "A Day Like Every Other…Almost." *D&C (D&C)*, November 28, 1971, p. 1A.

[11] "Girl Disappears in Brown St. Area." *Rochester Times-Union (T-U)*, November 17, 1971, p. 3B.

[12] Judy Adams. "Little Carmen Always Had a Smile." *T-U*, November 19, 1971, p. 1B.

[13] Crough, p. 307.

[14] Tom Ryan. "Nobody Stopped to Save Carmen." *D&C,* November 20, 1971, p. 1A.

[15] Michael Benson interview by phone with Michele Zuck, October 6, 2016.

[16] Crough, p. 238.

[17] "Could Motorists Have Saved Girl?" *T-U*, November 20, 1971, p. 8B.

[18] "Police Resume Hunt for Girl After All-Night Search Fails." *T-U*, November 18, 1971, p. 1B.

[19] Ibid.

[20] "Price for Tots: $7,000, Old Car." *D&C,* November 18, 1971, p. 10A

[21] "'Abused Child Needs Help.'" *D&C,* November 18, 1971, p. 10B

[22] Michael Benson interview with James Gillen, October 12, 2016.

[23] Monroe County Sheriff Albert W. Skinner had held the job since 1938. A bachelor who lived in the jailhouse, he was re-elected twelve times. He was a life-long cop and had grown into a big man, five-ten, 280. The man could hurt you just by leaning on you—and he'd leaned on a few. The Sheriff was a big man—54-inch waist, size 8 2/3 hat—but he was old, 78 in 1971. Skinner's record as a leader appeared progressive enough on the surface. During his tenure he founded the mounted patrol, the bomb squad, and the airport division. But in many ways the MCSO had developed into a staid organization under his leadership. Skinner lost the 1973 election to William Lombard, and died on October 27, 1975 at 81.

[24] Dick Cooper. "Police Hunt Girl's Slayer." *T-U*, November 19, 1971, p. 1A.

[25] "Can You Help Find a Killer?" *D&C,* November 21, 1971, p. 1A.

26 Dick Cooper. "Did Carmen Know Slayer?" *T-U*, November 24, 1971, p. 3B.

27 "More Clues to a Killer's Car." *D&C*, November 22, 1971, p. 1A.

28 "Police Report No Clues As Carmen, 10, Is Buried." *D&C*, November 23, 1971, p. 1B.

29 Sandy Flickner. "Silent Fear Invades Brown Street." *D&C*, November 24, 1971, p. 1B.

30 "Bull's Head Key To Slaying?" *D&C*, November 29, 1971, p. 1B.

31 Subject of the author's book, *The Devil at Genesee Junction* (Rowman & Littlefield, 2015).

32 "Funeral Held for Slain Girl." *T-U*, November 22, 1971, p. 2B.

33 "Girl on X-Way 'Definitely' Was Carmen." *T-U*, November 30, 1971, p. 2B.

34 Thom Akeman. "Carmen's Slacks Found in Riga." D&C, November 30, 1971, p. 1A.

35 Marion Rapp Recine. "As Readers See It: Girl's Death Shame of Rochester." *T-U*, November 30, 1971, p. 13B.

36 "3 Sheriff's Detectives Given Carmen's Case." *D&C*, December 21, 1971, p. 2B.

37 The billboards were located at Genesee and Clifton streets, Buffalo Road and West Avenue, Brown and Silver streets, Broad and Brown streets, and at 701 West Main Street.

38 Tom Ryan. "Billboards Seek Killer of Carmen Colon." *D&C*, February 23, 1972, p. 1B.

39 Tom Ryan. "Slaying in the Spotlight." *D&C*, March 2, 1972, p. 8B.

40 Tom Ryan. "Hunt for Carmen's Killer Goes to P.R." *D&C*, March 16, 1972, p. 1A.

41 "'Secret' Colon Quiz in P.R." *D&C*, March 17, 1972, p. 6B.

42 "Police Still Seek Suspect." *D&C*, March 19, 1972, p. 25A.

43 Crough, p. 238.

44 Tom Ryan. "Arrest Near in Slaying?" *D&C*, March 21, 1972, p. 1B.

45 "Slaying Suspect Search Futile." *D&C*, March 22, 1972, p. 1B.

46 "Lazarus Blames Press in Colon Case." D&C, March 23, 1972, p. 1B.

47 Tom Ryan. "'Hunted Man' Surrenders In Carmen Slaying Case." D&C, March 28, 1972, p. 1A.

48 Tom Ryan. "Carmen Slaying Suspect 'Cleared.'" *D&C,* March 29, 1972, p. 1B.

49 Crough, p. 238.

50 This location would become more interesting later in the case because of its proximity to the home and abduction of Michelle Maenza.

51 David Medina. "Colon Murder May Go Unsolved." D&C, November 27, 1972, p. 1B.

52 Steve Mills and Emil Venere. "Two separate family quarrels claim two lives." *D&C*, p. 1A.

53 Gary Craig. "Police still track leads into three 1970s slayings that shattered community's calm." *Rochester Democrat & Chronicle*, March 1, 2009, p. 1A.

54 Jack Jones. "Time refuses to heal a mom's double-initial agony." *D&C*, December 9, 1995, p. 1A.

55 Jack Jones. "City Man claims murder mix-up." *D&C*, April 9, 2002, p. 1B.

56 Caselaw website, accessed September 1, 2016.

57 Supreme Court, Monroe County, New York, Miguel Colon, Plaintiff, v. City of Rochester, City of Rochester Police Department, County of Monroe Sheriff's Department, The Discovery Channel, Film Garden Entertainment, The Academy, and Robert R. Hazelwood, Defendants. In his decision, Judge Andrew V. Siracuse said, "During the period of less than two years almost 30 years ago three young girls from poor neighborhoods in Rochester, New York, were kidnapped, raped and killed. Aside the horror of the crimes themselves, these attacks stood out because all three victims had first and last names beginning with the same letter, and the bodies of all three were found in outlining communities with the same initial letter; the first victim, for example, was Carmen Colon, and her body was found in Churchville. These crimes were never solved. A few years ago the producers of television shows that aired on the cable Discovery Channel

Nightmare in Rochester

approached the Rochester police with a proposal to broadcast a one-hour program on these so-called 'double initial murders." The investigative files would be supplied to a former FBI criminal profiler, Robert Hazelwood, without any information on suspects whom the police had identified. From information about the victims and the circumstances of the crimes themselves Hazelwood and a group of retired FBI personnel, The Academy, would attempt to generate a description of the assailant. This information would be supplied to the police department, to compare with any suspects and to suggest new avenues of investigation. In addition, it was hoped that broadcast of the show might elicit further leads from the public. Hazelwood's conclusions were, in part, that Carmen Colon had likely been killed by someone she knew, a relative or acquaintance, and that her death was unrelated to the other two. As it happened, police had suspected an uncle of Carmen's, one Miguel Colon, and in 1991 they were pursuing him when he committed suicide.…Television is a visual medium, and the producers of the program asked the City police department if there were any photographs available of the suspect Colon. The file had been discarded after Colon's death, but police noticed that he applied for a pistol permit in 1988. Pistol permit applications are stored in the Monroe County Clerk's office, so an officer contacted an employee of that office and asked for a photograph from Colon's application. It is clear from the affidavits supplied by the city that the officer furnished the clerk with significant identifying information in addition to the name. The clerk, unfortunately, did not pull the 1988 application by the Miguel Colon whose niece was murdered. Instead, she took out a 1967 application by the Plaintiff, another man named Miguel Colon with no connection at all with the double initial murders, or indeed any other crime. According to uncontradicted testimony from the officer, the clerk removed the photograph from the backing card which contained the information about the applicant and handed the photograph to him, telling him it did not need to be returned—"He's dead, anyway." She is reported to have said. At no time did the officer see the card itself. The photograph was duly forwarded to the producers of the program, and when it aired the plaintiff's image was shown five times, as the likely killer of Carmen Colon who himself committed suicide in 1991. Another image was shown once, this time of a group which apparently included the suspect Miguel Colon; the source of this photograph is unclear and the details difficult to make out."

[58] The top 10 songs on AM radio at the time of Wanda's demise were 1) "The Night the Lights Went Out in Georgia" by Vicki Lawrence, 2) "Neither One of Us Wants to Be the First to Say Goodbye" by Gladys Knight and the Pips, 3) "Killing Me Softly With His Song," Roberta Flack, 4) "Ain't No Woman Like the One I Got" by The Four Tops, 5) Break Up to Make Up" by The Stylistics, 6) "Tie a Yellow Ribbon Round he Ole Oak Tree" by Dawn, 7) "Sing" by The Carpenters, 8) "Danny's Song" by Anne Murray, 9) "Also Sprach Zarathustra" by Deodato, and 10) "The Cisco Kid" by War.

[59] "Second Rochester Girl Found Raped, Strangled on an Errand to a Store."

Schenectady Gazette, April 4, 1973, p. 16.

[60] Michael Benson interview with Joann Spock, October 13, 2016.

[61] Jack Marsh. "Wanda Was Halfway Home, Police Say." *T-U*, April 6, 1973, p. 1A.

[62] "Police Ask Tipster To Call Again." *T-U*, April 5, 1973, p. 1B.

[63] According to author Cheri Farnsworth, the railroad track stalker turned out to be a "known sex offender."

[64] When the railroad tracks were removed, the resulting pathway was converted into a 2.25-mile hiking and biking trail that ran from Mill Street in the High Falls area of Rochester northward to the Seneca Park pedestrian bridge.

[65] Bill O'Brien. "The Little Redhead of Avenue D: Mystery man in the bushes reported to police…too late." *D&C*, April 4, 1973, p. 1A.

[66] Jan Barber. "Wanda: Shy Type, Friendly, Pleasant." *T-U*, April 4, 1973, p. 8B.

[67] Jack Marsh and Terry Dillman. "Girl's Body Found in Webster: City Pupil, 11, Believed Murdered." *T-U*, April 3, 1973, p. 1A.

[68] Michael Benson interview with Mark Mariano, September 9, 2018.

[69] David Medina. "Missing Girl, 11, Found Slain: Died of Strangulation; Few Clues in Search." *D&C*, April 4, 1973, p. A1.

[70] "$2,500 Reward: Can You Help Solve This Crime?" *D&C*, April 4, 1973, p. A1.

[71] Jack Marsh and Dick Cooper. "Search on For Wanda's Killer." *T-U*, April 4, 1973, p. 1A.

[72] David Medina. "Wanda's Killer Still at Large, Police Stumped in Wide Search." *D&C*, April 5, 1973, p. 1A.

[73] That reward quickly bumped up to $6,000 after a hefty contribution from the Rochester Auto Dealers Association.

[74] David Medina. "Carmen-Wanda Link Doubted by Police." *D&C*, April 5, 1973, p. A3.

[75] Neva Flaherty. "Psychiatrist's View of Rapist-Slayer." *T-U*, April 4, 1973, p. 1B.

76 David Medina. "'Leads' But No Suspects in Slaying: Police Lean to Theory That Wanda Knew Her Killer." *D&C*, April 6, 1973, p. 1A.

77 Jack Marsh and Dick Cooper. "Search on for Wanda's Killer: Detectives Comb City's Northeast." *T-U*, April 4, 1973, p. 1A.

78 Dick Cooper and Jack Marsh. "Wanda Tipster Asked to Call Again." *T-U*, April 5, 1973, p. 1A.

79 Judy Adams. "200 Mourners Attend Funeral for Slain Girl." *T-U*, April 6, 1973, p. 1B.

80 David Medina. "Search for Killer 'Looks Brighter.'" *D&C*, April 7, 1973, p. 8B.

81 Paula Musto. "Murder Lead Falls Through." *D&C*, April 8, 1973, p. 1B.

82 Chuck Freadhoff. "'Best' Report Card Will Be Framed." *D&C*, April 9, 1973, p. 1B.

83 David Medina. "Wanda's Neighborhood Nervous Since Murder." *D&C*, April 9, 1973, p. 1B.

84 "No Progress in Hunt for Killer." *D&C,* April 10, 1973, p. 1B.

85 Chuck Freadhoff. "No 'Last Tango' Or 'Miss Jones' For This Group." *D&C*, April 20, 1973, p. 3B.

86 As far as we know, only one porn movie theme was ever played on Top 40 radio: "More, More, More" by the Andrea True Connection which went to #4 on the Billboard Hot 100 in 1976, the trick being that Andrea True was also the star of the movie.

87 Dan Lovely. "City Planners Reject 2 Housing Projects." *D&C*, June 26, 1973, p. 6B.

88 Paula Musto. "Wanda's Mother Cannot Forget…" *D&C*, July 16, 1973, p. 1A.

89 Joyce E. Walkowicz passed away on June 8, 2003 in Rochester at the age of 62.

90 "Wanda's Case Still Active." *D&C*, July 21, 1973, p. 6B.

91 Gerald Goldberg. "Program Asks Viewers to Solve Crime." *D&C*, September 26, 1973, p. 2C.

[92] Betty Utterbeck. "A Who-Done-It Where You May Know." *D&C,* October 20, 1973, 1C.

[93] "200 Tips from TV Show." *D&C,* October 24, 1973, p. 3C.

[94] The top 10 songs on AM radio at the time of Michelle Maenza's abduction were: 1) "Photograph" by Ringo Starr, 2) "Keep On Truckin'" by Eddie Kendricks, 3) "Top of the World" by The Carpenters, 4) "Space Race" by Billy Preston, 5) "Heartbeat—It's a Love Beat" by The DeFranco Family featuring Tony DeFranco, 6) "Midnight Train to Georgia" by Gladys Knight and the Pips, 7) "Just You'n'Me" by Chicago, 8) "Paper Roses" by Marie Osmond, 9) "Goodbye Yellow Brick Road" by Elton John, and 10) "The Love I Lost" by Harold Melvin and the Blue Notes.

[95] Of the three homes in which the double-initial victims lived, only 25 Webster Crescent, Michelle Maenza's home, was still standing in September 2018.

[96] "Police find body of missing girl; murder linked to earlier killings." *The Auburn Citizen-Advertiser,* November 29, 1973, p. 2.

[97] Mrs. Maenza's obituary in the D&C, November 10, 1985, said she had two kids, Michael and David Luciano from a previous marriage. She had a brother named Roy Vinton.

[98] Dick Cooper. "Shroud of Fear Descends on Neighbors of Michelle." *T-U,* November 29, 1973, p. 1B.

[99] Jack Marsh. "Hunt On for Missing Girl." *T-U,* November 27, 1973, p. 1A.

[100] In 2009 MM's uncle Stephen Maenza told *D&C* reporter Gary Craig that his brother Philip offered Michelle a ride home and she declined.

[101] Jack Marsh. "No Decent Leads Yet on Missing Girl, 11." *T-U,* November 28, 1973, p. 1B.

[102] Craig, Gary. "'Double Initials' Remain Mystery." *Democrat and Chronicle,* March 1, 2009, p. 1A.

[103] Michael Benson interview with Geanine Maenza, March 30, 2017.

[104] Gerald Goldberg. "Police: No Clues In Hunt for Girl." *Rochester Democrat & Chronicle,* November 28, 1973, p. 1A.

[105] Michael Zeigler. "Neighbors Fear Worst, Hope For The Best." *Rochester Democrat & Chronicle,* November 28, 1973, p. 1B.

[106] Gerald Goldberg and John McGinnis. "No Leads in Slaying of Girl, 11: Victim Strangled; Found Near Road." *Rochester Democrat & Chronicle*, November 29, 1973, p. 1A.

[107] Michael Benson interview with Gene VanDeWalle, October 18, 2018.

[108] Jack Jones. "No rest for innocent 'until we find this guy.'" *Rochester Democrat & Chronicle*, December 7, 1995, p. A1.

[109] Jack Marsh, John McGinnis and Del Ray. "Girl, 11, Strangled; Body Found in Wayne." *T-U*, November 28, 1973, p. 1A.

[110] Crough, p. 242.

[111] Steve Crosby. "Double-initial investigation: Wayne police offer aid." *D&C*, July 11, 1981, p. 1B.

[112] Bob Minzesheimer. "Killings Hauntingly Similar: Three girls are believed victims of the same attacker." *Rochester Democrat & Chronicle*, November 29, 1973, p. 1A.

[113] Jerry Goldberg. "Police Discount Slaying Coincidences." *D&C*, November 30, 1973, p. 1A.

[114] Jack Marsh. "Motorists Hold Key To Killing." *T-U*, December 3, 1973, p. 3B.

[115] Fred Eliason, Jack Marsh, and Del Ray. "3 Schoolgirls May Be Victims of Same Killer." *T-U*, November 29, 1973, p. 1A.

[116] Gerald Goldberg. "New Clues Checked in Slaying." *D&C*, December 1, 1973, p. 1A.

[117] Jack Marsh. "Police Quiz Witness Who 'Saw' Michelle." *T-U*, December 3, 1973, p. 1B.

[118] "Was It Michelle in Speeding Car?" *D&C*, December 2, 1973, p. 1A.

[119] "Police Get Michelle Half-Clue. *D&C*, December 3, 1973, p. 1A.

[120] Jack Marsh and Del Ray. "2 Leads Probed In Girl's Slaying." *T-U*, November 30, 1973, p. 1A.

[121] Jack Marsh. "Man Wanted; Have You Seen Him?" *T-U*, December 4, 1973, p. 1B.

[122] Gerald Goldberg. "Face-to-Face with Slayer, Girl?" *D&C*, December 4, 1973, p. 1A. (Goldberg won an award for this story, winning a New York State Associated Press Association's 1974 News Writing Contest in the "Spot News" category.)

[123] "Muted Rage at Wake: Michelle's Funeral Held." *T-U*, December 1, 1973, p. 1B.

[124] Mike Shore. "20 More Assigned to Slaying Probe." *T-U*, December 5, 1973, p. 1B.

[125] "Open Letter to Slayer: Turn Yourself In." *T-U*, December 6, 1973, p. 1B.

[126] Jack Marsh. "Third Witness Saw Killer?" *T-U*, December 6, 1973, p. 1B.

[127] Gerald Goldberg. "The Maenza Case: Song Delayed Witness." *D&C*, December 7, 1973, p. 8B.

[128] "Photo Brings Tips, But No Progress." *T-U*, p. 1B.

[129] Jack Marsh. "Hunting Michelle's Slayer: A Day with Two Detectives." *T-U*, December 11, 1973.

[130] Jack Marsh and John McGinnis. "Man Quizzed, Released in Michelle Slaying." *T-U*, December 12, 1973, p. 1B.

[131] "Suspect Quizzed in Girl's Death." *D&C*, December 12, 1973, p. 1A.

[132] "Police Give Suspect 'Benefit of the Doubt.'" *D&C*, December 13, 1973, p. 1B.

[133] The last two seemed pretty straightforward, but my 17-year-old mind, normally adept at prurience, struggled to come up with scenarios for a dirty movie named "Meatball". Hanky-panky at an Italian restaurant? I was stumped. In 2017 I looked it up. I was close. Scientist creates Swedish meatballs that act as an aphrodisiac.

[134] "Motion Rejected in X-Film Case." *D&C*, December 21, 1973, p. 1B.

[135] Gerald Goldberg. "Police Are Optimist They'll Solve Murder Case." *D&C*, December 15, 1973, p. 1B.

[136] "Maenza Murder Case: Suspect Is Cleared." *D&C*, December 22, 1973, p. 2B.

[137] Gerald Goldberg. "Search for Maenza Slayer Continues." *D&C*, January 12,

1974, p. 6B.

[138] Gerald Goldberg. "Suicide Ends Police Chase After Attack." *D&C,* January 2, 1974, p. 1B.

[139] Gerald Goldberg. "City Firefighter: He Got Job Despite Report." *D&C,* January 19, 1974, p.1A.

[140] Crough, p. 249.

[141] Crough, p. 250.

[142] Although it has been said by officials that the Wanda Walkowicz crime scene was the only one to yield readable DNA, Wayne County Sheriff's Investigator Kevin Kuntz told *D&C* reporter Gary Craig in 2009 that there was extant "physical evidence from all three crimes."

[143] Michael Benson interview with Mark Mariano, September 9, 2018.

[144] Michael Benson interview with Donna Bianchi, January 13, 2018.

[145] "Doctor aids probe." *D&C,* February 14, 1974, p. 1B.

[146] Michael Zeigler. "Patterns in the mind of a killer." *D&C,* March 3, 1974, p. 1E.

[147] Neva Flaherty. "3 Child Murders in 2 Years—All Unsolved: Killer May Desire To Get Caught—Doctor." *T-U,* November 29, 1973, p. 1B.

[148] Tom Buckley. "Three Rape-Murders Stir Rochester Area." *The New York Times*, December 24, 1973, p. 33.

[149] Dr. Barry pointed out in the article that the victims were all dumped exactly ten miles from their homes. Perhaps the number 10 had some significance to him, the psychiatrist opined—this despite the fact that it was at least eighteen miles from Michelle's home to her dumpsite. The distance from Wanda's home to her dumpsite was much closer.

[150] "Deputy off probe." *D&C,* February 22, 1974, p. 1B.

[151] "Abduction suspect sought." *Gates-Chili News*, August 6, 1974, p. 1.

[152] Thom Akeman. "4 men questioned, cleared in kidnap of 9-year-olds." *D&C,* August 6, 1974, p. 2B; Chief Roche was only 27 years old, and would go on to be the longest reigning police chief in Gates history, serving at the top spot in the department for 32 years, stepping down in 1996. He passed away on October 10,

2017.

[153] Gates Police Department Investigation and Supplemental Report 1974-A.

[154] "Rape suspect held for Grand Jury action." *Gates-Chili News*, August 13, 1974, p. 1.

[155] Don Tubman interview with Lieutenant Michael Wilcox, March 23, 2017.

[156] "Rabbit Prices Jumping." *D&C*, April 2, 1973, p. 1B. Interview with Joseph Jonger, proprietor of Jungle Trader Pet Shop at 3 Parsells Avenue.

[157] Sister Rita was unfortunately later a witness in the real-life "Agnes of God" case in which Sister Maureen Murphy gave birth and then suffocated her baby, a tragedy at a convent in the Rochester suburb of Brighton, N.Y. cite: Marcia Bullard. "Never heard baby cry, nun quoted," *D&C*, February 18, 1977, p. A1, A3.

[158] Don Tubman interview with Cynthia Nicoletti, October 3, 2018.

[159] "Rape suspect held for mental exam." *D&C*, August 7, 1974, p. 8B.

[160] Pete Prichard. "Out of Prison…2 Years Late." *D&C*, October 9, 1973, p. 1A. Written by the same guy who wrote the Sunday magazine overview of the double-initial case, although now bylined as Pete.

[161] Meryl Gordon. "Victim: Suspect didn't kidnap me." *D&C*, August 9, 1974, p.1A.

[162] "Kidmap suspect's release sought," *Rochester Democrat & Chronicle*, August 14, 1974, p. 1B.

[163] Phil Hand. "Judge: Suspect in rape, kidnap legally detained." *D&C*, August 20, 1972, p. 6B.

[164] "Grand Jury indicts Given on rape count." *D&C*, August 31, 1974, p. 1B.

[165] Keith Pritchard. "Witness: I saw marks on Given." *D&C*, January 21, 1975, p. 1B.

[166] Meryl Gordon. "Sheriff's officer beat him, rape suspect claims." *D&C,* January 23, 1975, p. 8B.

[167] Meryl Gordon. "Given was beaten, medical expert says." *D&C*, January 24, 1975, p. 1B.

168 "Jail official: Given had scratches on body." *D&C*, January 28, 1975, 5B.

169 Thom Akeman. "Girls' parents ask finish to sex case." *D&C*, July 21, 1975, p. 5B.

170 Sheridan Lyons. "Sentence angers victims' parents." *D&C*, September 13, 1975, p. 1B.

171 Caselaw website, accessed June 2, 2016.

172 Even then, an ancient facility, in use since 1878.

173 "Teen Escapees Arraigned." *D&C,* November 24, 1963, p. 15C.

174 "Escapees Held For Grand Jury." *The Geneva Times*, November 23, 1963, p. 8.

175 "In Yates Jail—Escapees Held for Grand Jury." *The Geneva Times*, November 25, 1963, p. 8.

176 Only a half-block from Lake Ontario in the Charlotte section of Rochester.

177 Debbie said, "I am not certain of the date but vividly recall how the story crept into my consciousness as I began to overhear adults in my life whispering about it. My parents are deaf. My brother and I often had to serve as conduits of information for them. They couldn't watch the TV news or hear other people talking in line at the grocery store, for example.

"The other adults in my life, from teachers to relatives, started talking about the fact that my name is double initials and that Dansville, which starts with the same initial, is close by. They wanted to be sure my parents knew about this and I don't think they realized how talking to me about it would scare the life out of me. The girls came from broken homes and my parents were not happily married at the time—they would later divorce—which also worried me.

"By the summer of 1974, it was deeply affecting. I was embarrassed that teachers, family members, and friends were talking about me because I have double initials—most girls at that age want to fly below the radar. I was too young to figure out how to engage my parents in my fears. Again, their deafness was a constant barrier to communication.

"The rape aspect of the crimes was particularly embarrassing to me—I was old enough to know something about sex but too young to understand that rape is not sex. The worst moment for me was in 1974 (I had recently turned 14) and my best friend Sarah Jones and I decided to walk down the railroad tracks behind my house.

"We both loved being outside and hunting for treasures. We were a long way from the nearest house when a man appeared out of nowhere, moving toward us. I was panicked but my friend didn't seem bothered, so I didn't say anything at first. As he moved closer, I saw that he had a long gun hanging by his side and I said something to Sarah—I honestly don't remember what—and she became as afraid as I was.

"We turned around to head away from the man and he started to sort of jog toward us. When I saw that he had picked up his pace, I sank to the ground, too terrified to move. My friend was pulling on my arm and urging me to get moving. I was literally frozen in fear and couldn't move or speak.

"My friend would move off a little ways to get away and then come back to tug on me. I am sure this happened over the course of just a few seconds, but it felt as if time had slowed to a crawl. It was excruciating.

"When the man was close enough to us that we could vaguely make out his features, he suddenly turned to the right about 90-degrees and headed towards a wooded area. We could just make out a hunting license pinned to his back.

"My friend was the first one to express relief, she said something like, 'He is just a hunter!' I got to my feet. My legs had never felt that wobbly before. And I just began walking towards home.

"We laughed nervously for a minute or so. When we told some of our friends about it later, I did share that I was afraid he was the double-initial killer and while no one mocked me, it did feel as if they thought it was funny that I was so afraid I couldn't move.

"I never told my parents, thinking I would get into trouble."

She told me that long before the double-initials murders she had been aware of herself as a potential target for perversion.

"When I was seven or eight, I found the big prize at a local Easter egg hunt and along with my photo, a newspaper published my name and address. I got home from school before any one else and would always bring in the mail. There was a letter addressed to me, so I opened it. Along with a hand-written note was a lewd drawing. I was much too young to understand what the drawing showed but it scared me. I showed my mother when she got home from work and it felt like my life blew apart. The police were called and for a time a patrol car regularly drove through my neighborhood. Rather than explaining things to me, the adults in my life gave a watered-down version, something like, 'A bad man wrote you an inappropriate letter. Don't worry but the police will try to find him.' Hearing about police, seeing a police car seemingly every time I went outside, and having everyone acting so frightened robbed me of my sense of safety in the world. I am not aware that they ever found out who it was. I did not think the same person who wrote me the letter was the double-initial killer but I do remember thinking that bad things really do happen and so it was conceivable I would be targeted by the killer."

Had the fear dissipated with adulthood?

"I have been surprised to find people talking about this case throughout my life, including again now! It came up among my friends in college (in Western New York) and many times in early adulthood. I told and retold the sorry about the hunter, but never felt I could adequately describe the paralyzing fear and most people laugh, finding it a humorous anecdote about a goofy teenage girl. It took many years before the haunting fear dissipated. I would often reflect on one piece of news I remembered that one of the victims was spotted naked running down a highway by many people, none of whom stopped to help. I am not sure if that is factual, but it was real in my mind and stoked my fears."

   Instead of becoming obsessed with the case, studying it, Debbie distanced herself from it.

[178] Darcy O'Brien. *Two of a Kind: The Hillside Stranglers*. New York: New American Library, 1985.

[179] Ted Schwartz. *The Hillside Strangler: A Murderer's Mind*. New York: Signet, 1982.

[180] Michael Zeigler and Michael Cordts. "City native suspect in murder of 2 women." *D&C*, January 18, 1979, p. 1B.

[181] "Theft interrupted." *D&C*, April 25, 1975, p. 1B.

[182] "Bianchi print interests police: Investigation rekindled in 'double initial' killings." *D&C*, July 9, 1981, p. 1B.

[183] Gary Gerew. "Bianchi print tests could take several weeks." *D&C*, July 10, 1981, p. 1B.

[184] Michael Zeigler. "Hillside Strangler asks to be cleared or charged in area deaths." *D&C,* March 9, 1993, p. 1A.

[185] Crough, p. 247.

[186] Jack Jones. "Girl, 6, strangled in Jay St. home." *D&C*, April 12, 1976, p. 1A.

[187] Jim Rowley. "Assailant rapes, strangles 6-year-old girl." *D&C*, April 12, 1976, p. 1B.

[188] John Stewart. "Few clues, suspects in rape killing." *D&C*, April 13, 1976, p. 1B.

[189] John Stewart. "Slayings of girls—related?" *D&C*, April 14, 1976, p. 1B.

[190] John Stewart. "Tragedy draws concern." *D&C*, April 15, 1976, p. 1B.

[191] John Stewart. "Police appealing for information." *D&C*, April 17, 1976, p. 6B.

[192] "Rape death probe keys on 1 man." *D&C*, April 18, 1976, p. 1B.

[193] John Stewart. "Slaying case witness held on drug count: Arrested after raid on home." *D&C*, April 20, 1976, p. 1B.

[194] Michael Zeigler. "Arrest in girl's 1976 death: Discarded cigarette links man, now 64, to slaying." *D&C*, October 4, 2007, p. 1A.

[195] Helen Kennedy. "DNA from cigarette butt may nail '76's 'Alphabet Killer.'" *New York Daily News*, October 4, 2007.

[196] "Inmate charged in 30-year-old N.Y. murder dies in Keys." *Heraldtribune.com*, posted November 12, 2007, accessed October 12, 2018.

[197] Ben Dobbin. "Double-initial murder case reopened: Authorities receive tip about deaths of girls in '70s near Rochester." *Milwaukee Journal Sentinel*, December 15, 1995.

[198] Jack Jones. "Investigation is rekindled in 3 killings of early '70s." *D&C*, December 7, 1995, p. 1A.

[199] Ibid.

[200] Gary Craig. "Police still track leads into three 1970s slayings that shattered community's calm." *D&C*, March 1, 2009, p. 1A.

[201] Crough, p. 247.

[202] "Butler Tops Rifle Tests." *D&C*, August 23, 1948, p. 21.

[203] "Fined on Lights Charge." *Rochester Democrat & Chronicle*, March 20, 1953, p. 29.

[204] "Woman Accuses E. Rochesterian." *Rochester Democrat & Chronicle*, April 26, 1958, p. 19.

[205] Central Park is a eight-block long street with a mall in its center, running east-west in Rochester's east side. The eastern end of Central Park is about 200 yards from the home of Michelle Maenza.

[206] Gary Craig. "Perinton Attack is Proof in Calif. Serial Killing Trial," *D&C*, July 3, 2013.

[207] "Sentencing Date Set for 3 Youths In Theft at School." *D&C*, September 11, 1958, p. 31.

[208] "Man Gets Probation, Suspended Sentence." *D&C*, September 25, 1958, p. 29.

[209] Gary Klien. "Naso murder arrest brings Fairfax victim's family 'a little closer.'" *Marin Independent Journal* website, posted April 17, 2011, accessed June 3, 2016.

[210] C.L. Swinney. *List of 10*. USA: RJ Parker Publishing, 2017, p. 20.

[211] Ibid, p. 123.

[212] Ibid, p. 125.

[213] "Missing Mother? Healdsburg body probably female." *The Santa Rosa Press-Democrat*, January 26, 1983, p. 12.

[214] Ibid, p. 139.

[215] Ibid, p. 161.

[216] On April 11, 2011, at 5:00 PM, Ryan Petersen, a peace officer employed by the Marin County Sheriff's Office, signed a "Statement of Probable Cause for Arrests Made Without a Warrant And Arrestee Booked Into Jail" in regards to the arrest of Joseph Naso on four counts of murder. The statement read, "On August 6, 1994 Tracy Tafoya went missing from the Yuba City area. Tafoya was working as a prostitute in the area at the time of her death. Tafoya was located dumped on the side of Highway 70, next to the Marysville Cemetery, deceased near Joe Naso's residence. Tracy's death was deemed suspicious and labeled as a homicide due to the location of the body and the condition. During a probation search of Joe Naso's residence in Reno, Nevada, he was found in possession of a handwritten list which had the reference to ten different women and ten different locations. The last entry on the list made reference to a girl from Marysville, with (cemetery) written next to it. Nevada DPS conducted a search of Joe Naso's safety deposit box. Inside the safety deposit box was newspaper clippings and photos related to the death of Tracy Tafoya. Located in Joe Naso's home were writings referring to Tafoya's disappearance."

[217] "California: Woman recalls multiple murder suspect trying to buy underwear from her." *RGJ.com*, April 14, 2011, accessed June 22, 2016.

[218] *D&C* website, posted April 4, 2017, accessed November 22, 2018.

[219] Shannon Moore. "A Close Encounter with the Suspected Serial Killer." *Foxreno.com*, April 14, 2011, accessed June 22, 2016.

[220] Was this a clue as to the nature of the DNA sample, a message that it was not semen, or were police open to the notion that the DIK, like "The Hillside Strangler" might turn out to be more than one guy?

[221] Gary Craig. "Calif. Deaths parallel double-initial murders here." *D&C*, April 13, 2011, p. 1B.

[222] Karl Fischer and Robert Salonga. "'I guess you never know'": suspect's portrait begins to emerge." *Marin.ij.com*, posted April 13, 2011, accessed August 31, 2015.

[223] Matthias Gafni. "Serial killing suspect had boxes of notebooks detailing how he would torture women, investigator told former neighbor." *Contra Costa Times*, April 16, 2011.

[225] "'Double initial' serial killer suspect 'had boxes of notes detailing grisly plans to torture and kill women.'" *Daily Mail Reporter*, April 18, 2011.

[226] Justin Burton. "No Naso plea in 'double initial' killings." *Sfgate.com*, April 14, 2011, accessed June 22, 2016.

[227] "Naso Letter: Arrest Without Warrant." MSNBC website, June 6, 2012, accessed May 16, 2016.

[228] Rob Young. "Yuba woman recalls 'creepy' encounter with suspected killer Naso." *Appealdemocrat.com*, April 18, 2011, accessed June 23, 2016.

[229] Ibid.

[230] Gary Klien. "At preliminary hearing, accused killer Naso reminisces with former girlfriend." *Marin Independent Journal*, January 13, 2012. Accessed via *Marinij.com*, July 22, 2016.

[231] Keri Brenner. "UPDATE: "girl' in Healdsburg." *Healdsburg Patch*, January 18, 2012, unknown page.

[232] "Prosecution rests in N. Calif. Serial killing case." *San Francisco Chronicle*, January 20, 2012, page unknown.

[233] Jason Dearen (Associated Press). "Prosecutor and murder suspect give final remarks. Mercury News website, posted January 20, 2012, accessed July 26, 2016.

[234] Jay Barmann. "Joseph Naso Might Have Murdered Someone in the Tenderloin." SFist website, posted January 24, 2012, accessed July 26, 2016.

[235] Gary Klien. "Serial-killing suspect Naso, in closing pitch, says women voluntarily disrobe for him." *Marin Independent Journal*, January 21, 2012, accessed at Mercury News website on July 26, 2016.

236 "Naso Hearing Expected to Wrap Up on Monday." *Bay City News*, January 20, 2013, accessed at Piedmont Patch website, accessed July 26, 2016.

237 Dylan Silver. "Cold cases share similarities to alleged Naso crimes." *tahoedailytribune.com*, posted January 20, 2012, accessed October 30, 2018.

238 "Naso's re-entry of pleas to four murders off until next week." *Ktvu.com*, posted February 3, 2012, accessed July 26, 2016.

239 Raymond Cohen. "Woman says accused California serial killer raped her in 1961." *Chicago Tribune*, March 23, 2012, accessed via *chicagotribune.com*, July 27, 2016.

240 Dan Noyes. "I-Team receives letter from accused 'Alphabet Killer'." *Abc7news.com*, posted June 5, 2012, accessed July 28, 2016.

241 "Naso contacts News 4 by mail for second time." MyNews4 website, posted August 27, 2012, accessed July 29, 2016.

242 "Serial Murder Suspect Interviews Possible Jurors." KTVN website, posted June 4, 2013, accessed July 29, 2016.

243 Jason Dearen. "Jurors brought to tear up at murder trial." Bakersfield Now website, posted June 17, 2013, accessed July 30, 2016.

244 "Jurors tear up as Naso serial murder trial begins." KTVU website, posted June 17, 2013, accessed July 30, 2016.

245 Nicole Baptista. "Naso refutes incriminating letter." *Novato Advance*, July 17, 2013.

246 Justin Berton. "Prosecutors link 6th victim to serial killer Naso." *San Francisco Chronicle*, August 28, 2013.

247 "Reputed Marin Serial Killer Ordered to Pony Up." *San Rafael Patch*, December 17, 2013.

248 Swinney, p. 258.

249 "Police: Burglaries." *Star-Gazette* (Elmira, NY), July 31, 1986, p. 15.

250 "Man is sought as the rapist of Parma girl, 11." *D&C,* October 1, 1986, p. 6B.

251 Todd Lightly. "Parolee sought in Parma rape." *D&C*, October 3, 1986, p. 1B.

252 Katie Kilfoyle. "Man charged with raping girl, 11: Suspect eluded police 2 months before capture." *D&C*, November 30, 1986, p. 4B.

253 Michael Zeigler. "High-risk sex offender to be freed May 27," *D&C*, May 16, 2010, p. 9B.

254 Caselaw website, accessed November 22, 2018.

255 "X-Mass" was also the way the Zodiac killer spelled Christmas in his taunting letters to California journalists and law enforcement.

256 Jeff Wilkin. "Teen-ager's murder isn't forgotten." *D&C*, November 23, 1989, p. 1B.

257 Jon Hand. "Mother won't give up on decades-old cold case." *D&C*, December 16, 2014.

258 Mark Pittman. "Body of teen-age girl is found at School 33." *Rochester Democrat & Chronicle*, November 23, 1984, p. 1A.

259 Todd Lighty. "Neighbors to start fund to find killer: Residents still shaken by teen-age girl's death." *D&C*, February 1, 1985, p. 1B.

260 Todd Lighty. "Group offers $1,700 reward for lead to killer of girl, 14." *D&C*, February 23, 1985, p. 1B.

261 Todd Lighty. "Posters remind city of slaying." *D&C*, April 19, 1985, p. 1B.

262 "Lights-on rule urged at school where body found." *D&C,* May 6, 1985, p. 4B.

263 Michael Benson interview with Cynthia Nicoletti, October 15, 2016.

264 Michael Benson interview with Cynthia Nicoletti, October 17, 2016.

CPSIA information can be obtained
at www.ICGtesting.com
Printed in the USA
LVHW081915060219
606607LV00015B/1130/P